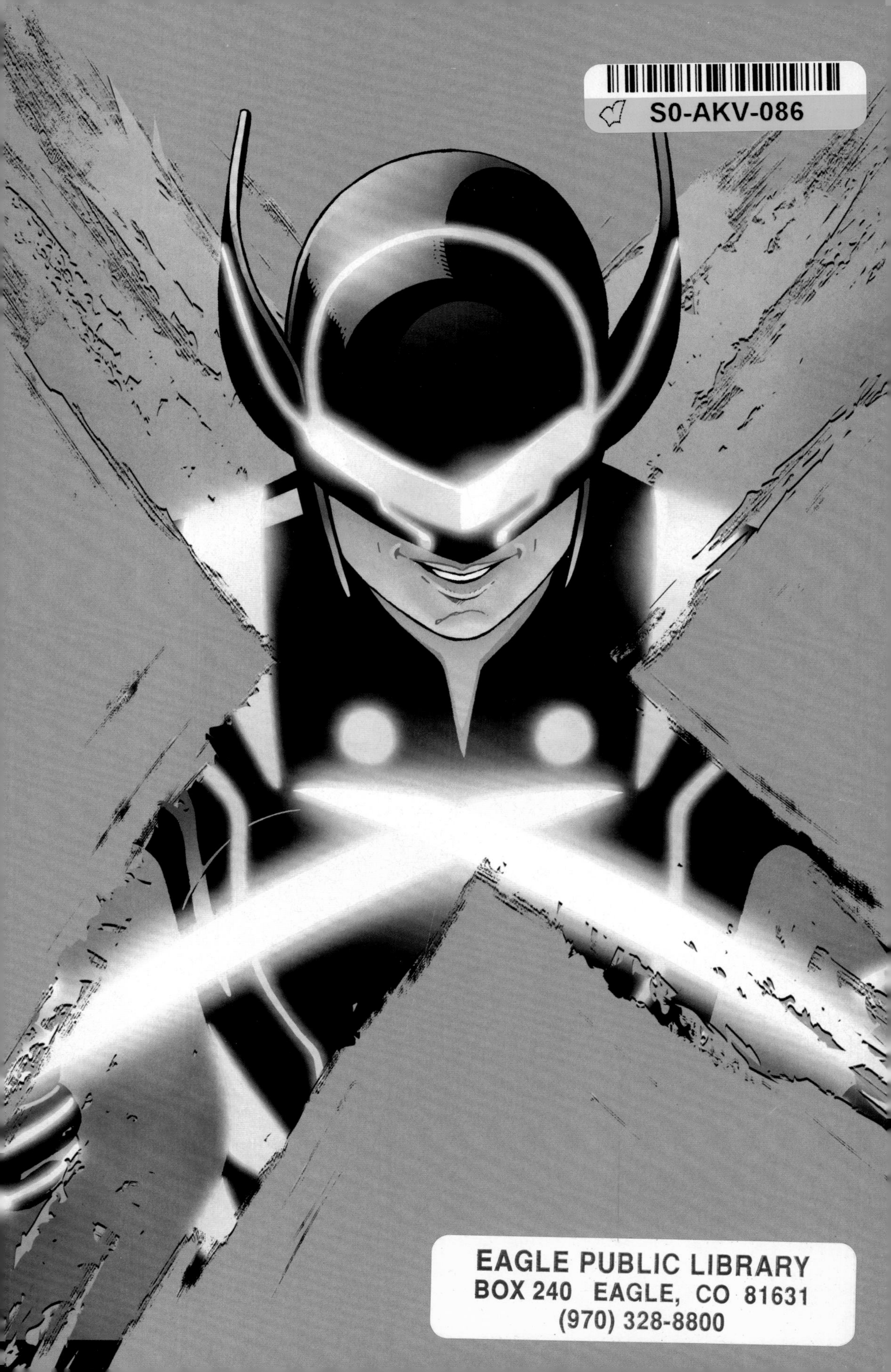

collection editor **JENNIFER GRÜNWALD**
assistant editor **CAITLIN O'CONNELL**
associate managing editor **KATERI WOODY**
editor, special projects **MARK D. BEAZLEY**
vp production & special projects **JEFF YOUNGQUIST**
svp print, sales & marketing **DAVID GABRIEL**
book designers **JAY BOWEN** & **ADAM DEL RE**

editor in chief **C.B. CEBULSKI**
chief creative officer **JOE QUESADA**
president **DAN BUCKLEY**
executive producer **ALAN FINE**

ALL-NEW WOLVERINE VOL. 6: OLD WOMAN LAURA. Contains material originally published in magazine form as ALL-NEW WOLVERINE #31-35. First printing 2018. ISBN 978-1-302-91110-2. Published by MARVEL WORLDWIDE, INC., a subsidiary of MARVEL ENTERTAINMENT, LLC. OFFICE OF PUBLICATION: 135 West 50th Street, New York, NY 10020. Copyright © 2018 MARVEL No similarity between any of the names, characters, persons, and/or institutions in this magazine with those of any living or dead person or institution is intended, and any such similarity which may exist is purely coincidental. **Printed in Canada.** DAN BUCKLEY, President, Marvel Entertainment; JOHN NEE, Publisher; JOE QUESADA, Chief Creative Officer; TOM BREVOORT, SVP of Publishing; DAVID BOGART, SVP of Business Affairs & Operations, Publishing & Partnership; DAVID GABRIEL, SVP of Sales & Marketing, Publishing; JEFF YOUNGQUIST, VP of Production & Special Projects; DAN CARR, Executive Director of Publishing Technology; ALEX MORALES, Director of Publishing Operations; DAN EDINGTON, Managing Editor; SUSAN CRESPI, Production Manager; STAN LEE, Chairman Emeritus. For information regarding advertising in Marvel Comics or on Marvel.com, please contact Vit DeBellis, Custom Solutions & Integrated Advertising Manager, at vdebellis@marvel.com. For Marvel subscription inquiries, please call 888-511-5480. **Manufactured between 5/18/2018 and 6/19/2018 by SOLISCO PRINTERS, SCOTT, QC, CANADA.**

10 9 8 7 6 5 4 3 2 1

X-23 WAS CREATED TO BE A WEAPON.
For a time, that's all she was. But Laura Kinney escaped that life with the help of the man she was cloned from, the man who became her mentor: THE WOLVERINE. Tragically, the original Wolverine has fallen, but Laura will live as his legacy, and fight for her better future. She is the...

ALL-NEW WOLVERINE

OLD WOMAN LAURA

Gabby Kinney, A.K.A. Honey Badger, is a preteen clone of Laura Kinney. Gabby does not feel pain, is able to heal quickly and has a single claw in each hand. Gabby is as deadly as she is cute, and loves to spend time with her pet wolverine named Jonathan.

Deadpool, A.K.A. the Merc with the Mouth, A.K.A. Wade Wilson, is one of the best and most annoying mercenaries in the world. Wade has an incredible healing factor and skin like Swiss cheese. Deadpool is as deadly as he is disgusting, and loves to spendtime with all of his guns.

Despite their differences, Gabby and Wade are friends.Best friends, in fact.

writer
TOM TAYLOR

artists
**MARCO FAILLA (#31),
DJIBRIL MORISSETTE-PHAN (#32)
& RAMON ROSANAS (#33-35)**

color artist
NOLAN WOODARD

letterer
VC's CORY PETIT

cover art
DAVID LOPEZ

assistant editor
TOM GRONEMAN

editors
CHRISTINA HARRINGTON & MARK PANICCIA

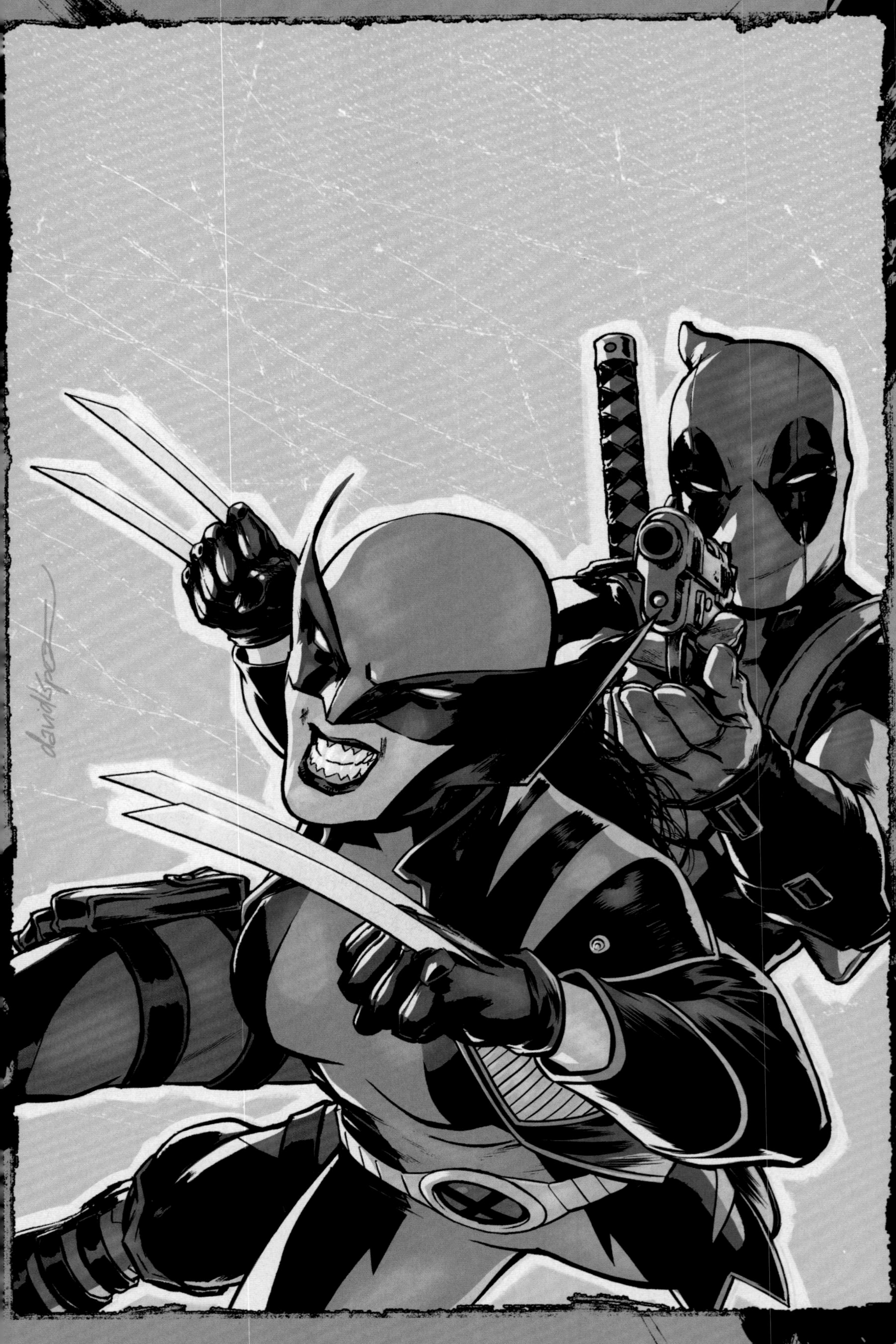

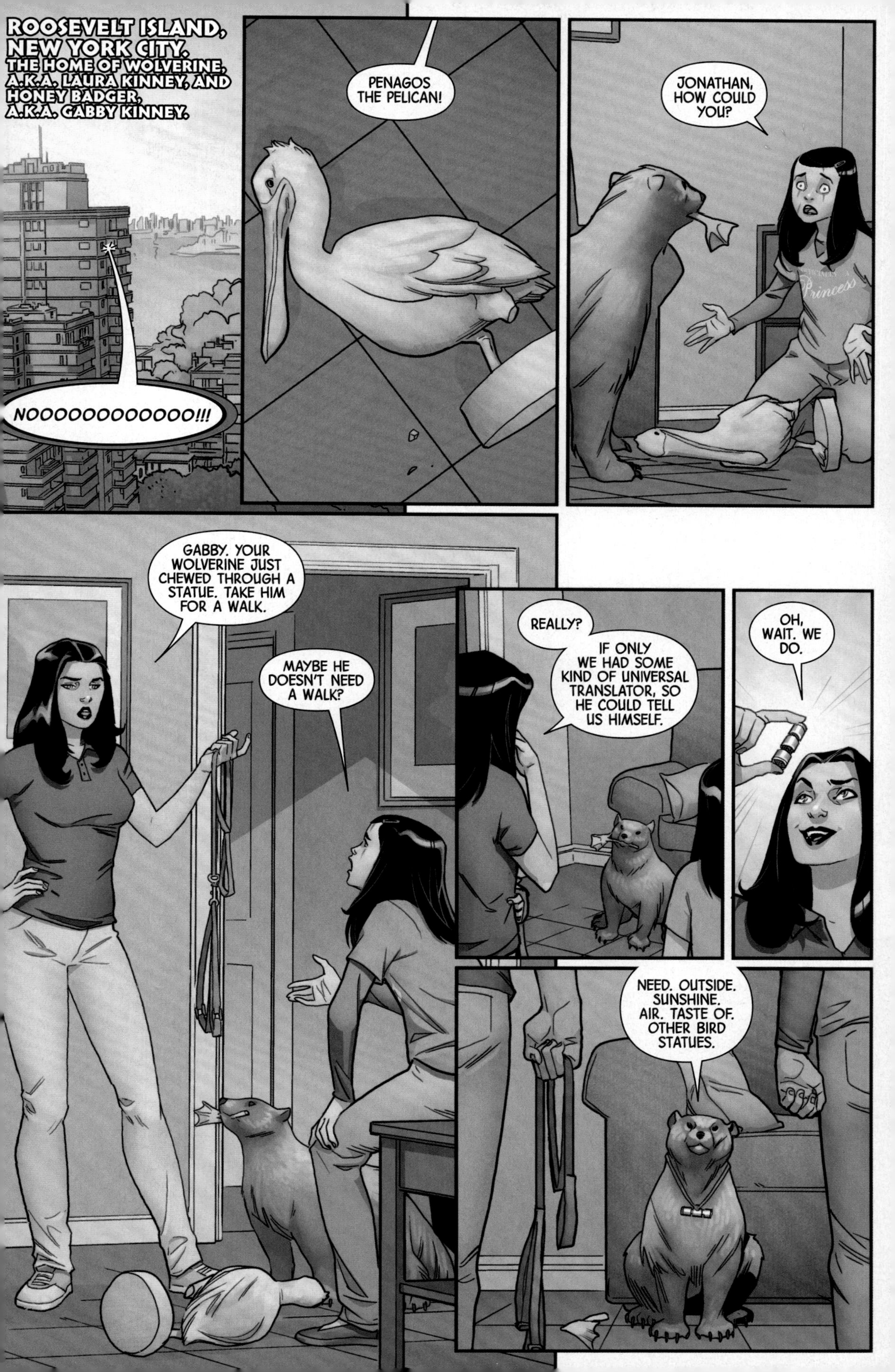
ROOSEVELT ISLAND, NEW YORK CITY.
THE HOME OF WOLVERINE, A.K.A. LAURA KINNEY, AND HONEY BADGER, A.K.A. GABBY KINNEY.
NOOOOOOOOOOOO!!!
PENAGOS THE PELICAN!
JONATHAN, HOW COULD YOU?
GABBY. YOUR WOLVERINE JUST CHEWED THROUGH A STATUE. TAKE HIM FOR A WALK.
MAYBE HE DOESN'T NEED A WALK?
REALLY?
IF ONLY WE HAD SOME KIND OF UNIVERSAL TRANSLATOR, SO HE COULD TELL US HIMSELF.
OH, WAIT. WE DO.
NEED. OUTSIDE. SUNSHINE. AIR. TASTE OF. OTHER BIRD STATUES.

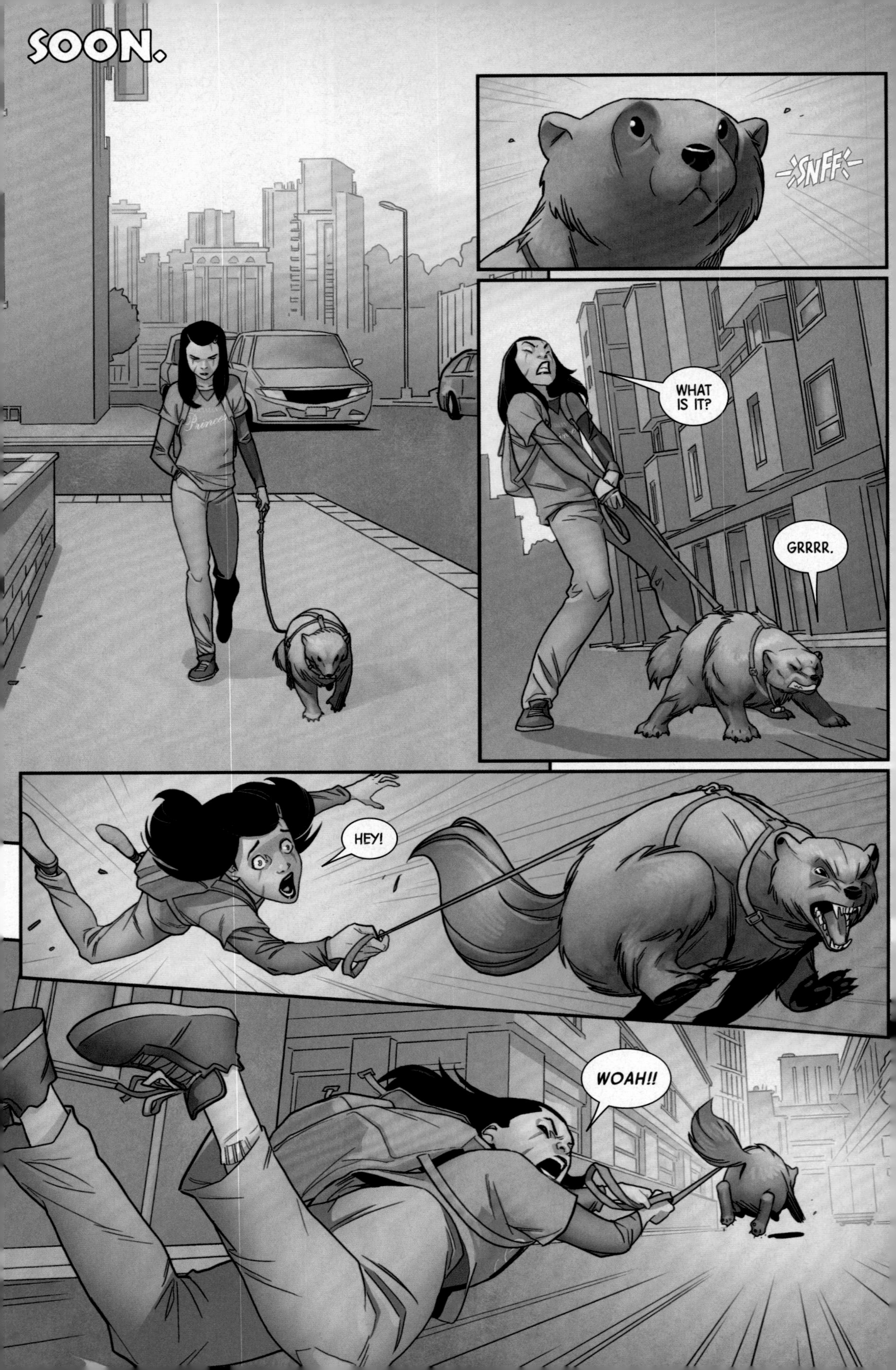
SOON.
SNFF
WHAT IS IT?
GRRRR.
HEY!
WOAH!!

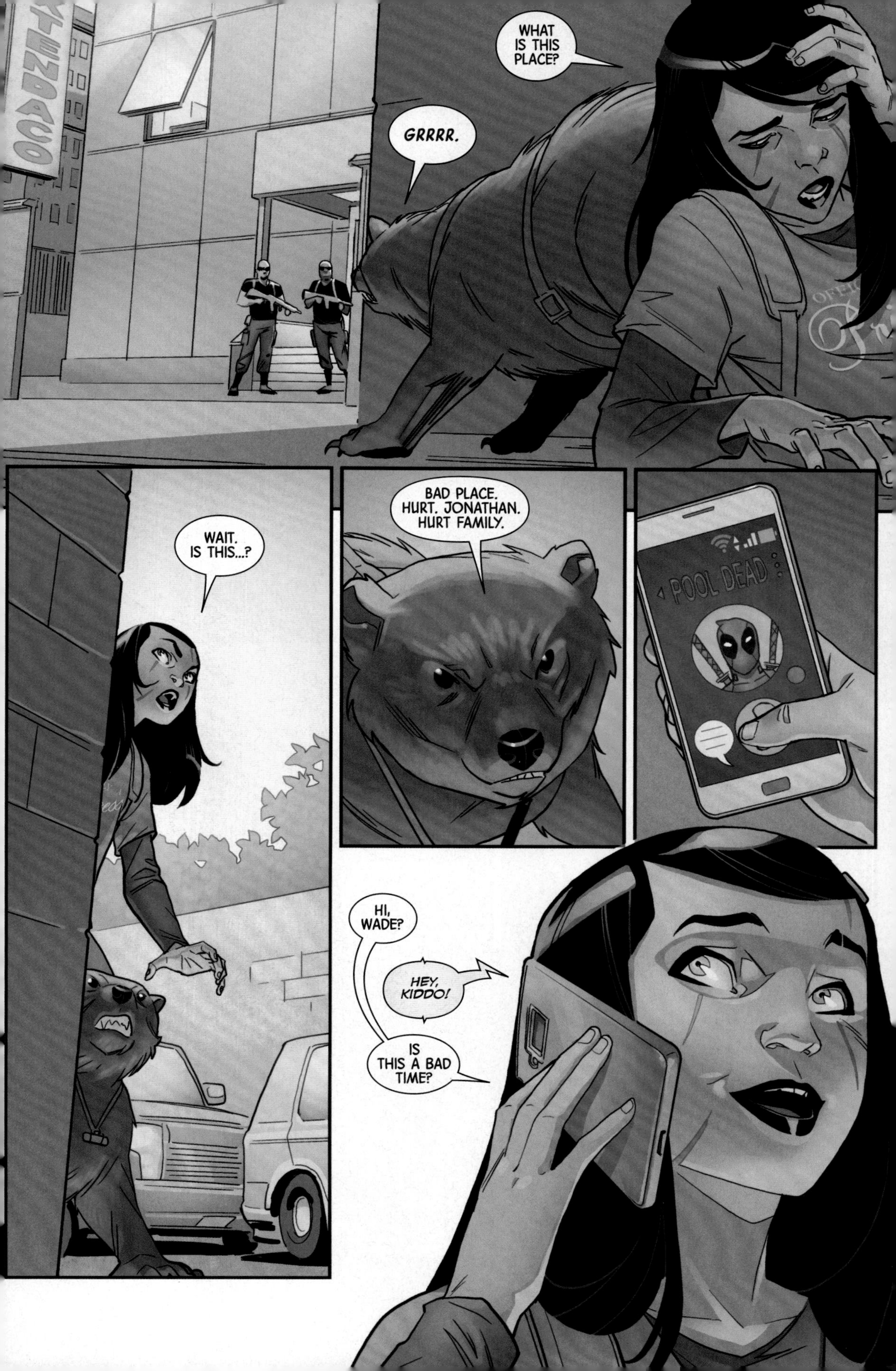

WHAT IS THIS PLACE?
GRRRR.
WAIT. IS THIS...?
BAD PLACE. HURT. JONATHAN. HURT FAMILY.
POOL DEAD
HI, WADE?
HEY, KIDDO!
IS THIS A BAD TIME?

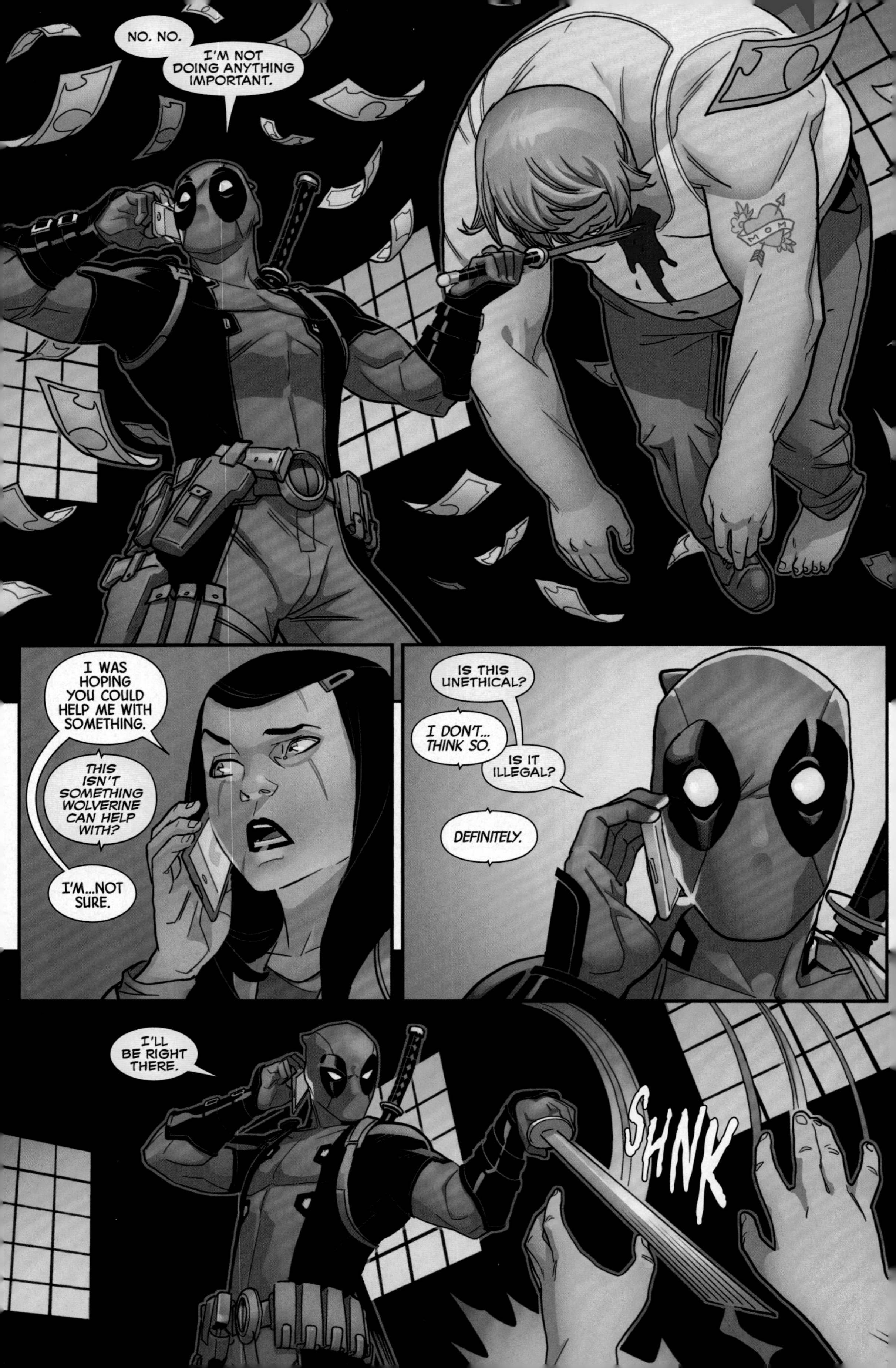
NO. NO.
I'M NOT DOING ANYTHING IMPORTANT.
I WAS HOPING YOU COULD HELP ME WITH SOMETHING.
THIS ISN'T SOMETHING WOLVERINE CAN HELP WITH?
I'M...NOT SURE.
IS THIS UNETHICAL?
I DON'T... THINK SO.
IS IT ILLEGAL?
DEFINITELY.
I'LL BE RIGHT THERE.
SHNK

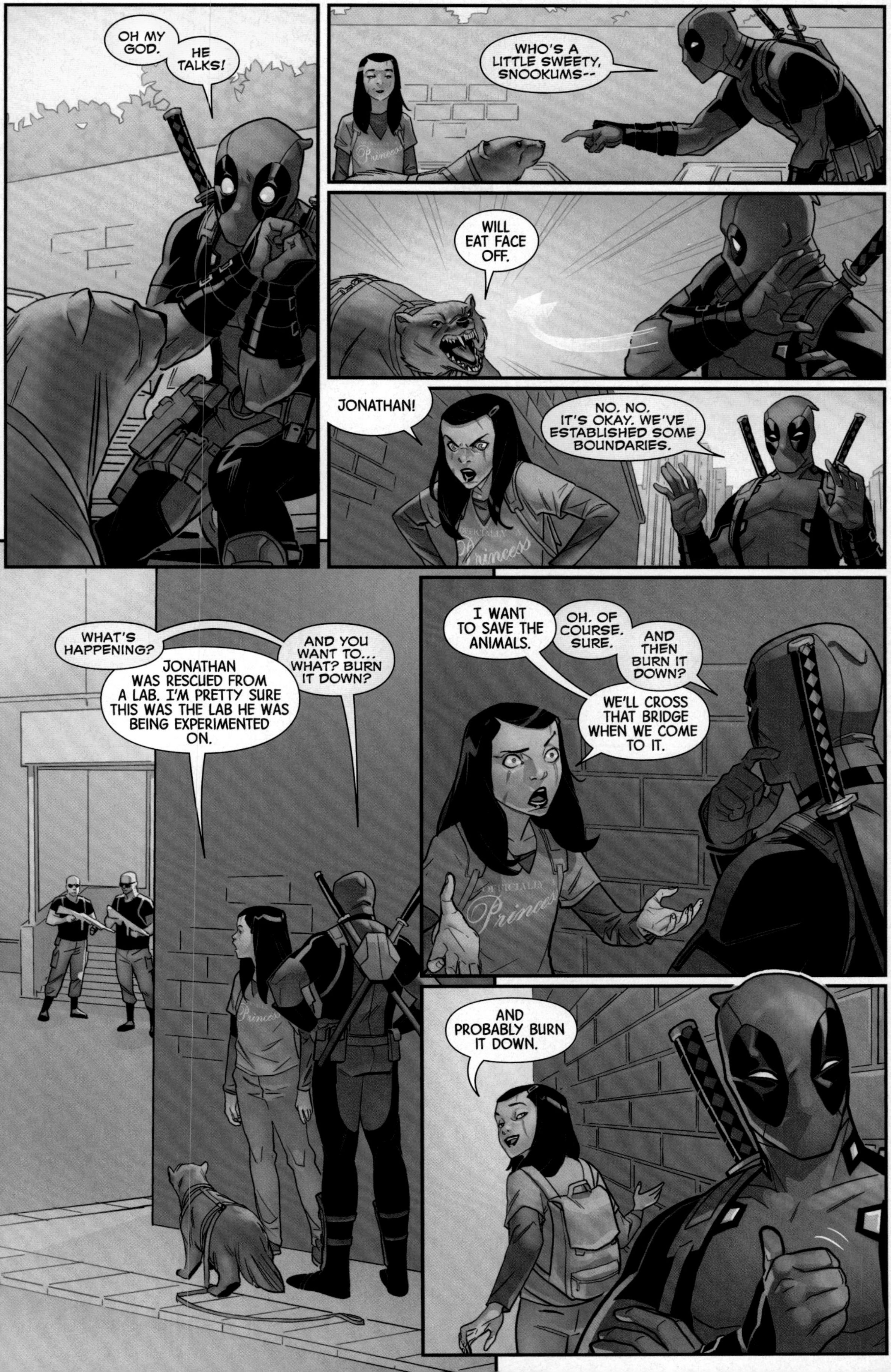

OH MY GOD.
HE TALKS!
WHO'S A LITTLE SWEETY, SNOOKUMS--
WILL EAT FACE OFF.
JONATHAN!
NO. NO. IT'S OKAY. WE'VE ESTABLISHED SOME BOUNDARIES.
WHAT'S HAPPENING?
JONATHAN WAS RESCUED FROM A LAB. I'M PRETTY SURE THIS WAS THE LAB HE WAS BEING EXPERIMENTED ON.
AND YOU WANT TO... WHAT? BURN IT DOWN?
I WANT TO SAVE THE ANIMALS.
OH. OF COURSE. SURE.
AND THEN BURN IT DOWN?
WE'LL CROSS THAT BRIDGE WHEN WE COME TO IT.
AND PROBABLY BURN IT DOWN.

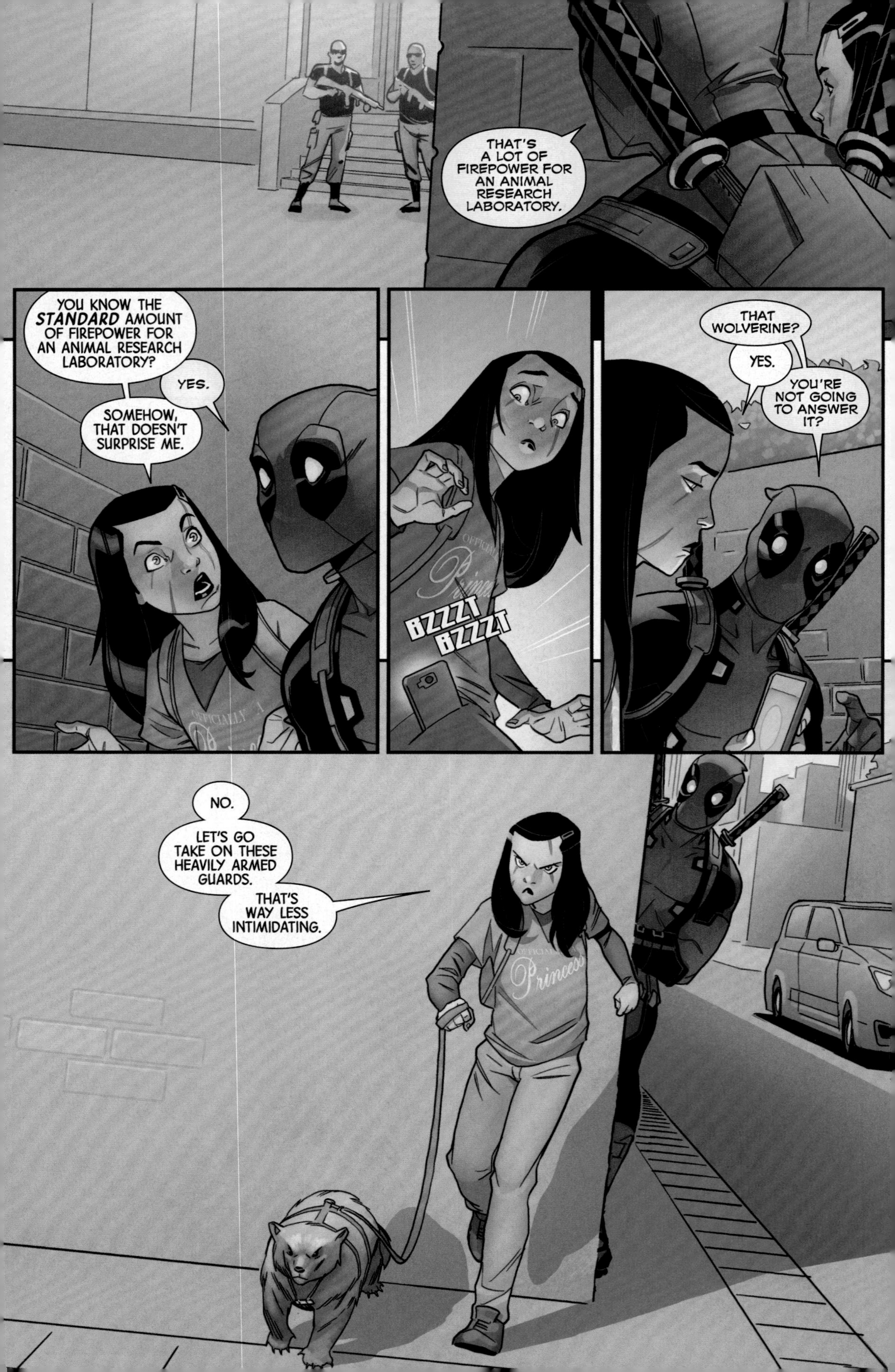
THAT'S A LOT OF FIREPOWER FOR AN ANIMAL RESEARCH LABORATORY.
YOU KNOW THE STANDARD AMOUNT OF FIREPOWER FOR AN ANIMAL RESEARCH LABORATORY?
YES.
SOMEHOW, THAT DOESN'T SURPRISE ME.
BZZZT BZZZT
THAT WOLVERINE?
YES.
YOU'RE NOT GOING TO ANSWER IT?
NO.
LET'S GO TAKE ON THESE HEAVILY ARMED GUARDS.
THAT'S WAY LESS INTIMIDATING.

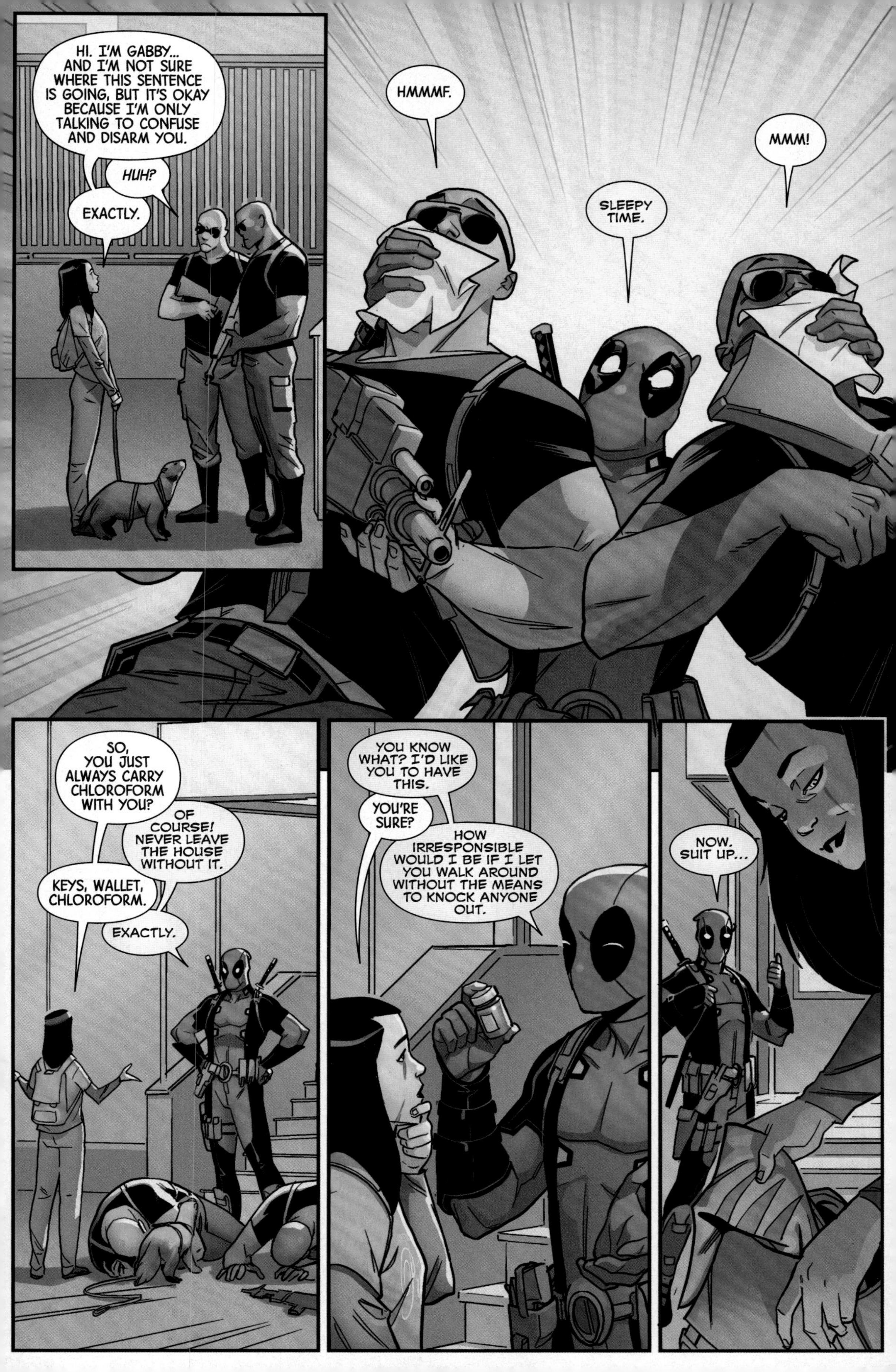
HI. I'M GABBY... AND I'M NOT SURE WHERE THIS SENTENCE IS GOING, BUT IT'S OKAY BECAUSE I'M ONLY TALKING TO CONFUSE AND DISARM YOU.
HUH?
EXACTLY.
HMMMF.
SLEEPY TIME.
MMM!
SO, YOU JUST ALWAYS CARRY CHLOROFORM WITH YOU?
OF COURSE! NEVER LEAVE THE HOUSE WITHOUT IT.
KEYS, WALLET, CHLOROFORM.
EXACTLY.
YOU KNOW WHAT? I'D LIKE YOU TO HAVE THIS.
YOU'RE SURE?
HOW IRRESPONSIBLE WOULD I BE IF I LET YOU WALK AROUND WITHOUT THE MEANS TO KNOCK ANYONE OUT.
NOW. SUIT UP...

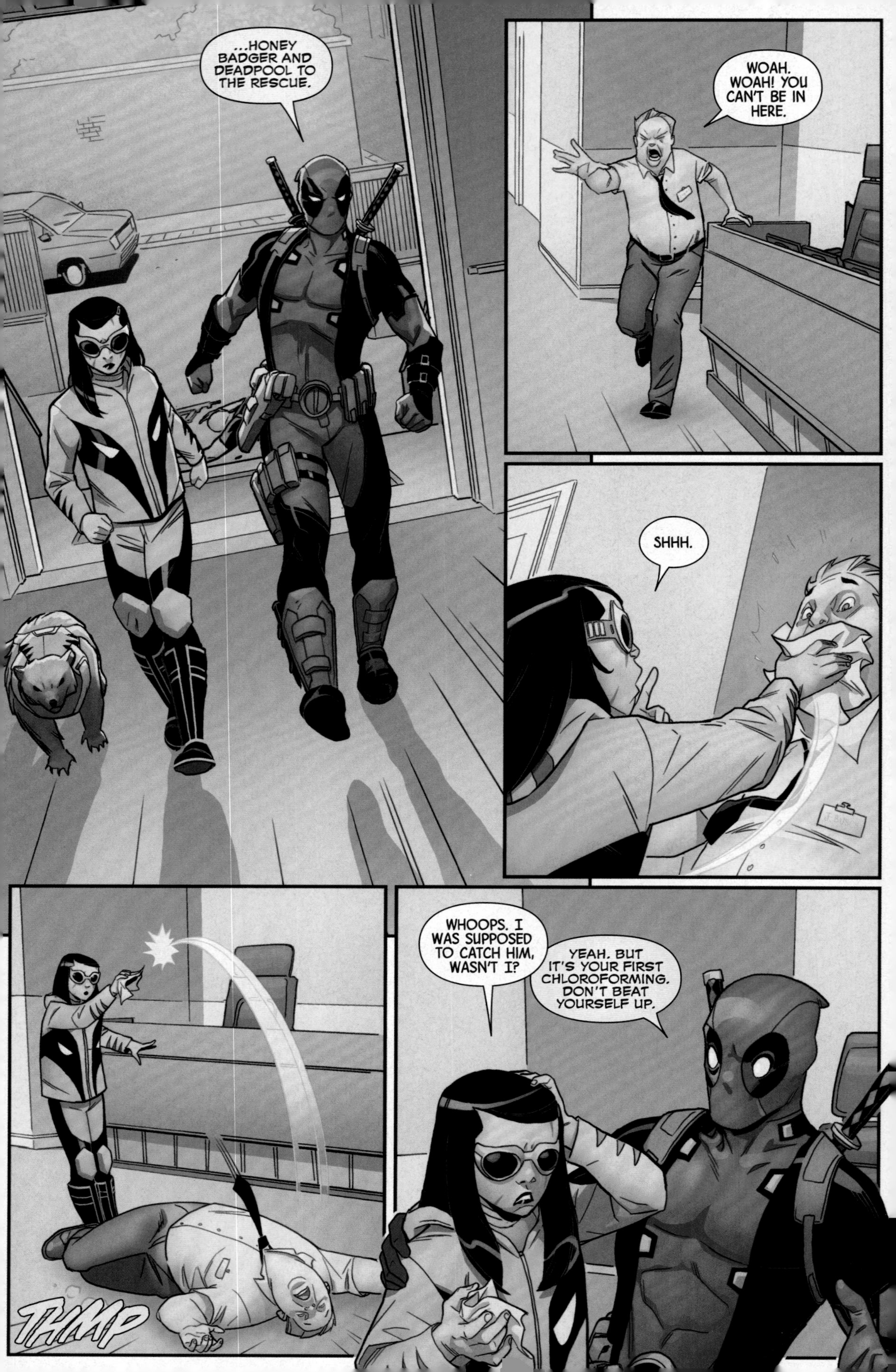
...HONEY BADGER AND DEADPOOL TO THE RESCUE.
WOAH. WOAH! YOU CAN'T BE IN HERE.
SHHH.
THMP
WHOOPS. I WAS SUPPOSED TO CATCH HIM, WASN'T I?
YEAH. BUT IT'S YOUR FIRST CHLOROFORMING. DON'T BEAT YOURSELF UP.

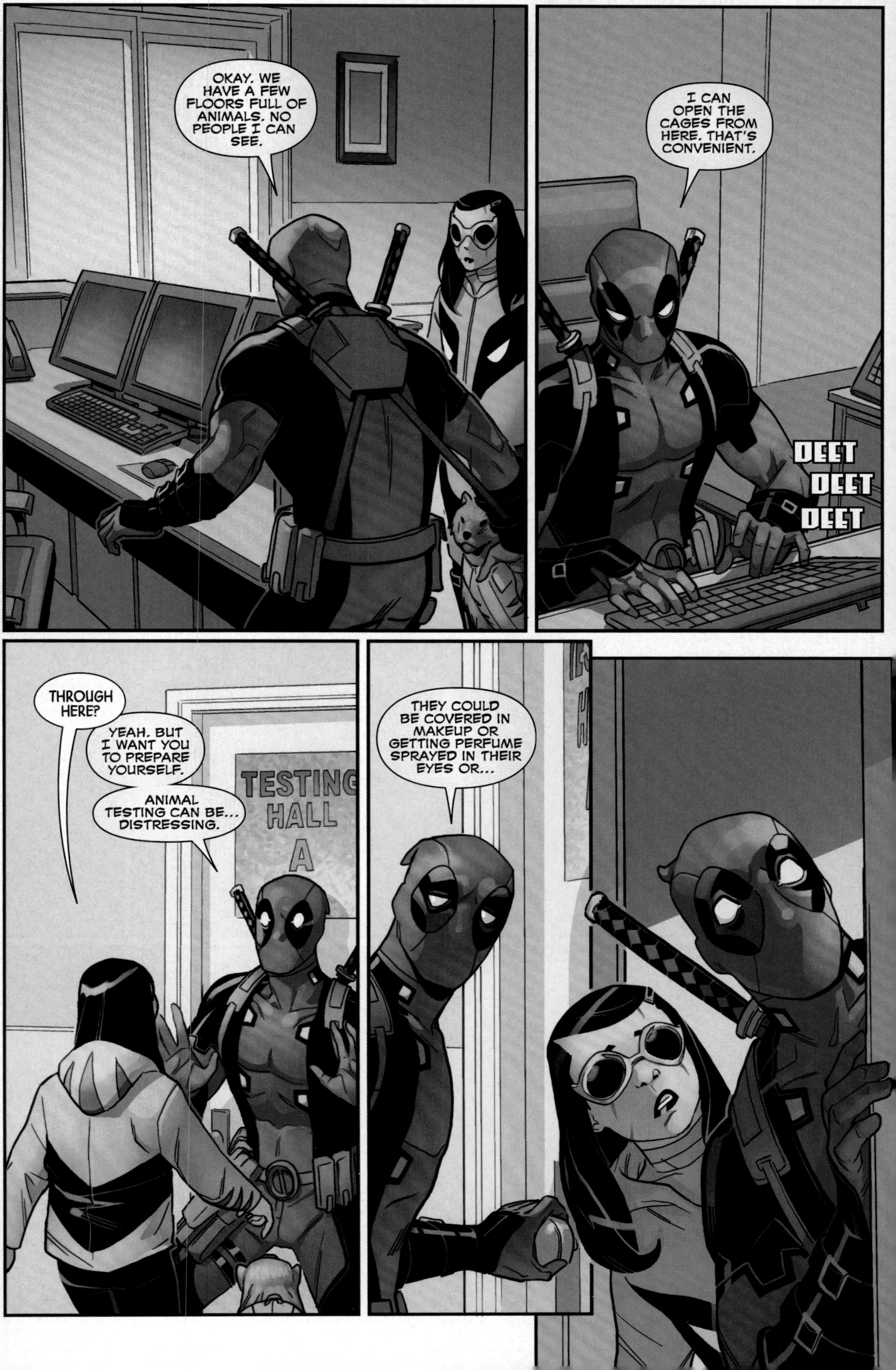
OKAY. WE HAVE A FEW FLOORS FULL OF ANIMALS. NO PEOPLE I CAN SEE.
I CAN OPEN THE CAGES FROM HERE. THAT'S CONVENIENT.
DEET
DEET
DEET
THROUGH HERE?
YEAH. BUT I WANT YOU TO PREPARE YOURSELF.
ANIMAL TESTING CAN BE... DISTRESSING.
TESTING HALL A
THEY COULD BE COVERED IN MAKEUP OR GETTING PERFUME SPRAYED IN THEIR EYES OR...

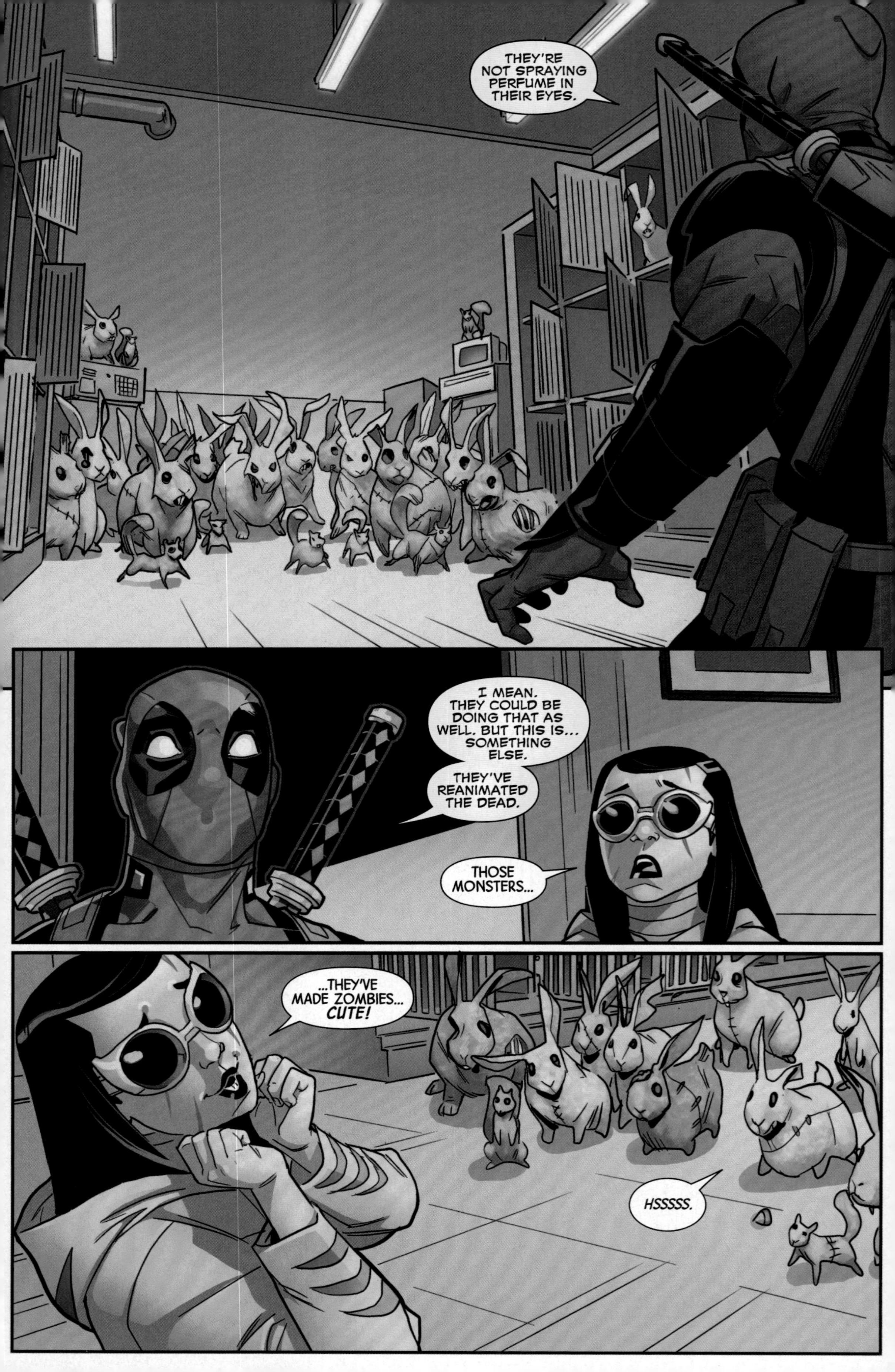
THEY'RE NOT SPRAYING PERFUME IN THEIR EYES.
I MEAN. THEY COULD BE DOING THAT AS WELL. BUT THIS IS... SOMETHING ELSE.
THEY'VE REANIMATED THE DEAD.
THOSE MONSTERS...
...THEY'VE MADE ZOMBIES... CUTE!
HSSSSS.

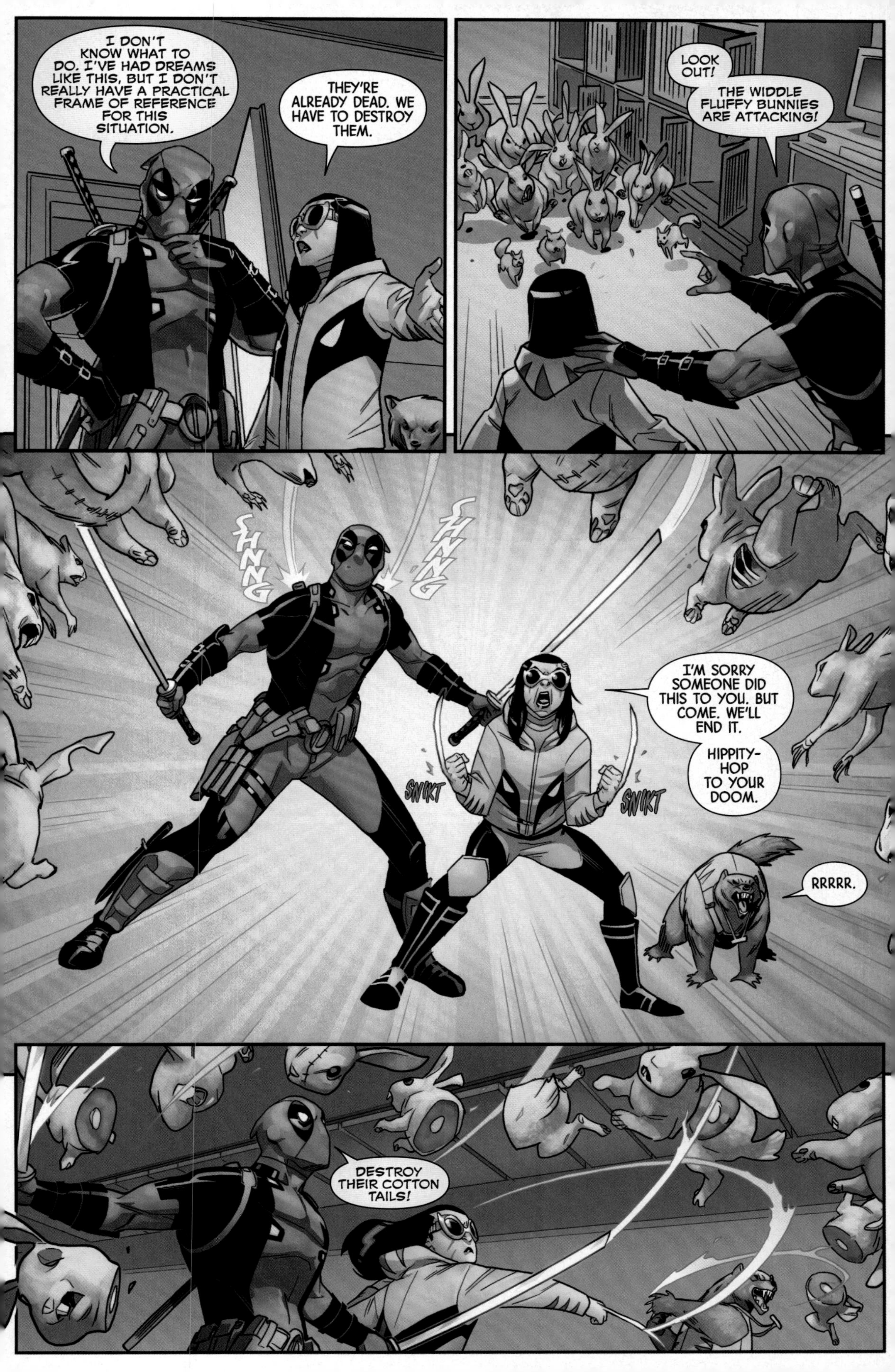
I DON'T KNOW WHAT TO DO. I'VE HAD DREAMS LIKE THIS, BUT I DON'T REALLY HAVE A PRACTICAL FRAME OF REFERENCE FOR THIS SITUATION.
THEY'RE ALREADY DEAD. WE HAVE TO DESTROY THEM.
LOOK OUT!
THE WIDDLE FLUFFY BUNNIES ARE ATTACKING!
SHNNG
SHNNG
SNIKT
SNIKT
I'M SORRY SOMEONE DID THIS TO YOU. BUT COME. WE'LL END IT.
HIPPITY-HOP TO YOUR DOOM.
RRRRR.
DESTROY THEIR COTTON TAILS!

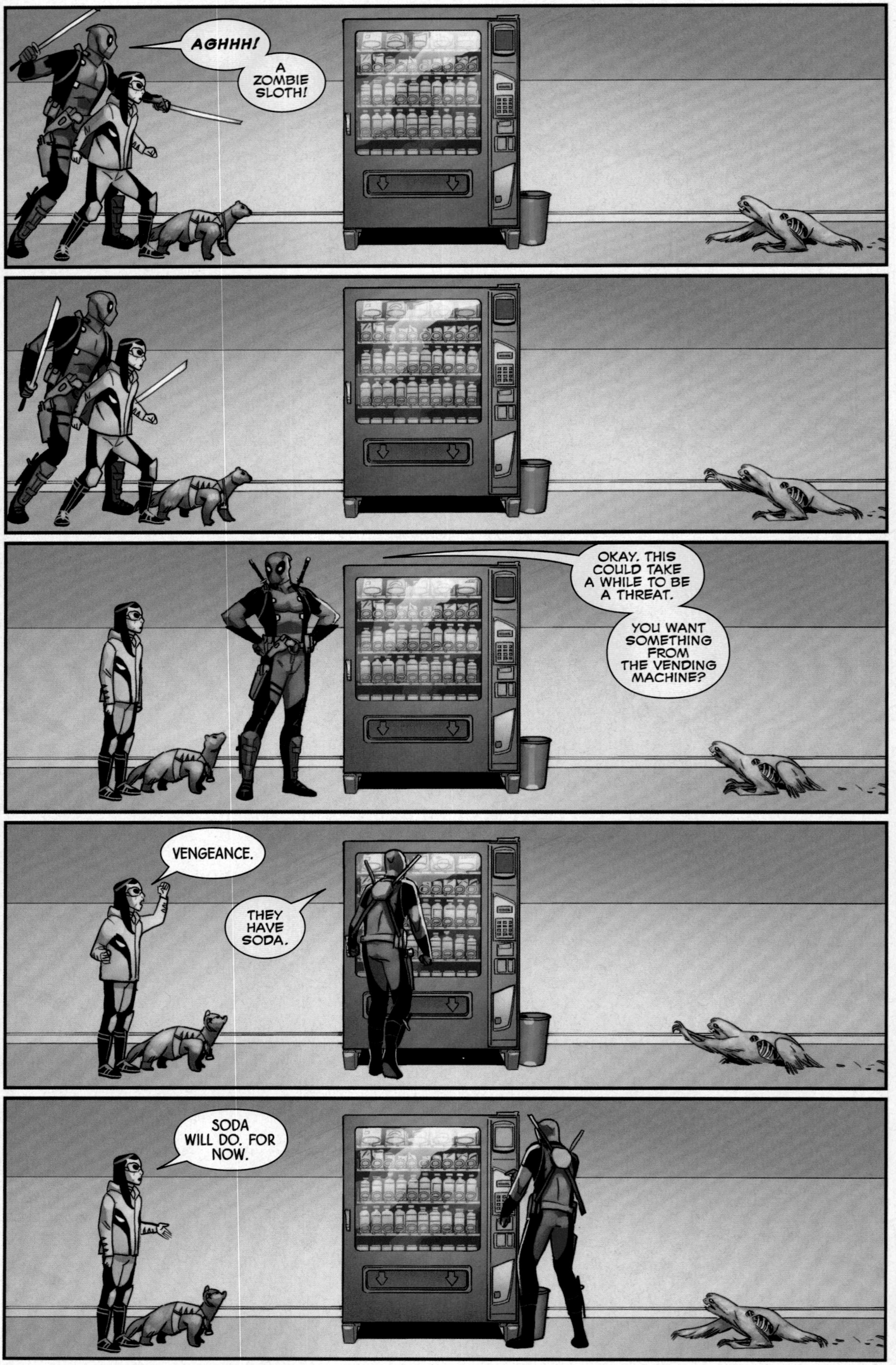

AGHHH!
A ZOMBIE SLOTH!
OKAY. THIS COULD TAKE A WHILE TO BE A THREAT.
YOU WANT SOMETHING FROM THE VENDING MACHINE?
VENGEANCE.
THEY HAVE SODA.
SODA WILL DO. FOR NOW.

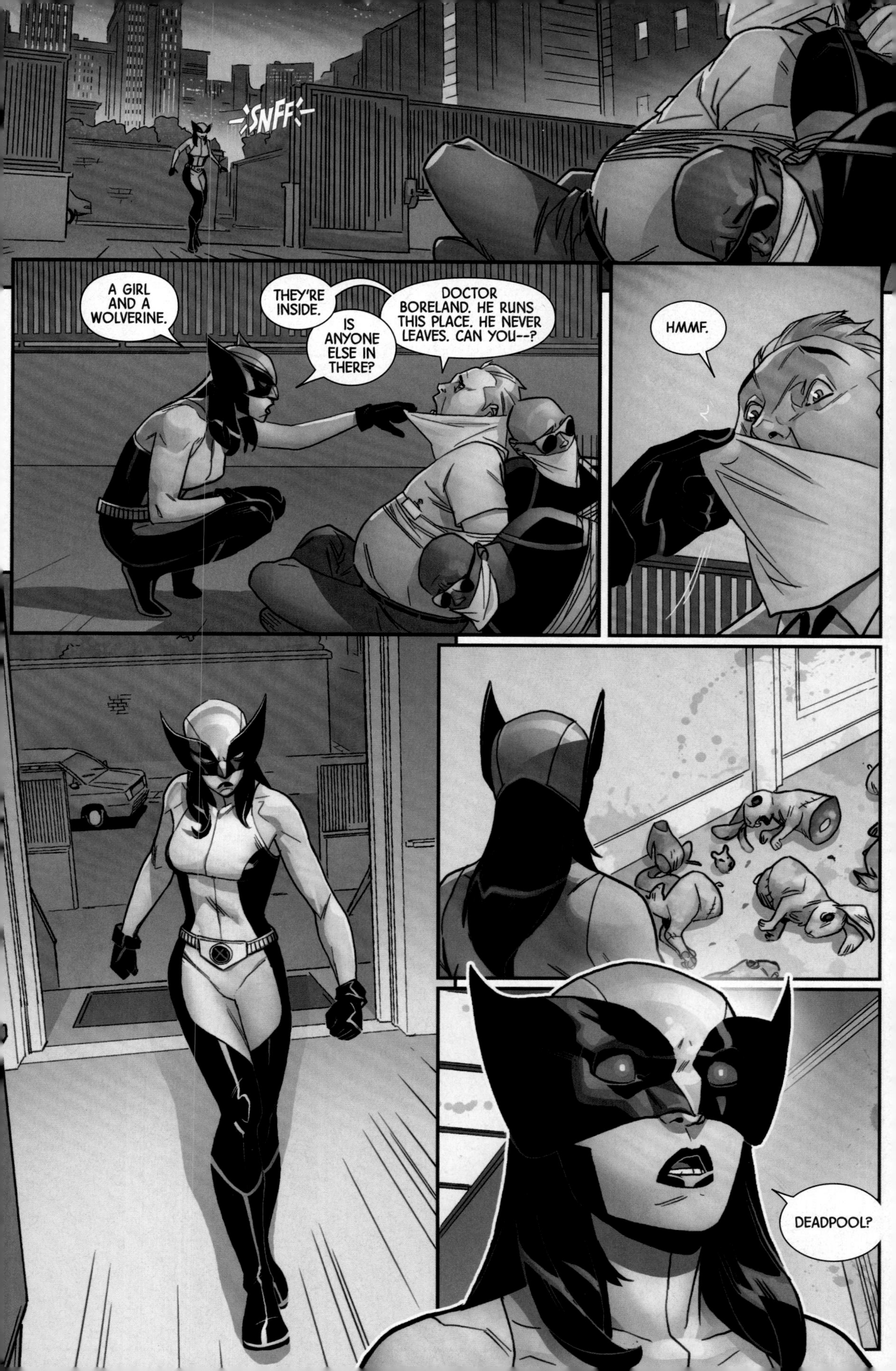

SNFF
A GIRL AND A WOLVERINE.
THEY'RE INSIDE.
IS ANYONE ELSE IN THERE?
DOCTOR BORELAND. HE RUNS THIS PLACE. HE NEVER LEAVES. CAN YOU--?
HMMF.
DEADPOOL?

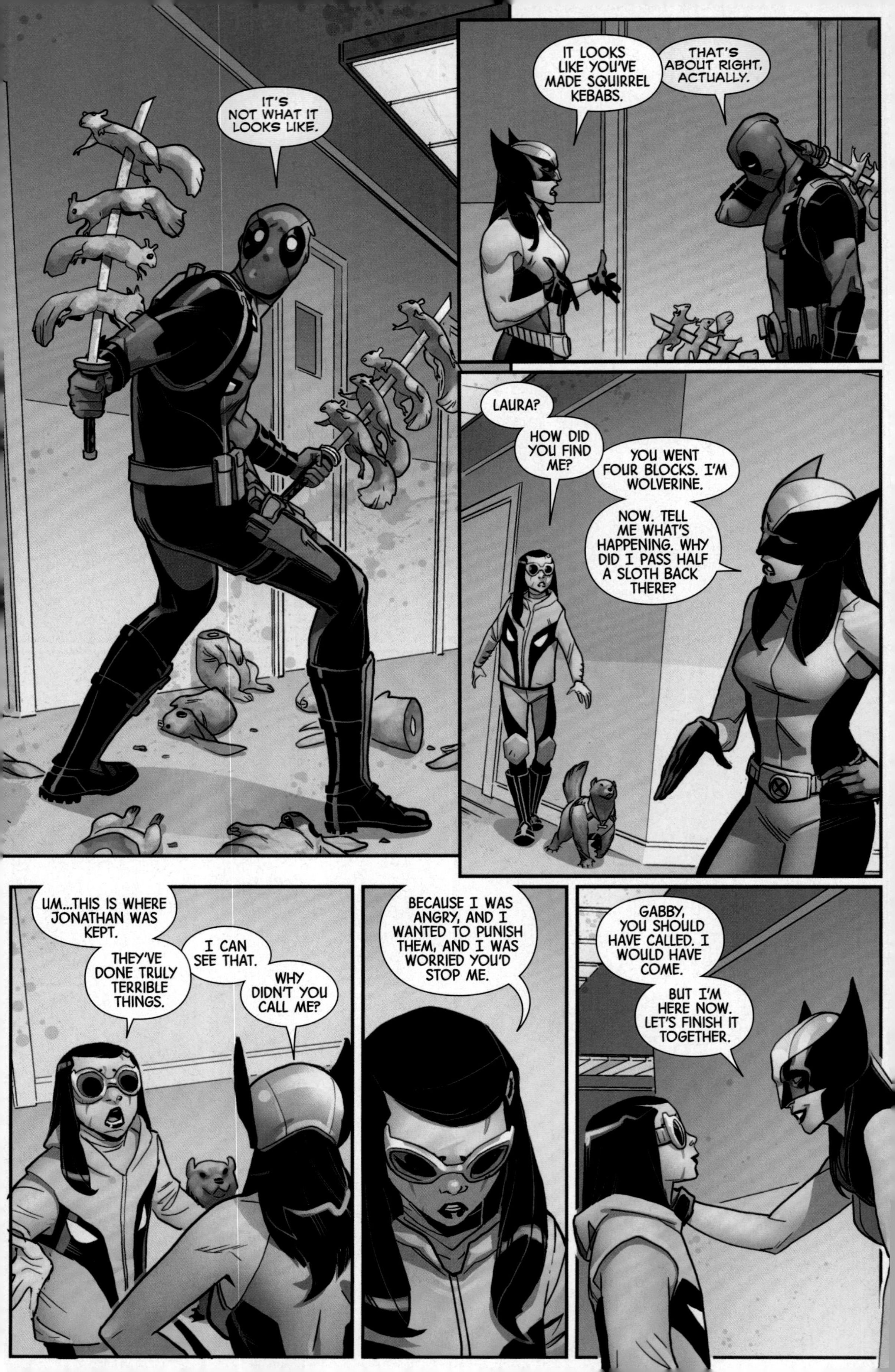

IT'S NOT WHAT IT LOOKS LIKE.
IT LOOKS LIKE YOU'VE MADE SQUIRREL KEBABS.
THAT'S ABOUT RIGHT, ACTUALLY.
LAURA?
HOW DID YOU FIND ME?
YOU WENT FOUR BLOCKS. I'M WOLVERINE.
NOW. TELL ME WHAT'S HAPPENING. WHY DID I PASS HALF A SLOTH BACK THERE?
UM...THIS IS WHERE JONATHAN WAS KEPT.
THEY'VE DONE TRULY TERRIBLE THINGS.
I CAN SEE THAT.
WHY DIDN'T YOU CALL ME?
BECAUSE I WAS ANGRY, AND I WANTED TO PUNISH THEM, AND I WAS WORRIED YOU'D STOP ME.
GABBY, YOU SHOULD HAVE CALLED. I WOULD HAVE COME.
BUT I'M HERE NOW. LET'S FINISH IT TOGETHER.

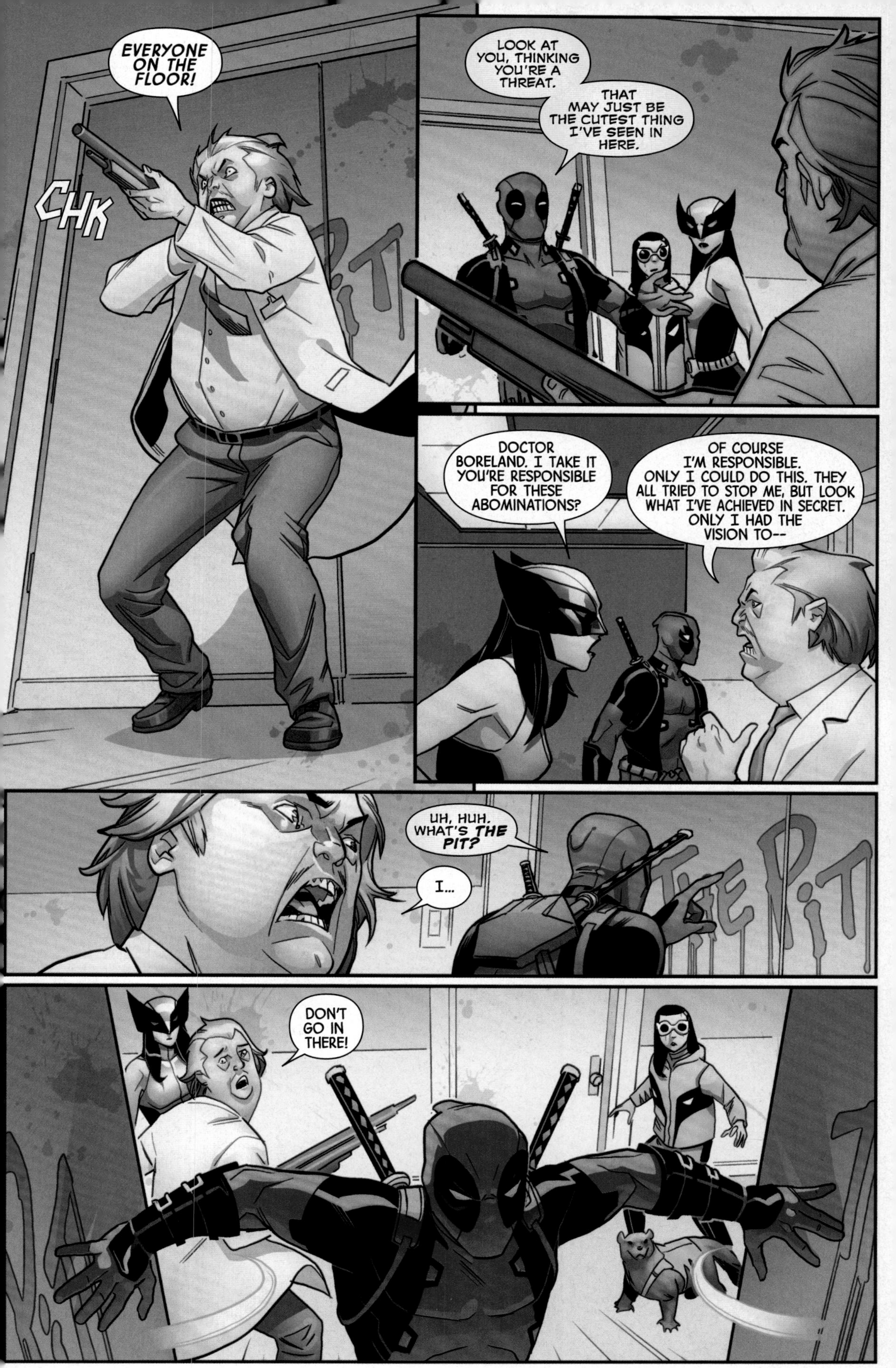
EVERYONE ON THE FLOOR!
CHK
LOOK AT YOU, THINKING YOU'RE A THREAT.
THAT MAY JUST BE THE CUTEST THING I'VE SEEN IN HERE.
DOCTOR BORELAND. I TAKE IT YOU'RE RESPONSIBLE FOR THESE ABOMINATIONS?
OF COURSE I'M RESPONSIBLE. ONLY I COULD DO THIS. THEY ALL TRIED TO STOP ME, BUT LOOK WHAT I'VE ACHIEVED IN SECRET. ONLY I HAD THE VISION TO--
UH, HUH. WHAT'S THE PIT?
I...
DON'T GO IN THERE!

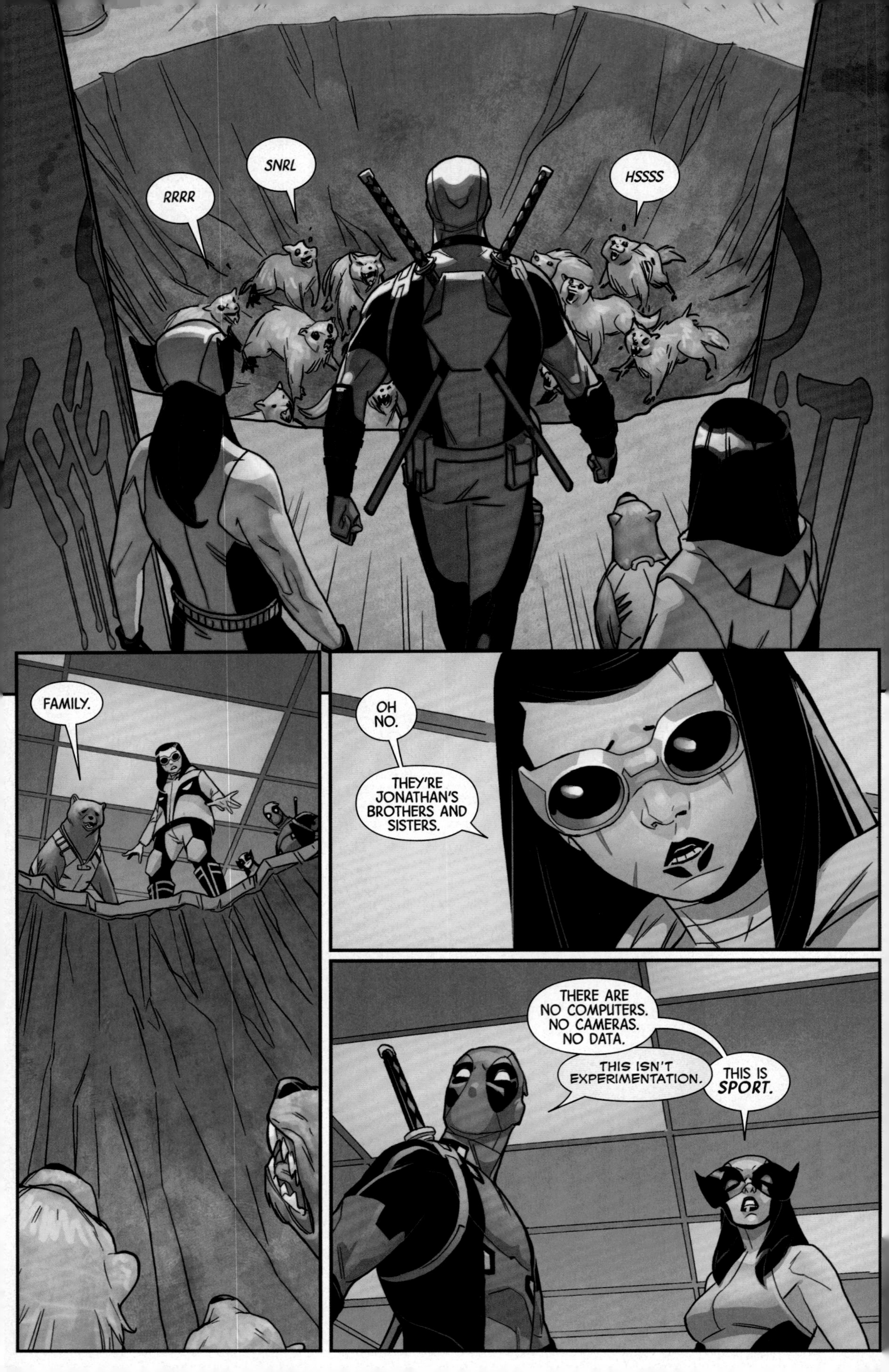
RRRR
SNRL
HSSSS
FAMILY.
OH NO.
THEY'RE JONATHAN'S BROTHERS AND SISTERS.
THERE ARE NO COMPUTERS. NO CAMERAS. NO DATA.
THIS ISN'T EXPERIMENTATION.
THIS IS SPORT.

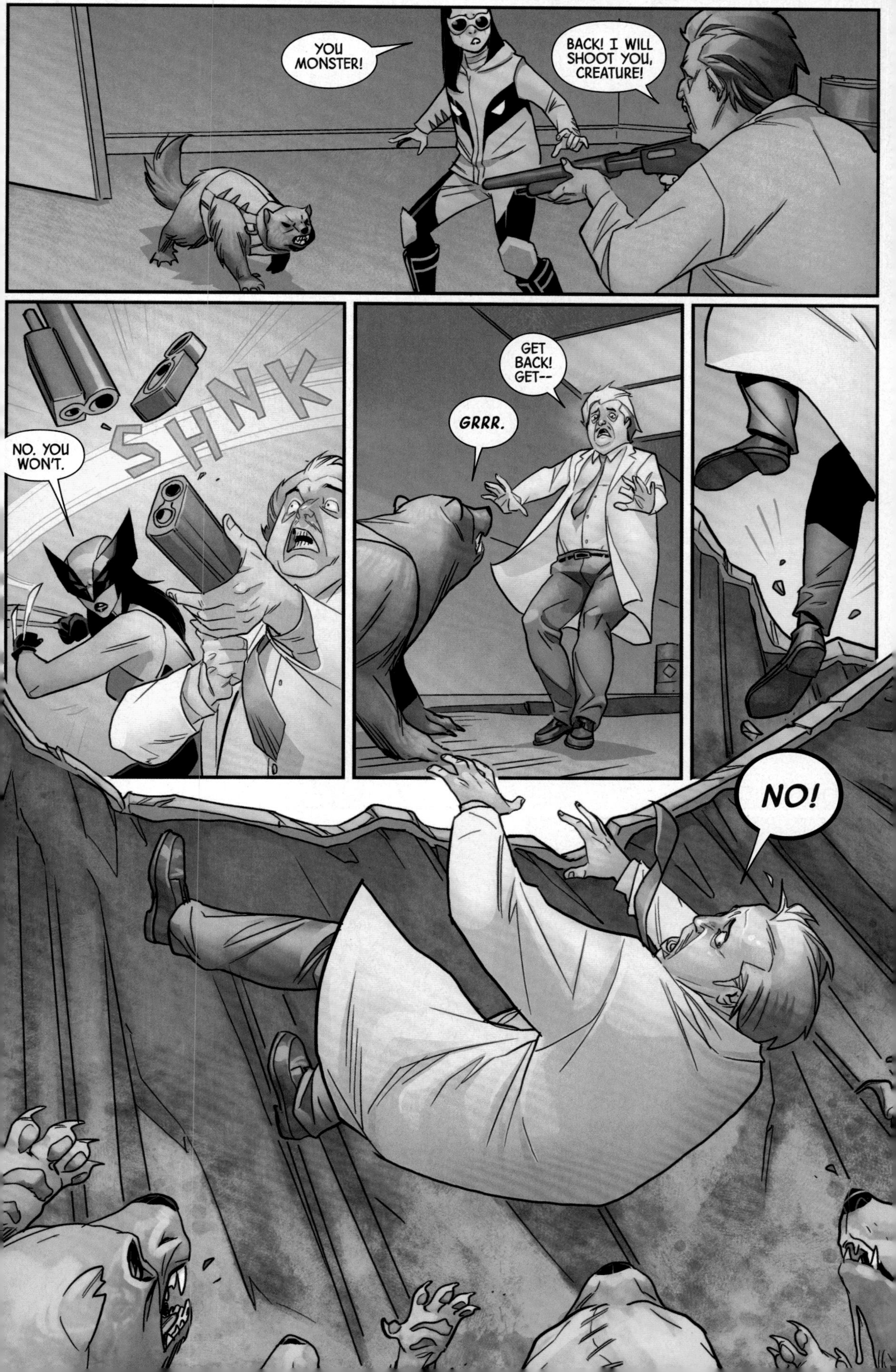
YOU MONSTER!
BACK! I WILL SHOOT YOU, CREATURE!
SHNK
NO. YOU WON'T.
GET BACK! GET--
GRRR.
NO!

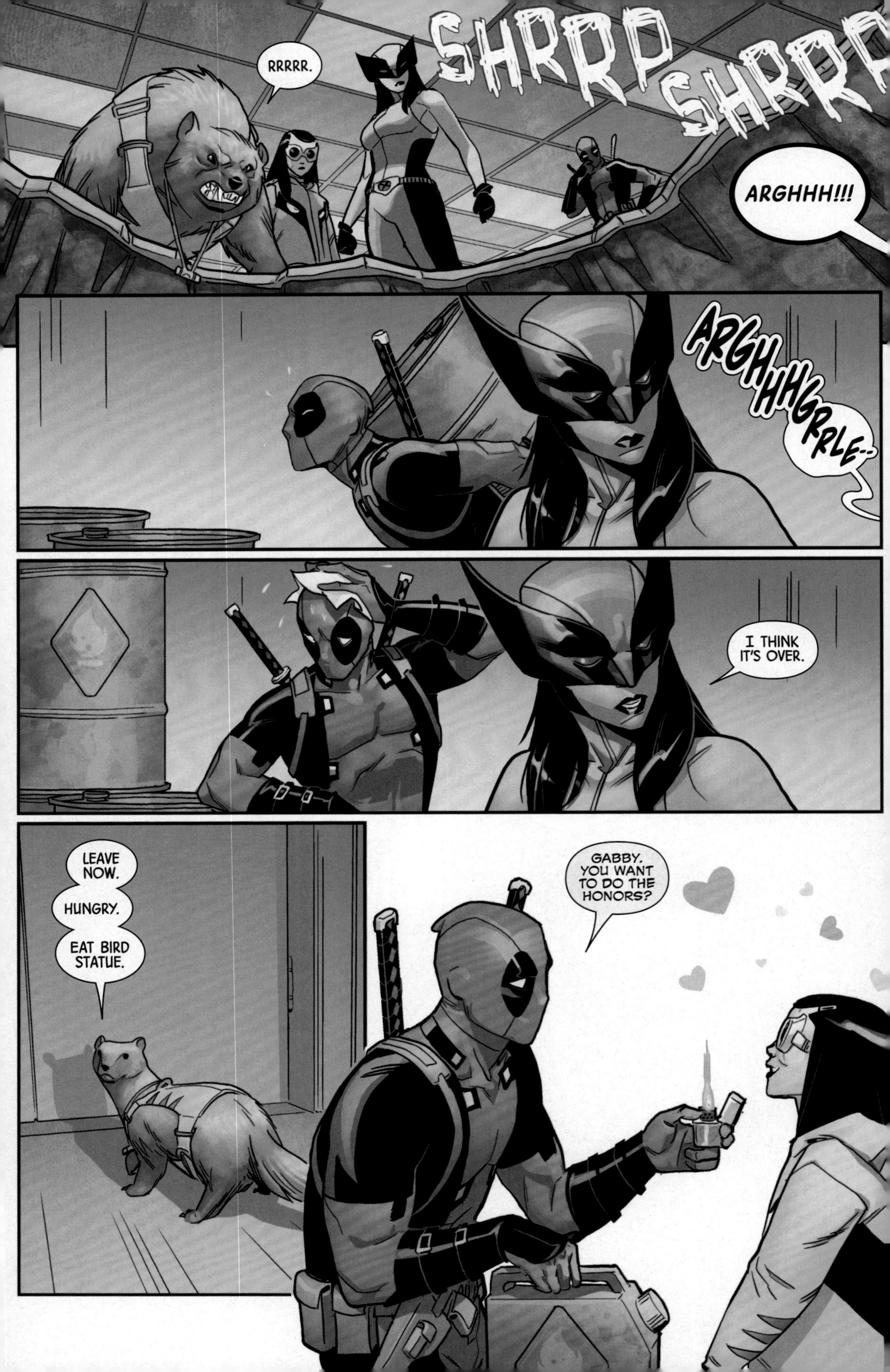
SHRRP SHRRP
RRRRR.
ARGHHH!!!
ARGHHHGRRLE--
I THINK IT'S OVER.
LEAVE NOW.
HUNGRY.
EAT BIRD STATUE.
GABBY. YOU WANT TO DO THE HONORS?

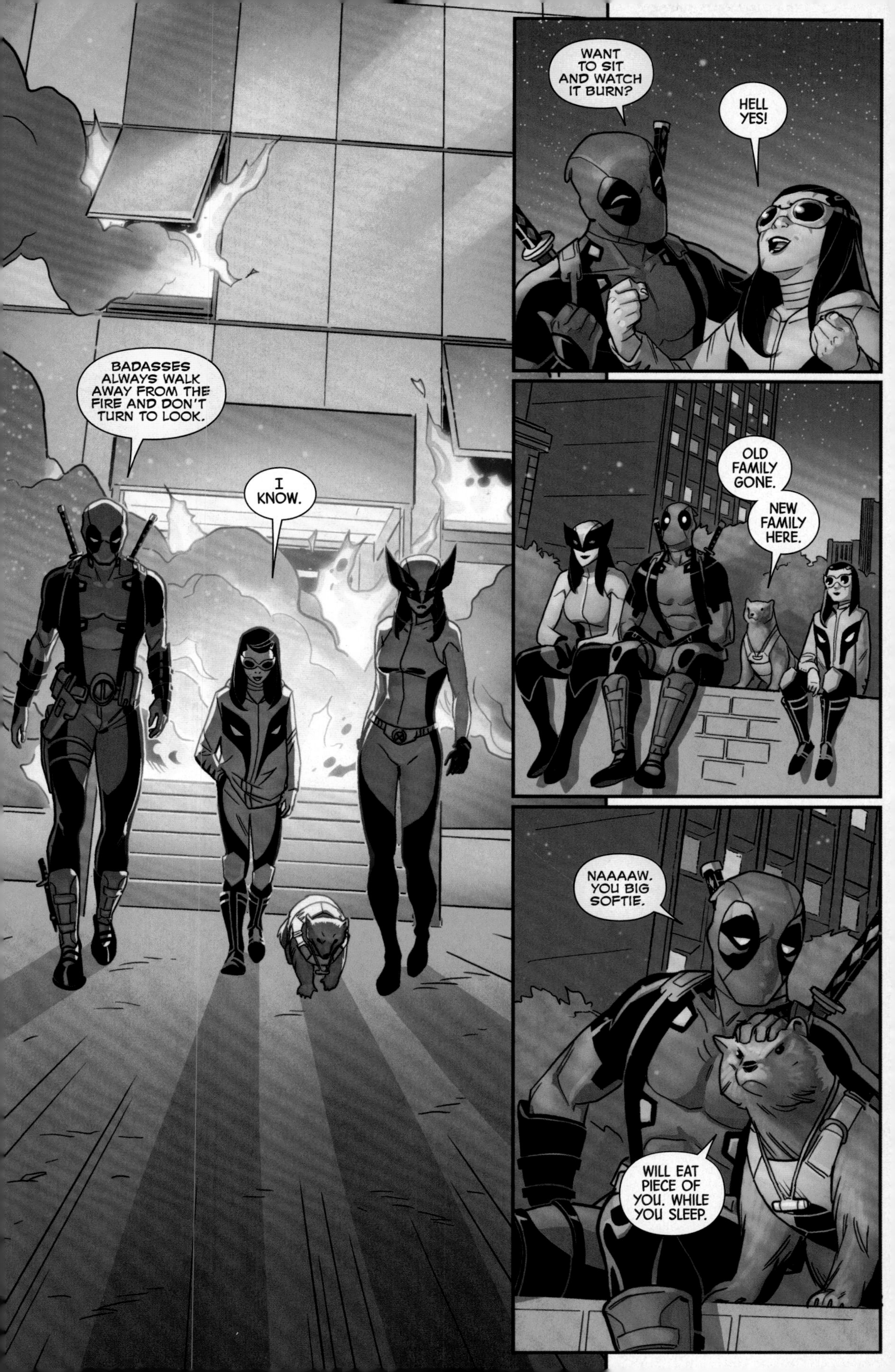
BADASSES ALWAYS WALK AWAY FROM THE FIRE AND DON'T TURN TO LOOK.
I KNOW.
WANT TO SIT AND WATCH IT BURN?
HELL YES!
OLD FAMILY GONE.
NEW FAMILY HERE.
NAAAAW. YOU BIG SOFTIE.
WILL EAT PIECE OF YOU. WHILE YOU SLEEP.

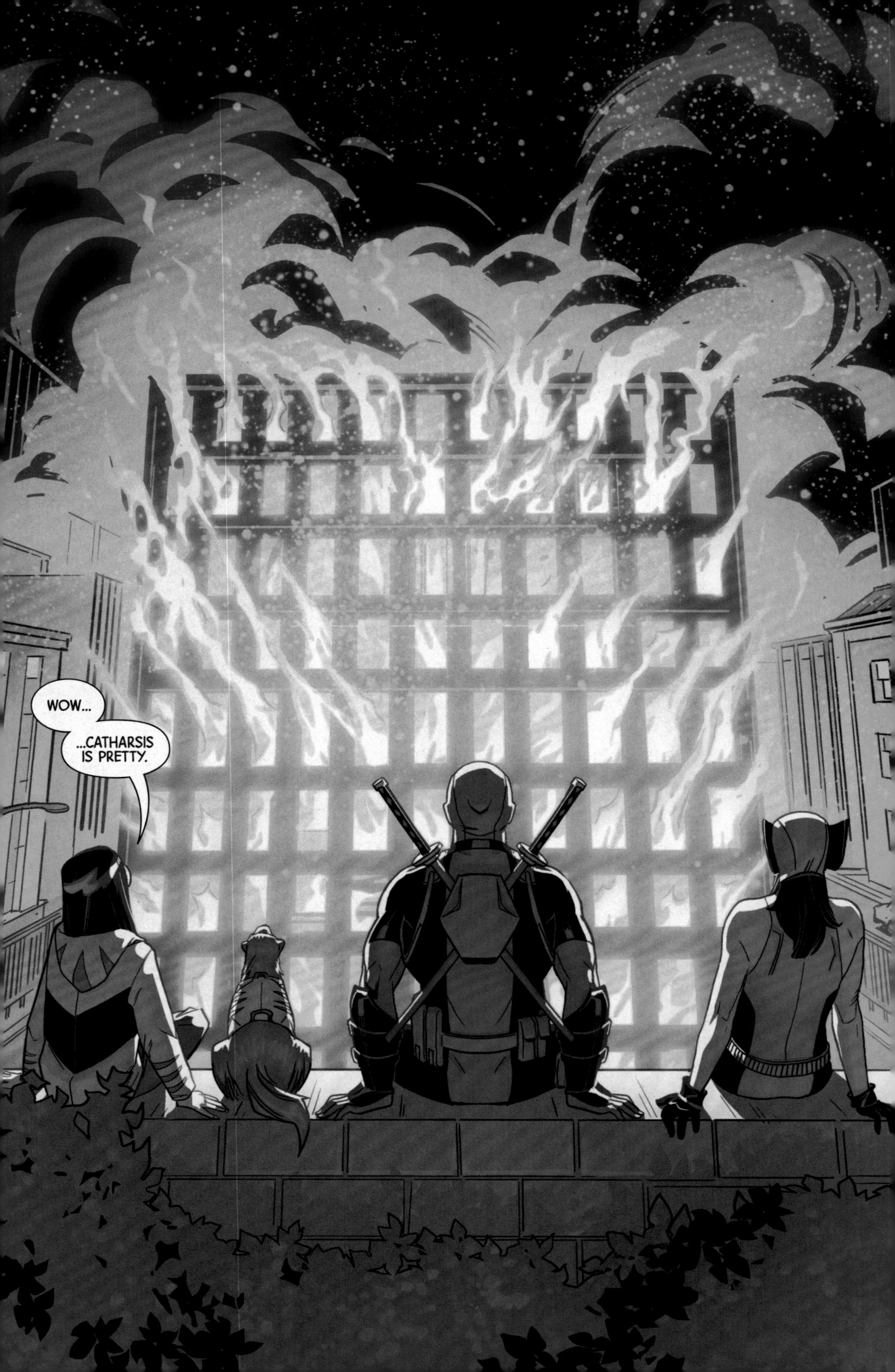
WOW...
...CATHARSIS IS PRETTY.

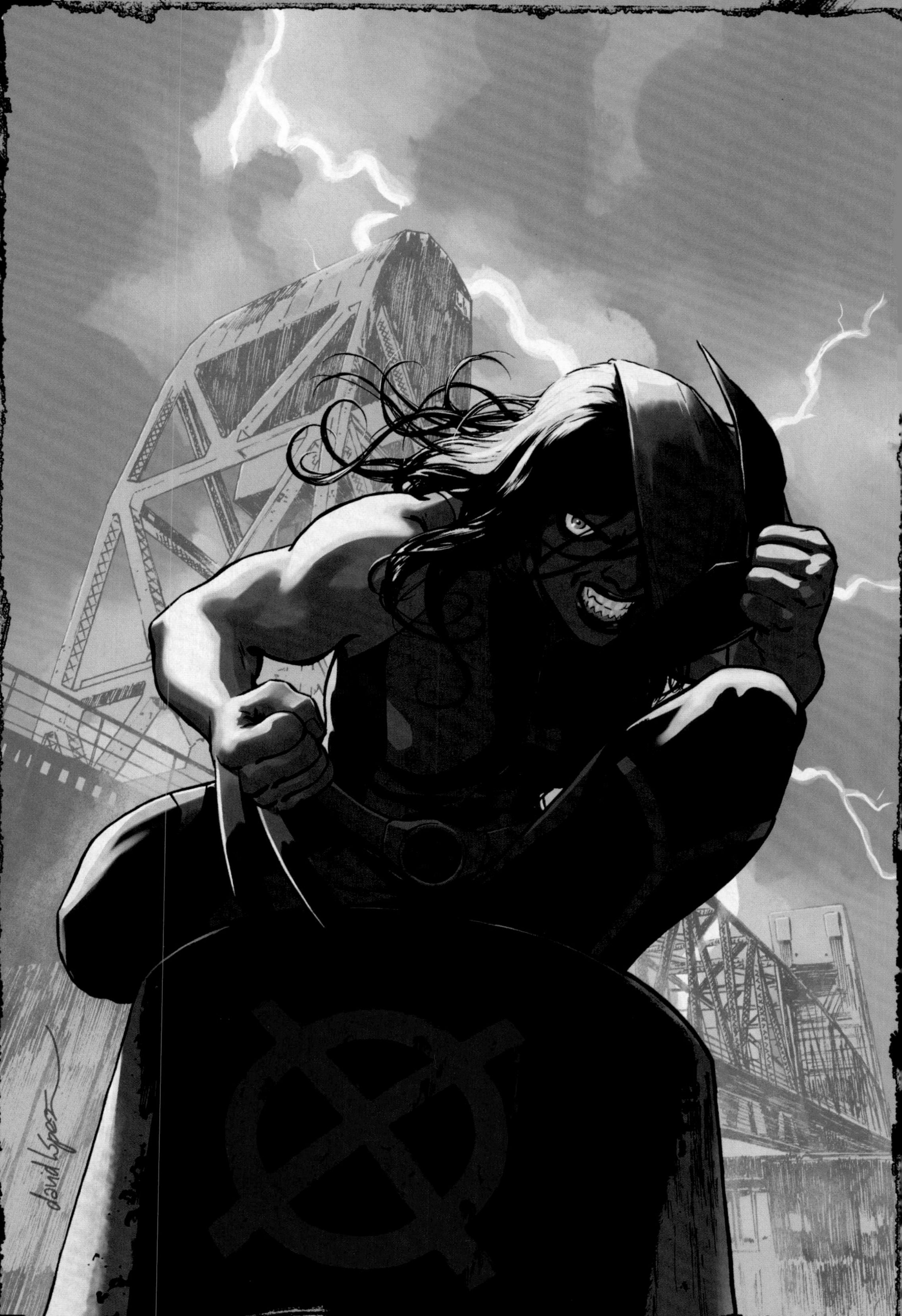

32

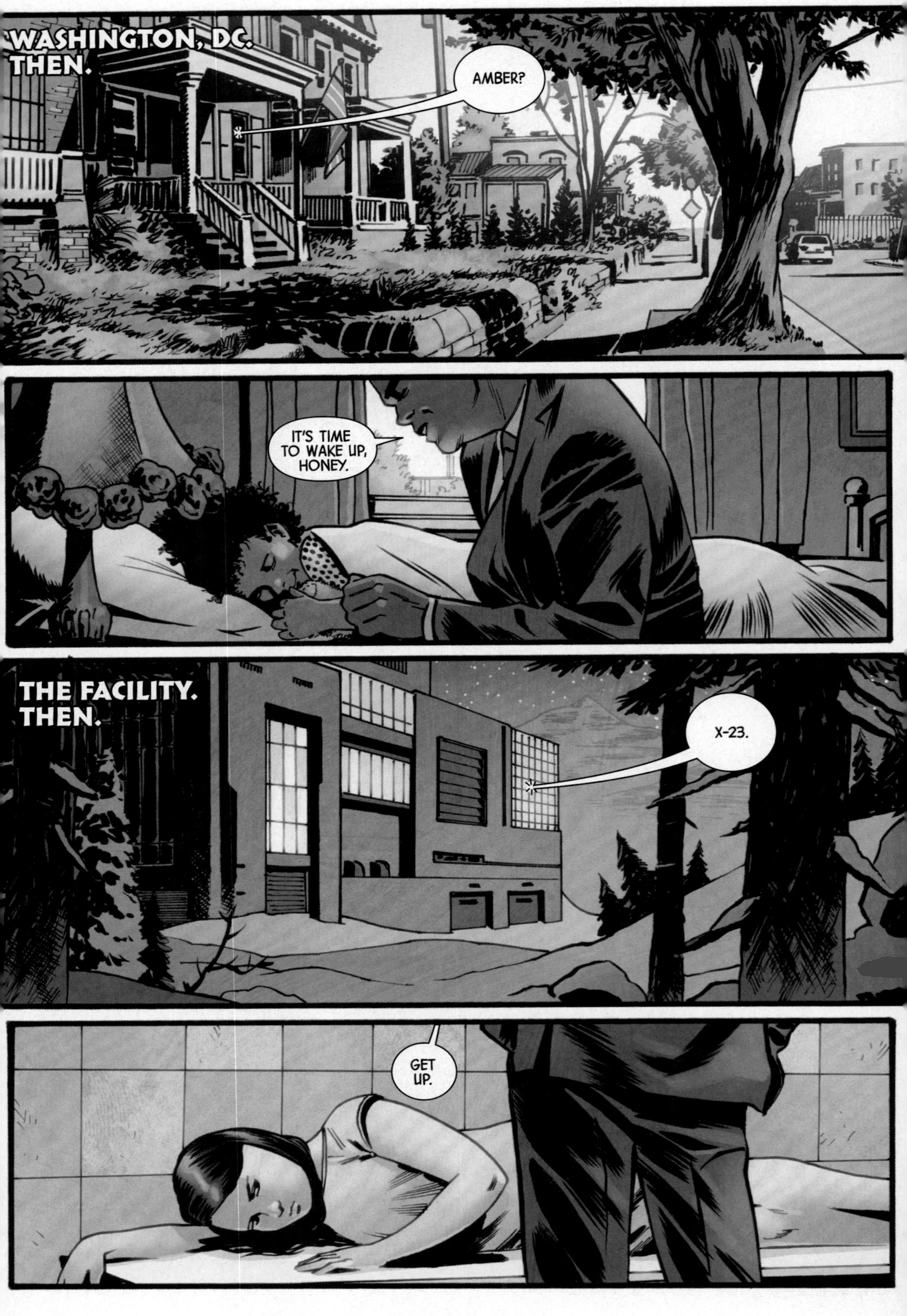
WASHINGTON, DC.
THEN.
AMBER?
IT'S TIME TO WAKE UP, HONEY.
THE FACILITY.
THEN.
X-23.
GET UP.

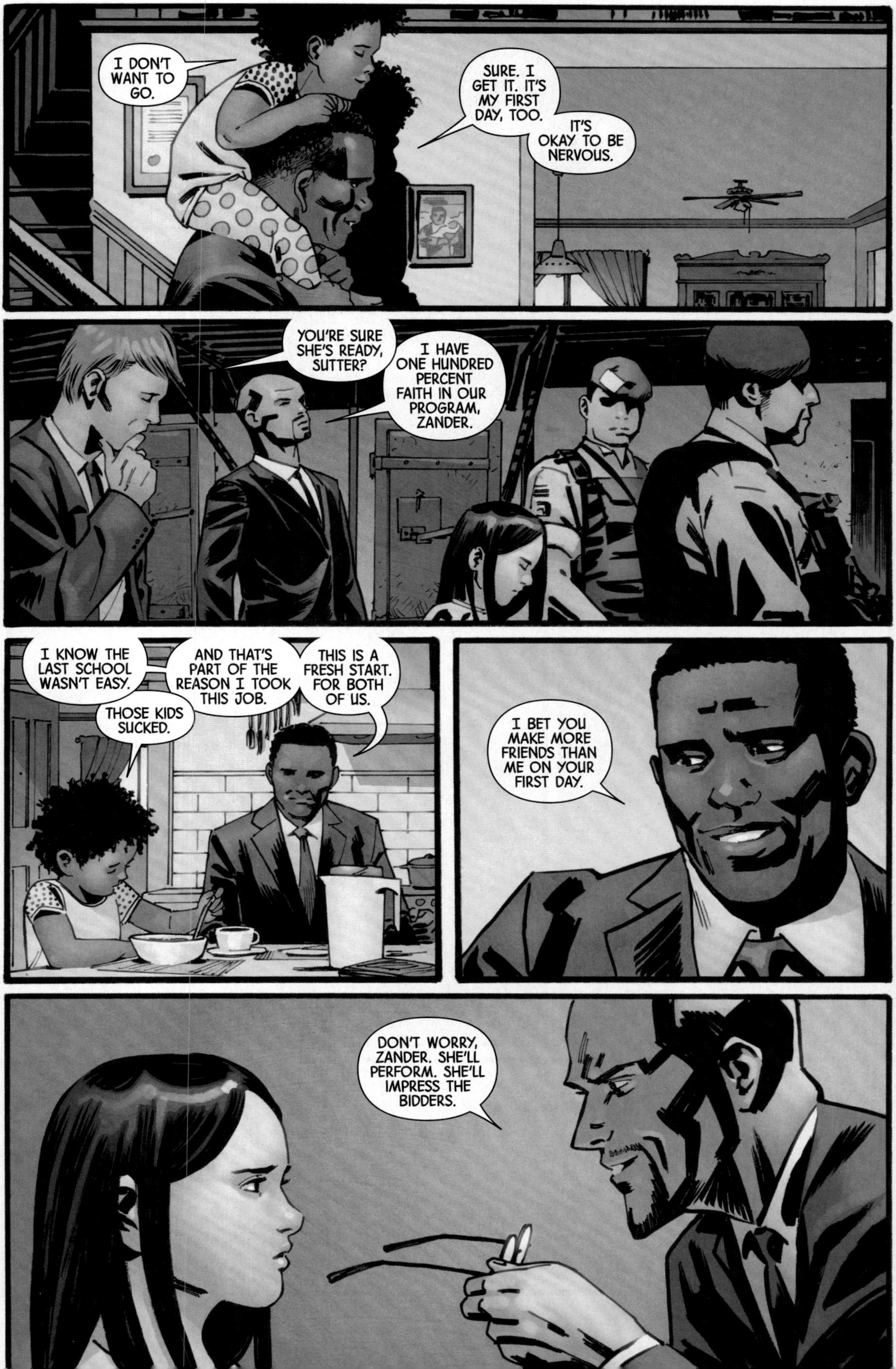
I DON'T WANT TO GO.
SURE. I GET IT. IT'S MY FIRST DAY, TOO.
IT'S OKAY TO BE NERVOUS.
YOU'RE SURE SHE'S READY, SUTTER?
I HAVE ONE HUNDRED PERCENT FAITH IN OUR PROGRAM, ZANDER.
I KNOW THE LAST SCHOOL WASN'T EASY.
THOSE KIDS SUCKED.
AND THAT'S PART OF THE REASON I TOOK THIS JOB.
THIS IS A FRESH START. FOR BOTH OF US.
I BET YOU MAKE MORE FRIENDS THAN ME ON YOUR FIRST DAY.
DON'T WORRY, ZANDER. SHE'LL PERFORM. SHE'LL IMPRESS THE BIDDERS.

CLASS.

WE HAVE A NEW STUDENT JOINING US TODAY.

HI.

MEET AMBER.

HONEY. I'VE GOT SOMEONE WHO WANTS TO MEET THE NEXT PRESIDENT.

WELL, HELLO THERE. I HOPE YOUR PARENTS ARE VOTING JOHNSON.

LET'S GET A PHOTO, SHALL WE?

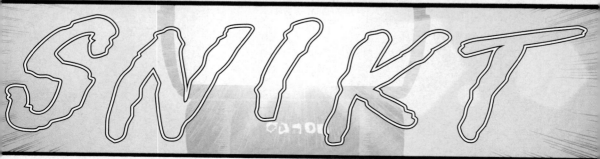

SNIKT

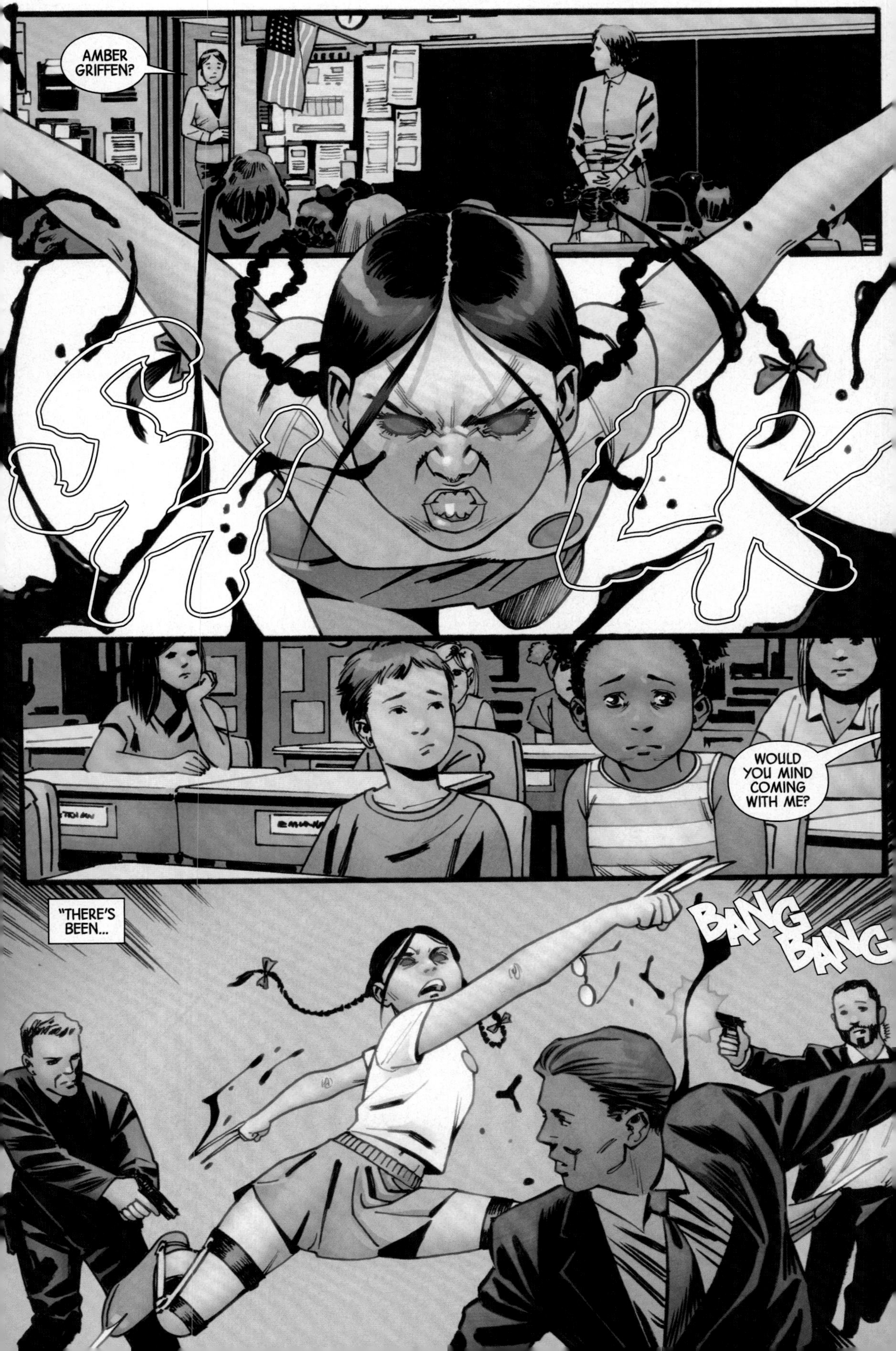
AMBER GRIFFEN?
WOULD YOU MIND COMING WITH ME?
"THERE'S BEEN...
BANG BANG

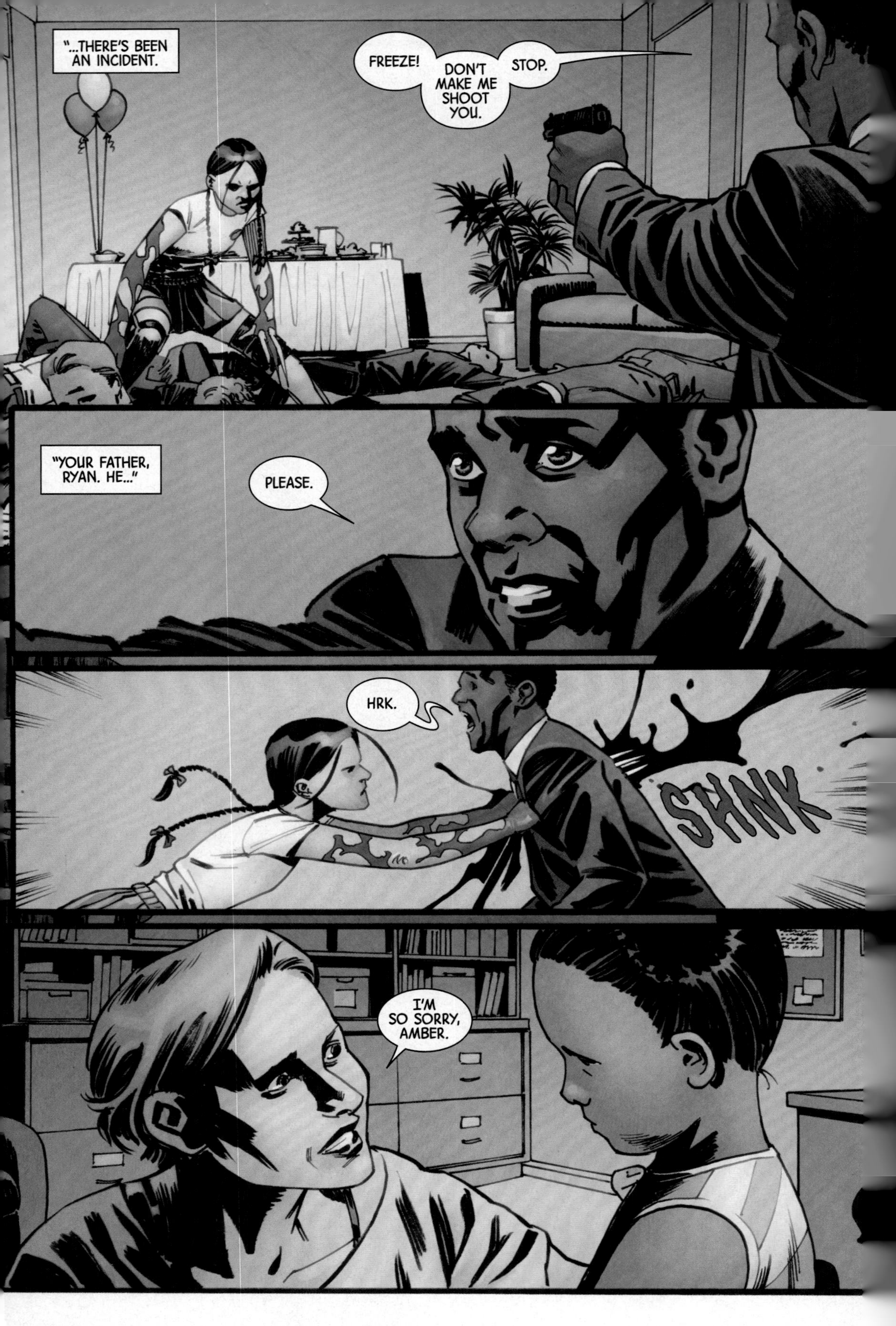
"...THERE'S BEEN AN INCIDENT.
FREEZE!
DON'T MAKE ME SHOOT YOU.
STOP.
"YOUR FATHER, RYAN. HE..."
PLEASE.
HRK.
SHNK
I'M SO SORRY, AMBER.

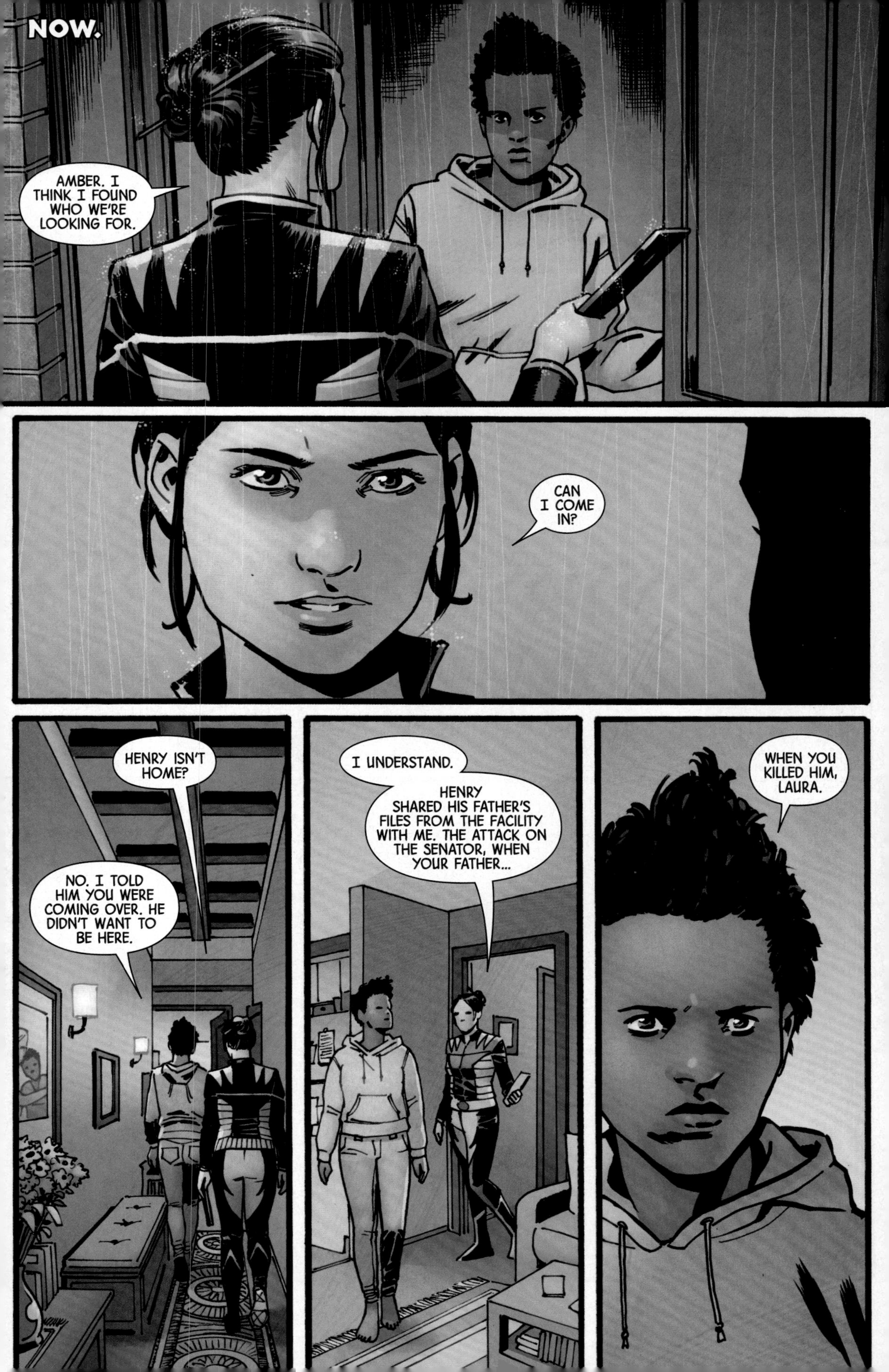
NOW.
AMBER. I THINK I FOUND WHO WE'RE LOOKING FOR.
CAN I COME IN?
HENRY ISN'T HOME?
NO. I TOLD HIM YOU WERE COMING OVER. HE DIDN'T WANT TO BE HERE.
I UNDERSTAND.
HENRY SHARED HIS FATHER'S FILES FROM THE FACILITY WITH ME. THE ATTACK ON THE SENATOR, WHEN YOUR FATHER...
WHEN YOU KILLED HIM, LAURA.

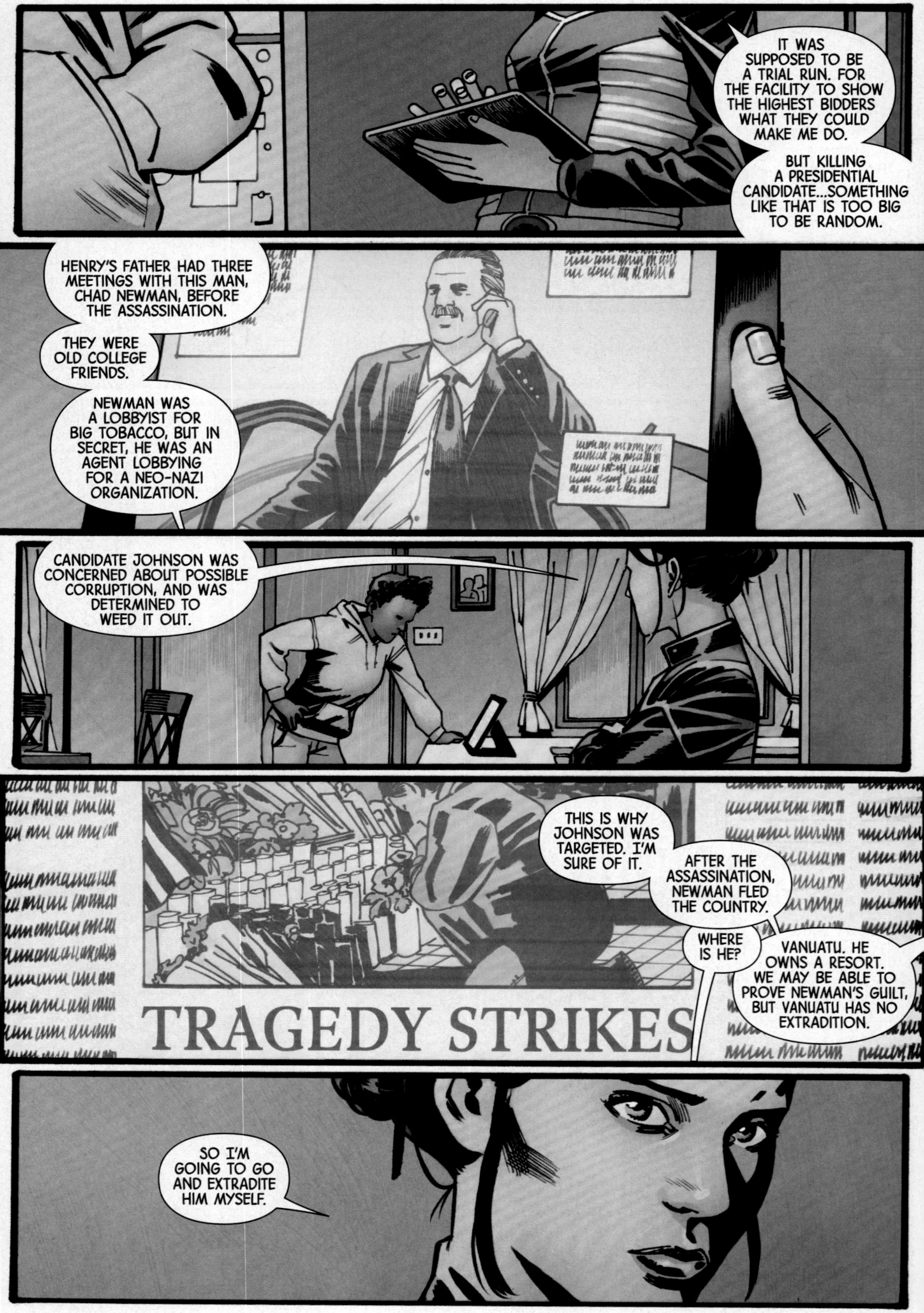
IT WAS SUPPOSED TO BE A TRIAL RUN. FOR THE FACILITY TO SHOW THE HIGHEST BIDDERS WHAT THEY COULD MAKE ME DO.
BUT KILLING A PRESIDENTIAL CANDIDATE...SOMETHING LIKE THAT IS TOO BIG TO BE RANDOM.
HENRY'S FATHER HAD THREE MEETINGS WITH THIS MAN, CHAD NEWMAN, BEFORE THE ASSASSINATION.
THEY WERE OLD COLLEGE FRIENDS.
NEWMAN WAS A LOBBYIST FOR BIG TOBACCO, BUT IN SECRET, HE WAS AN AGENT LOBBYING FOR A NEO-NAZI ORGANIZATION.
CANDIDATE JOHNSON WAS CONCERNED ABOUT POSSIBLE CORRUPTION, AND WAS DETERMINED TO WEED IT OUT.
TRAGEDY STRIKES
THIS IS WHY JOHNSON WAS TARGETED. I'M SURE OF IT.
AFTER THE ASSASSINATION, NEWMAN FLED THE COUNTRY.
WHERE IS HE?
VANUATU. HE OWNS A RESORT. WE MAY BE ABLE TO PROVE NEWMAN'S GUILT, BUT VANUATU HAS NO EXTRADITION.
SO I'M GOING TO GO AND EXTRADITE HIM MYSELF.

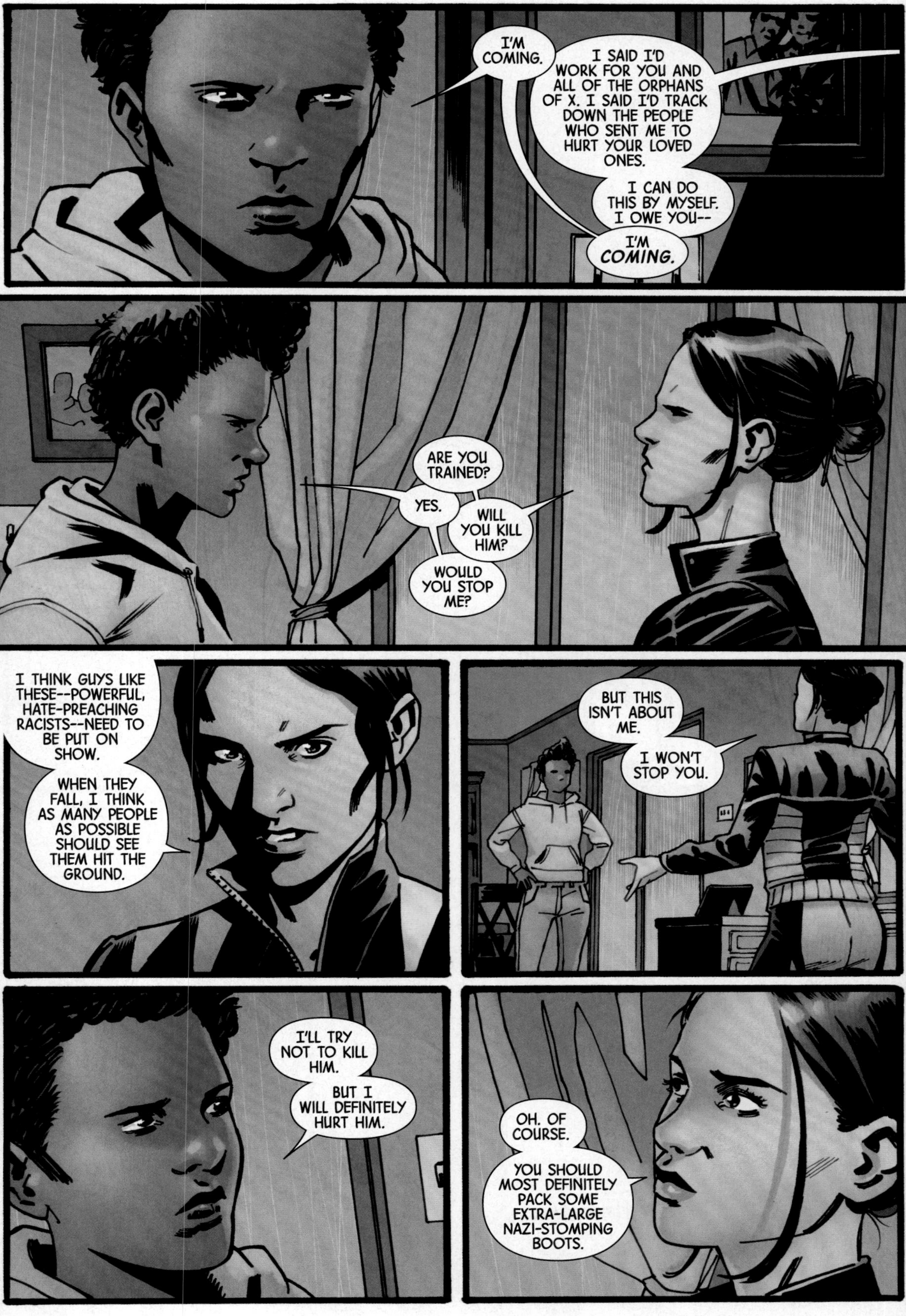
I'M COMING.
I SAID I'D WORK FOR YOU AND ALL OF THE ORPHANS OF X. I SAID I'D TRACK DOWN THE PEOPLE WHO SENT ME TO HURT YOUR LOVED ONES.
I CAN DO THIS BY MYSELF. I OWE YOU--
I'M COMING.
ARE YOU TRAINED?
YES.
WILL YOU KILL HIM?
WOULD YOU STOP ME?
I THINK GUYS LIKE THESE--POWERFUL, HATE-PREACHING RACISTS--NEED TO BE PUT ON SHOW.
WHEN THEY FALL, I THINK AS MANY PEOPLE AS POSSIBLE SHOULD SEE THEM HIT THE GROUND.
BUT THIS ISN'T ABOUT ME.
I WON'T STOP YOU.
I'LL TRY NOT TO KILL HIM.
BUT I WILL DEFINITELY HURT HIM.
OH. OF COURSE.
YOU SHOULD MOST DEFINITELY PACK SOME EXTRA-LARGE NAZI-STOMPING BOOTS.

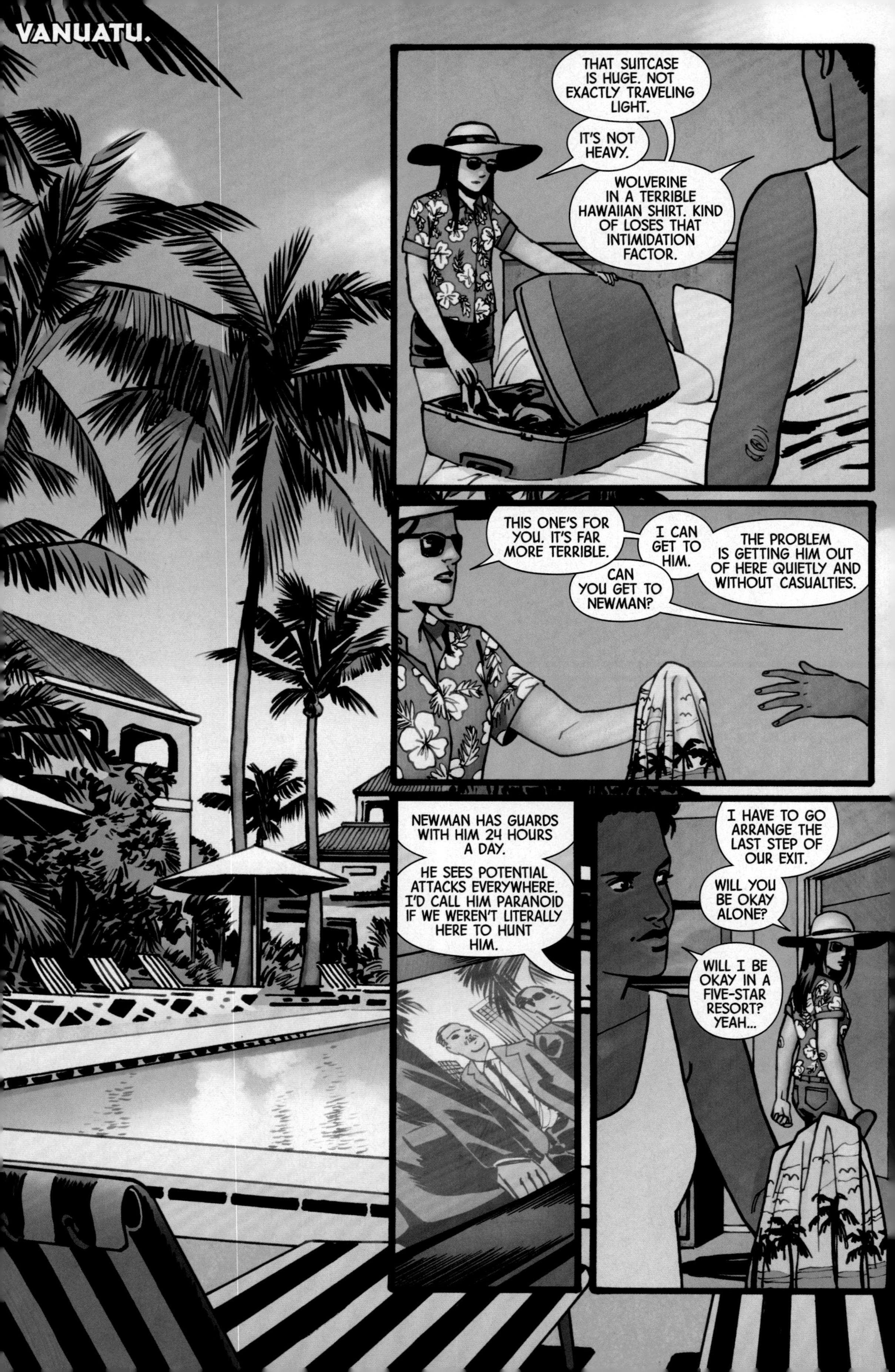
VANUATU.
THAT SUITCASE IS HUGE. NOT EXACTLY TRAVELING LIGHT.
IT'S NOT HEAVY.
WOLVERINE IN A TERRIBLE HAWAIIAN SHIRT. KIND OF LOSES THAT INTIMIDATION FACTOR.
THIS ONE'S FOR YOU. IT'S FAR MORE TERRIBLE.
CAN YOU GET TO NEWMAN?
I CAN GET TO HIM.
THE PROBLEM IS GETTING HIM OUT OF HERE QUIETLY AND WITHOUT CASUALTIES.
NEWMAN HAS GUARDS WITH HIM 24 HOURS A DAY.
HE SEES POTENTIAL ATTACKS EVERYWHERE. I'D CALL HIM PARANOID IF WE WEREN'T LITERALLY HERE TO HUNT HIM.
I HAVE TO GO ARRANGE THE LAST STEP OF OUR EXIT.
WILL YOU BE OKAY ALONE?
WILL I BE OKAY IN A FIVE-STAR RESORT? YEAH...

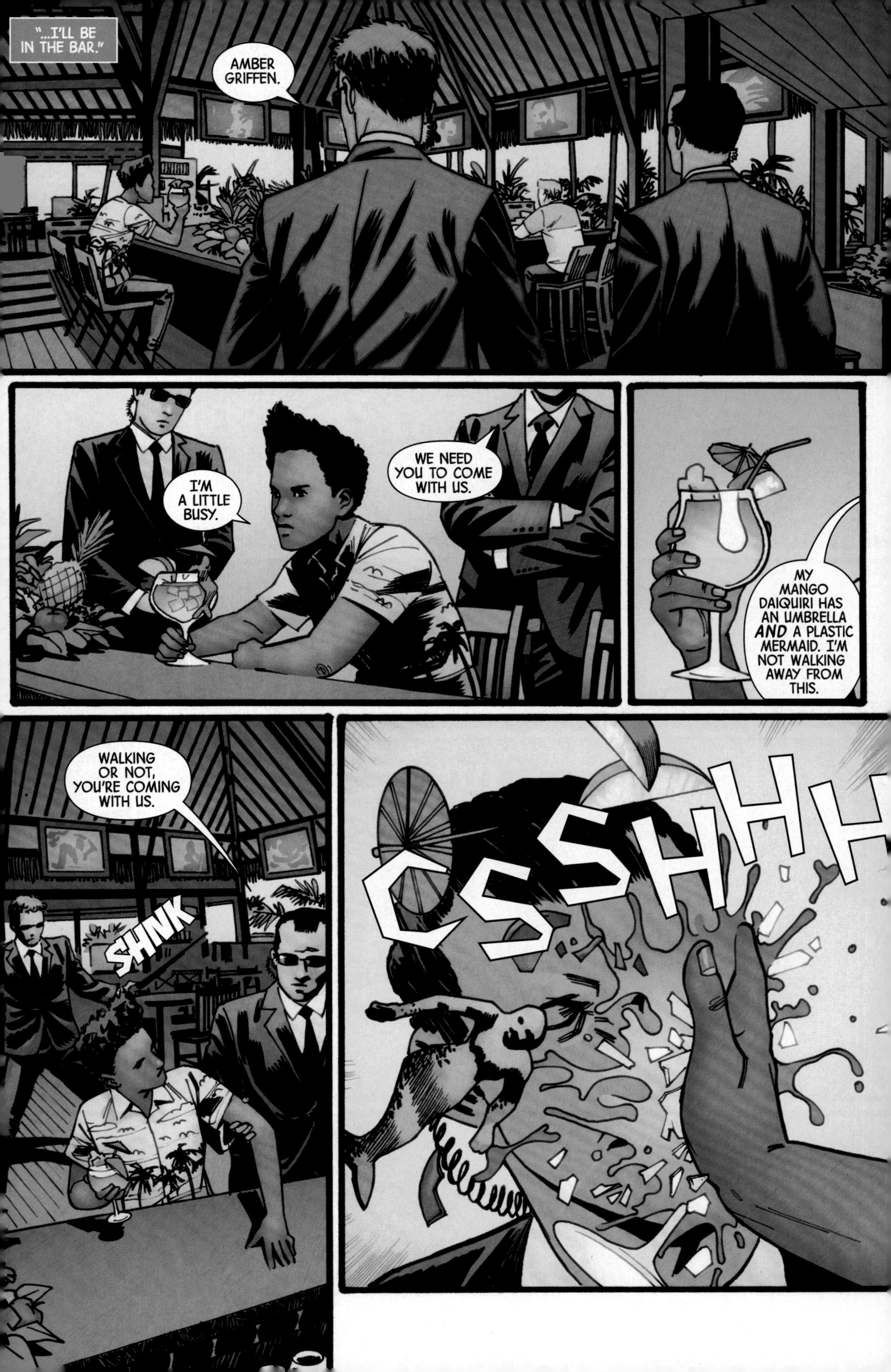
"...I'LL BE IN THE BAR."
AMBER GRIFFEN.
I'M A LITTLE BUSY.
WE NEED YOU TO COME WITH US.
MY MANGO DAIQUIRI HAS AN UMBRELLA AND A PLASTIC MERMAID. I'M NOT WALKING AWAY FROM THIS.
WALKING OR NOT, YOU'RE COMING WITH US.
SHNK
CSSHHH

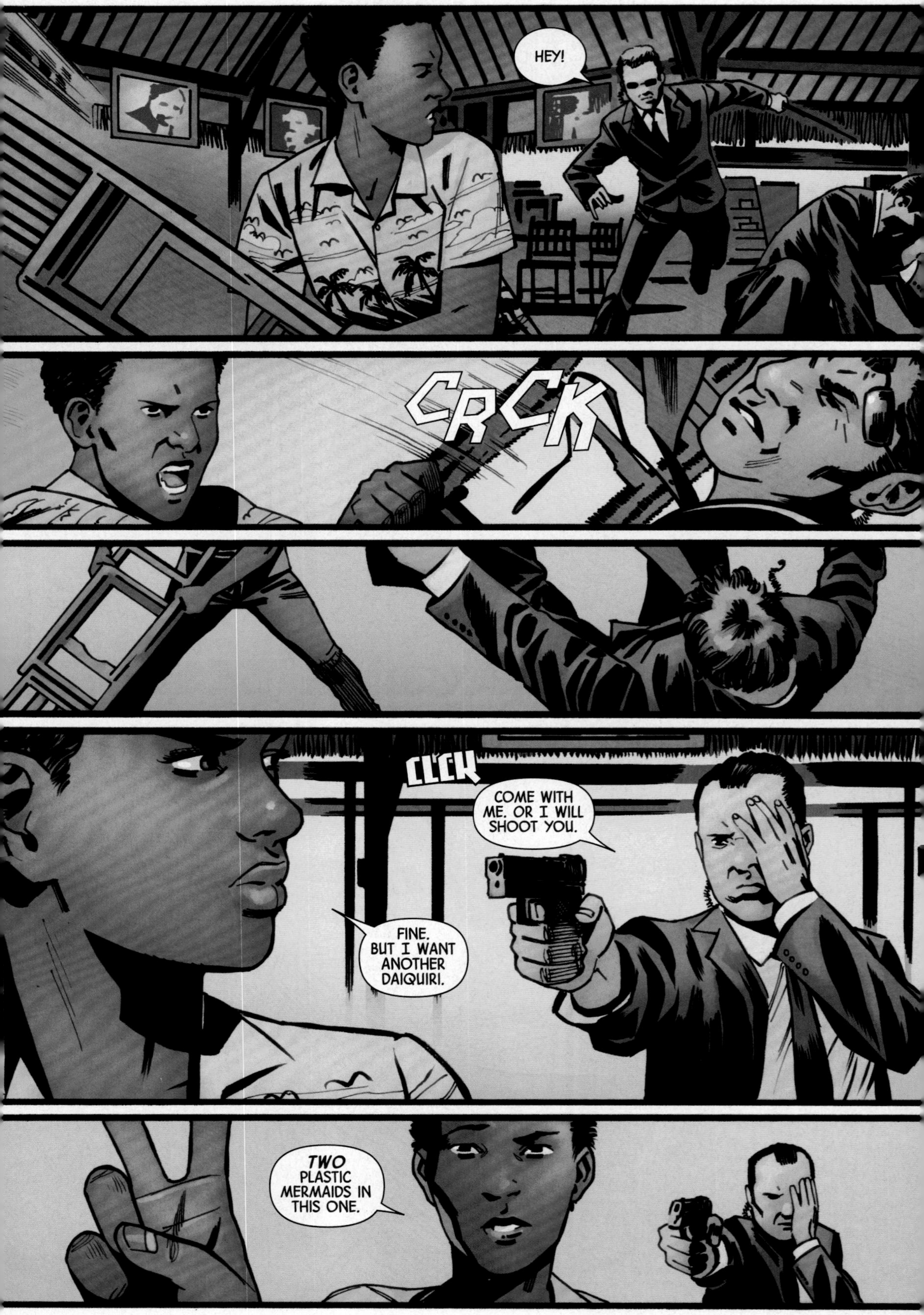
HEY!
CRCK
CLCK
COME WITH ME. OR I WILL SHOOT YOU.
FINE. BUT I WANT ANOTHER DAIQUIRI.
TWO PLASTIC MERMAIDS IN THIS ONE.

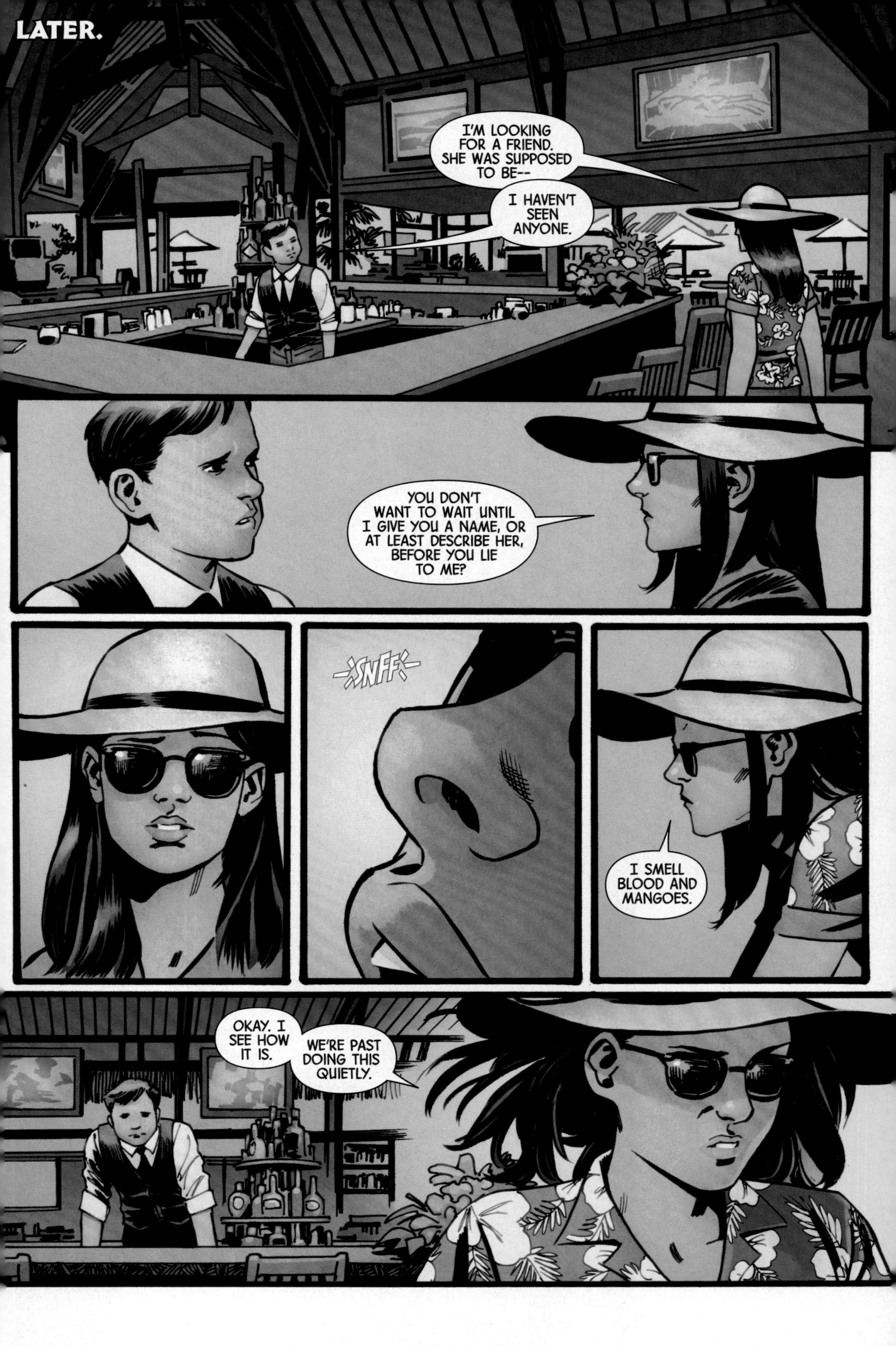
LATER.
I'M LOOKING FOR A FRIEND. SHE WAS SUPPOSED TO BE--
I HAVEN'T SEEN ANYONE.
YOU DON'T WANT TO WAIT UNTIL I GIVE YOU A NAME, OR AT LEAST DESCRIBE HER, BEFORE YOU LIE TO ME?
SNFF
I SMELL BLOOD AND MANGOES.
OKAY. I SEE HOW IT IS.
WE'RE PAST DOING THIS QUIETLY.

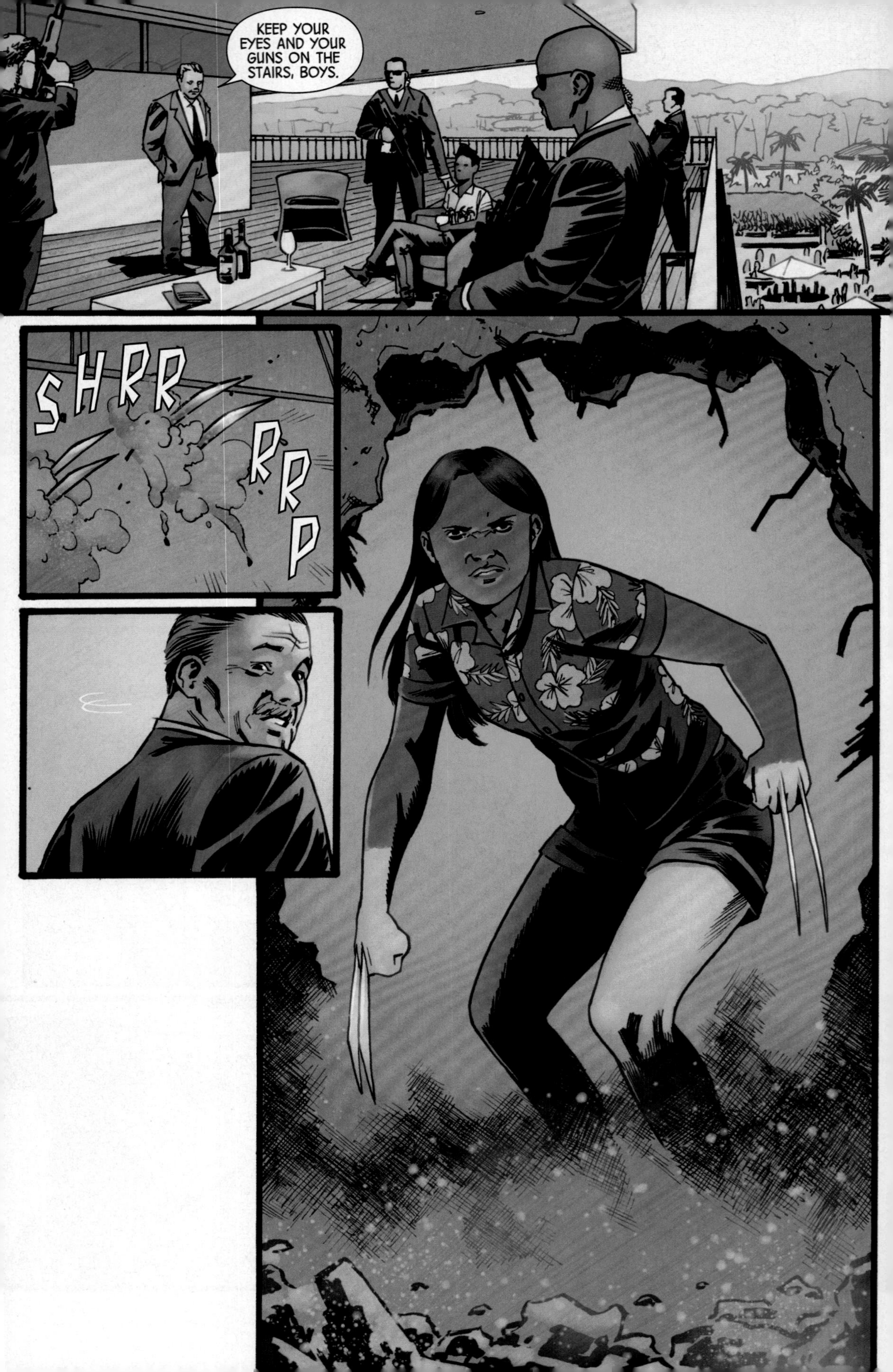
KEEP YOUR EYES AND YOUR GUNS ON THE STAIRS, BOYS.
SHRR RRRP

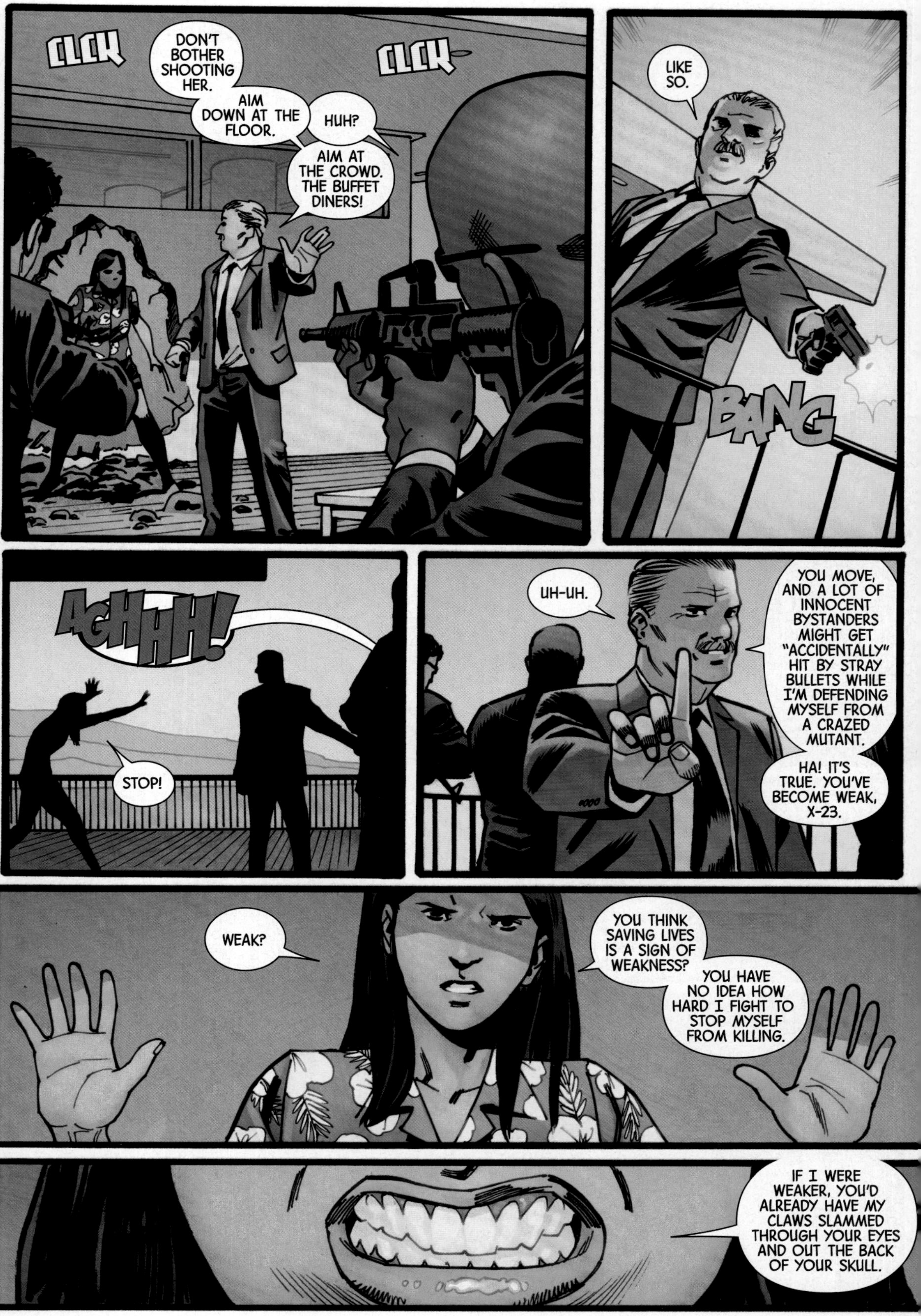
CLCK
DON'T BOTHER SHOOTING HER.
AIM DOWN AT THE FLOOR.
CLCK
HUH?
AIM AT THE CROWD. THE BUFFET DINERS!
LIKE SO.
BANG
AGHHH!
STOP!
UH-UH.
YOU MOVE, AND A LOT OF INNOCENT BYSTANDERS MIGHT GET "ACCIDENTALLY" HIT BY STRAY BULLETS WHILE I'M DEFENDING MYSELF FROM A CRAZED MUTANT.
HA! IT'S TRUE. YOU'VE BECOME WEAK, X-23.
WEAK?
YOU THINK SAVING LIVES IS A SIGN OF WEAKNESS?
YOU HAVE NO IDEA HOW HARD I FIGHT TO STOP MYSELF FROM KILLING.
IF I WERE WEAKER, YOU'D ALREADY HAVE MY CLAWS SLAMMED THROUGH YOUR EYES AND OUT THE BACK OF YOUR SKULL.

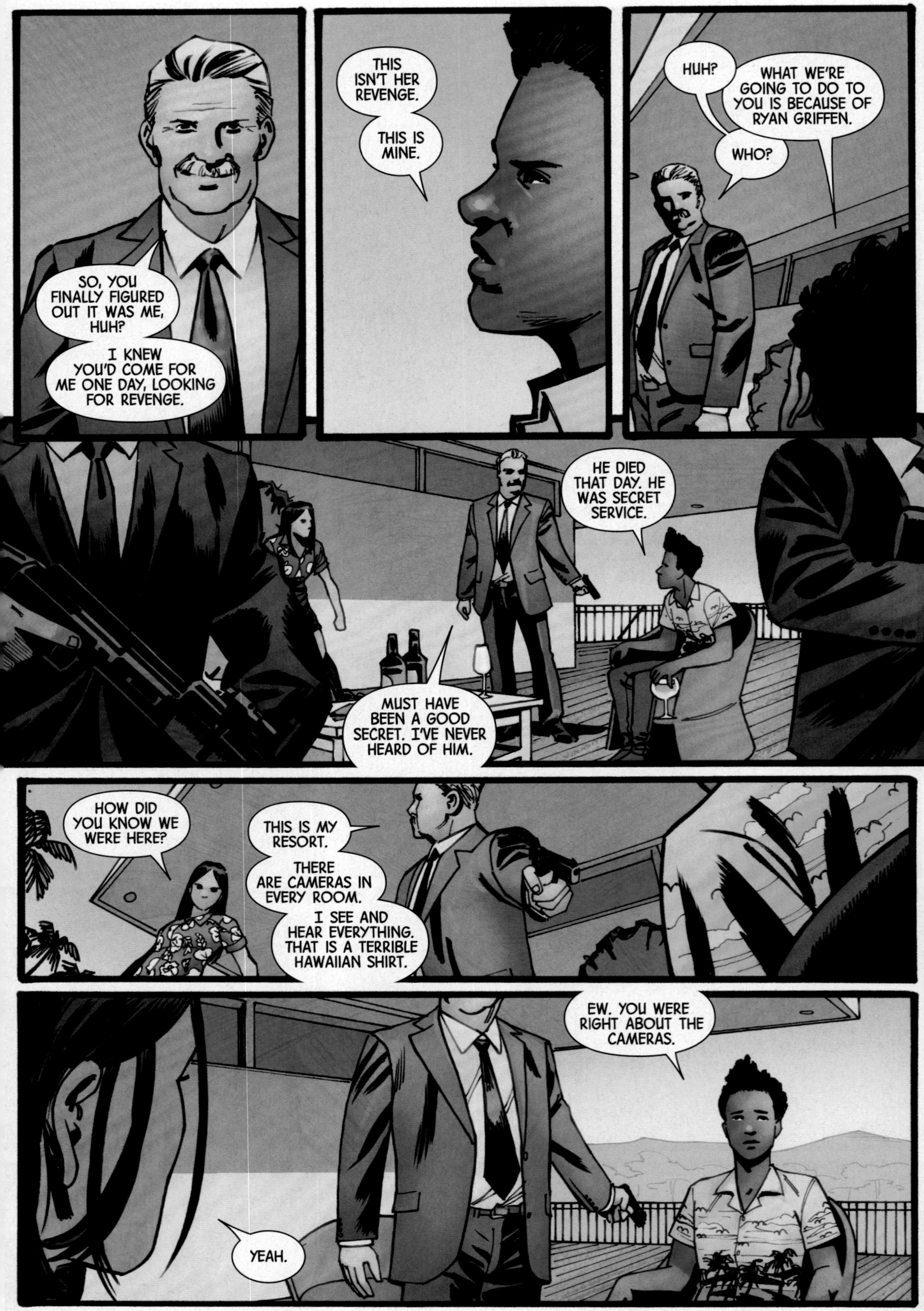
SO, YOU FINALLY FIGURED OUT IT WAS ME, HUH?
I KNEW YOU'D COME FOR ME ONE DAY, LOOKING FOR REVENGE.
THIS ISN'T HER REVENGE.
THIS IS MINE.
HUH?
WHAT WE'RE GOING TO DO TO YOU IS BECAUSE OF RYAN GRIFFEN.
WHO?
HE DIED THAT DAY. HE WAS SECRET SERVICE.
MUST HAVE BEEN A GOOD SECRET. I'VE NEVER HEARD OF HIM.
HOW DID YOU KNOW WE WERE HERE?
THIS IS MY RESORT.
THERE ARE CAMERAS IN EVERY ROOM.
I SEE AND HEAR EVERYTHING. THAT IS A TERRIBLE HAWAIIAN SHIRT.
EW. YOU WERE RIGHT ABOUT THE CAMERAS.
YEAH.

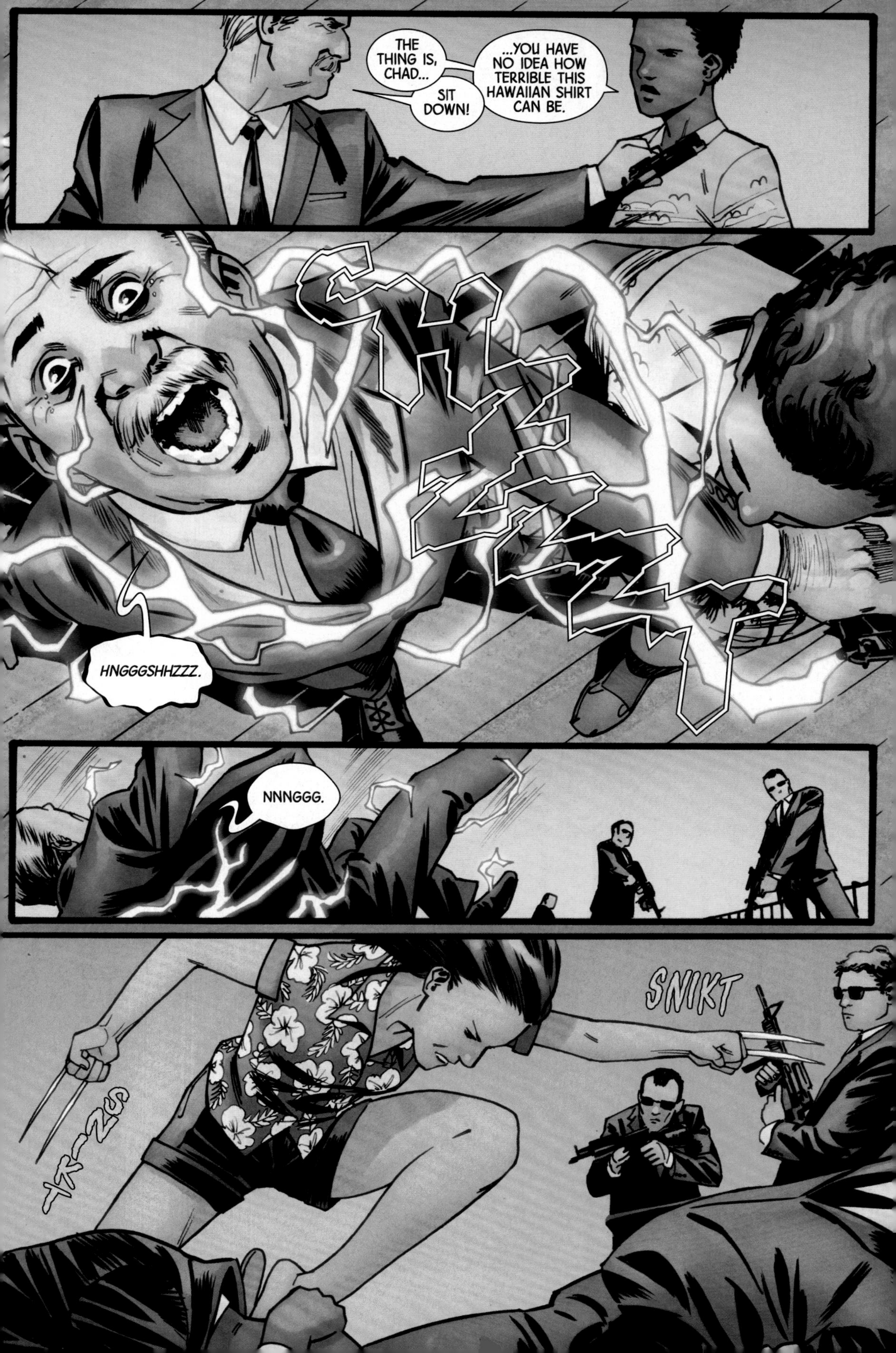
THE THING IS, CHAD...
SIT DOWN!
...YOU HAVE NO IDEA HOW TERRIBLE THIS HAWAIIAN SHIRT CAN BE.
HNGGGSHHZZZ.
NNNGGG.
SNIKT

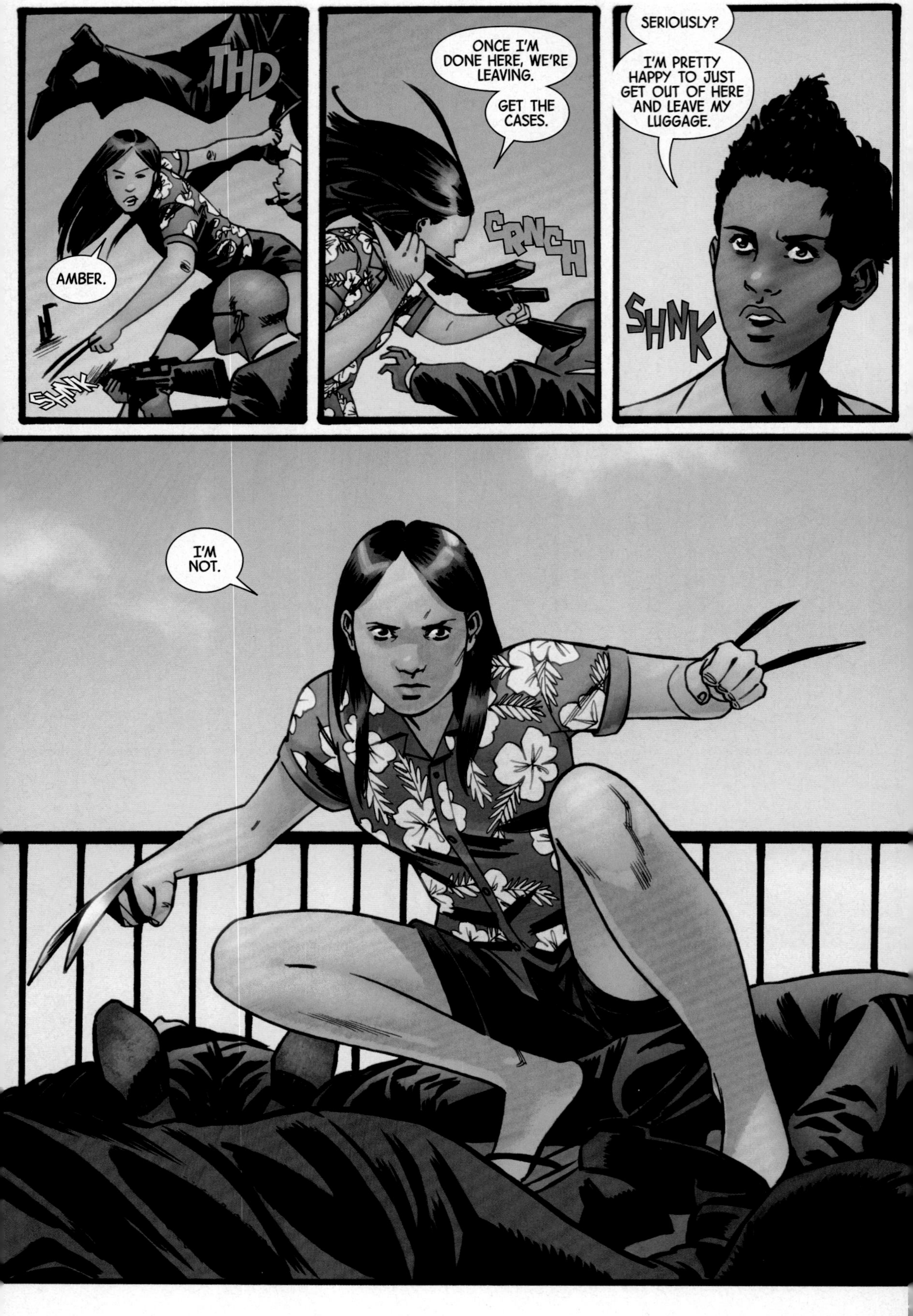
THD
AMBER.
SHNK
ONCE I'M DONE HERE, WE'RE LEAVING.
GET THE CASES.
CRNCH
SERIOUSLY?
I'M PRETTY HAPPY TO JUST GET OUT OF HERE AND LEAVE MY LUGGAGE.
SHNK
I'M NOT.

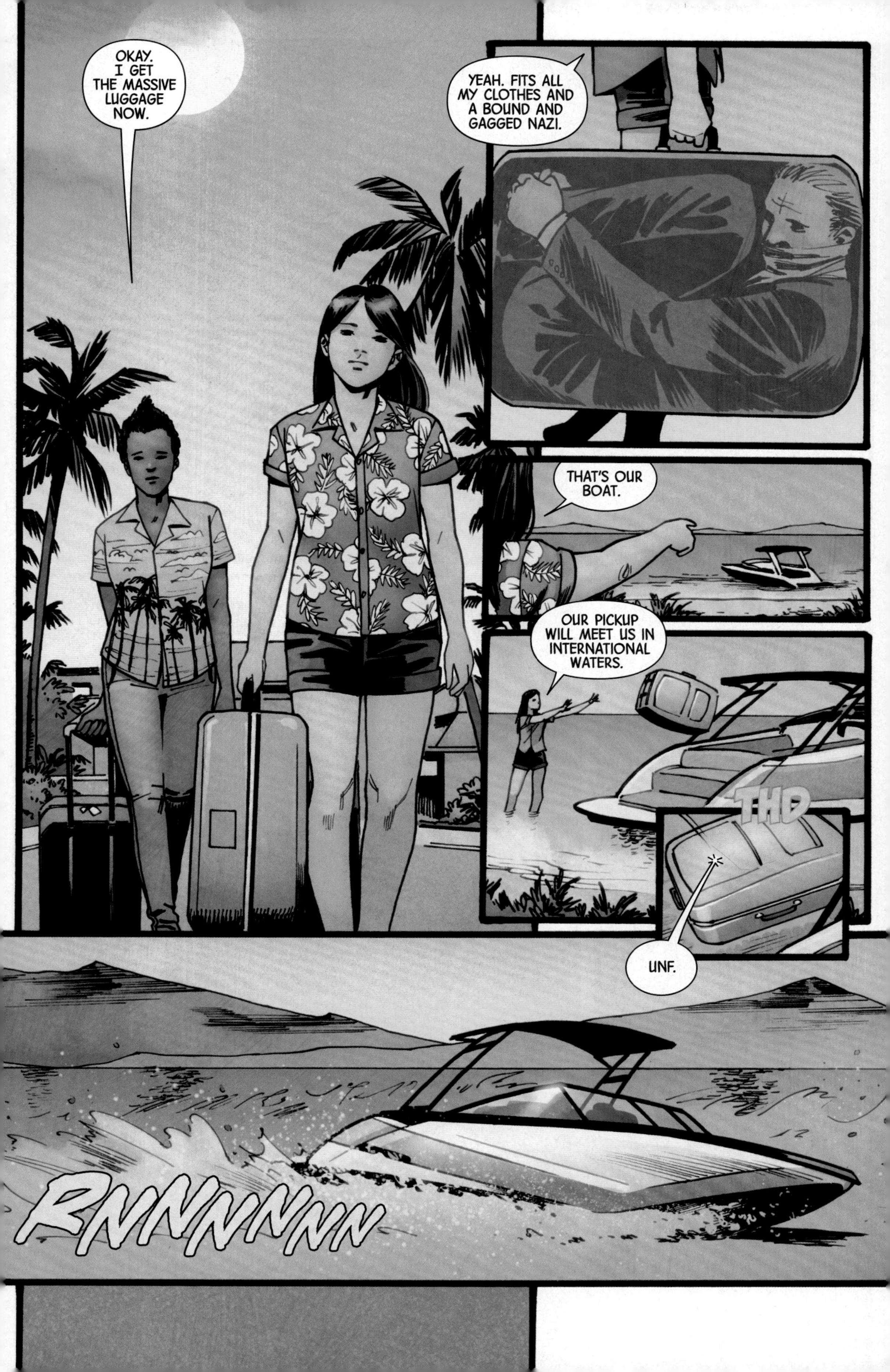
OKAY. I GET THE MASSIVE LUGGAGE NOW.
YEAH. FITS ALL MY CLOTHES AND A BOUND AND GAGGED NAZI.
THAT'S OUR BOAT.
OUR PICKUP WILL MEET US IN INTERNATIONAL WATERS.
THD
UNF.
RNNNNNN

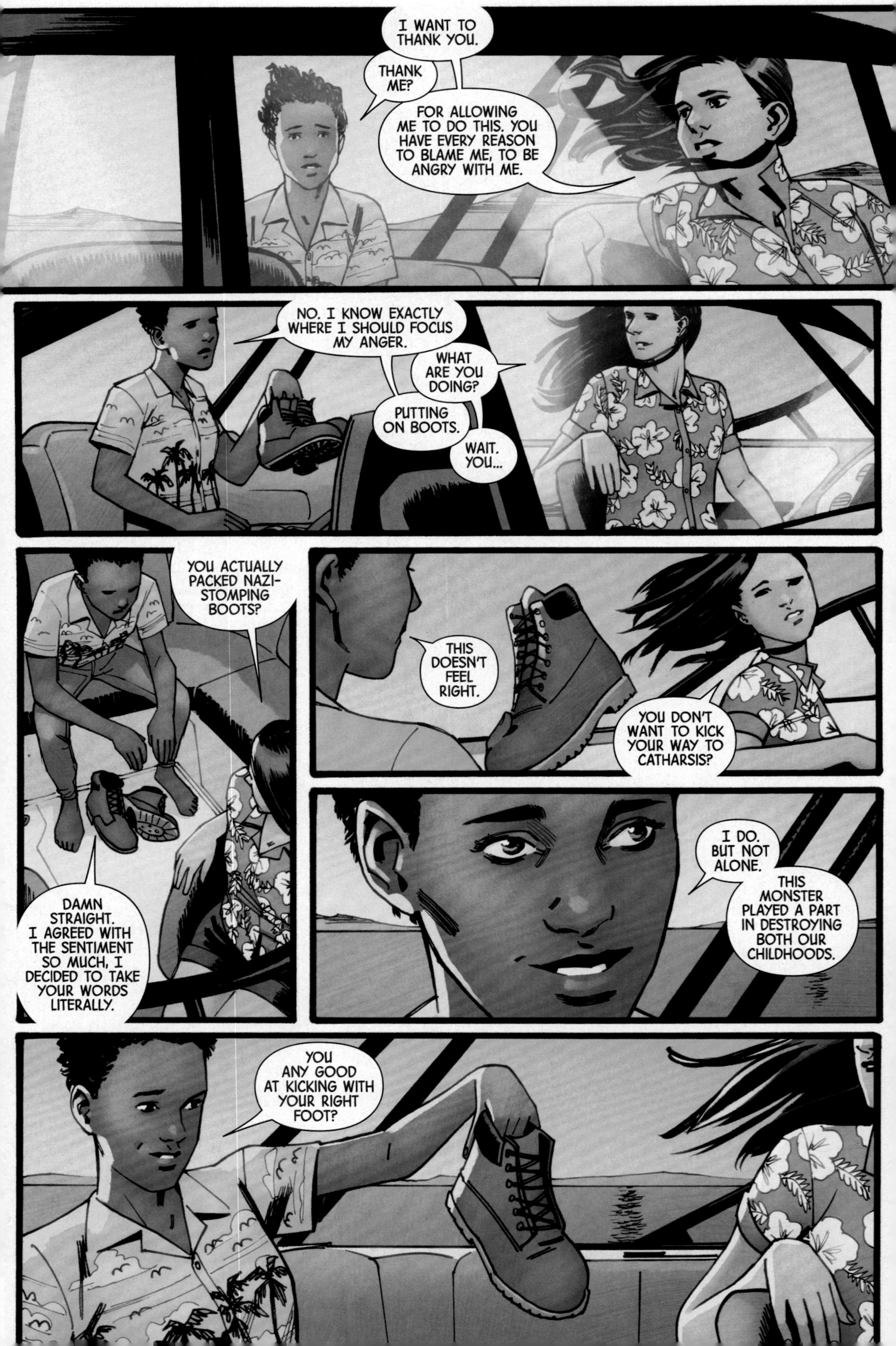
I WANT TO THANK YOU.
THANK ME?
FOR ALLOWING ME TO DO THIS. YOU HAVE EVERY REASON TO BLAME ME, TO BE ANGRY WITH ME.
NO. I KNOW EXACTLY WHERE I SHOULD FOCUS MY ANGER.
WHAT ARE YOU DOING?
PUTTING ON BOOTS.
WAIT. YOU...
YOU ACTUALLY PACKED NAZI-STOMPING BOOTS?
DAMN STRAIGHT. I AGREED WITH THE SENTIMENT SO MUCH, I DECIDED TO TAKE YOUR WORDS LITERALLY.
THIS DOESN'T FEEL RIGHT.
YOU DON'T WANT TO KICK YOUR WAY TO CATHARSIS?
I DO. BUT NOT ALONE.
THIS MONSTER PLAYED A PART IN DESTROYING BOTH OUR CHILDHOODS.
YOU ANY GOOD AT KICKING WITH YOUR RIGHT FOOT?

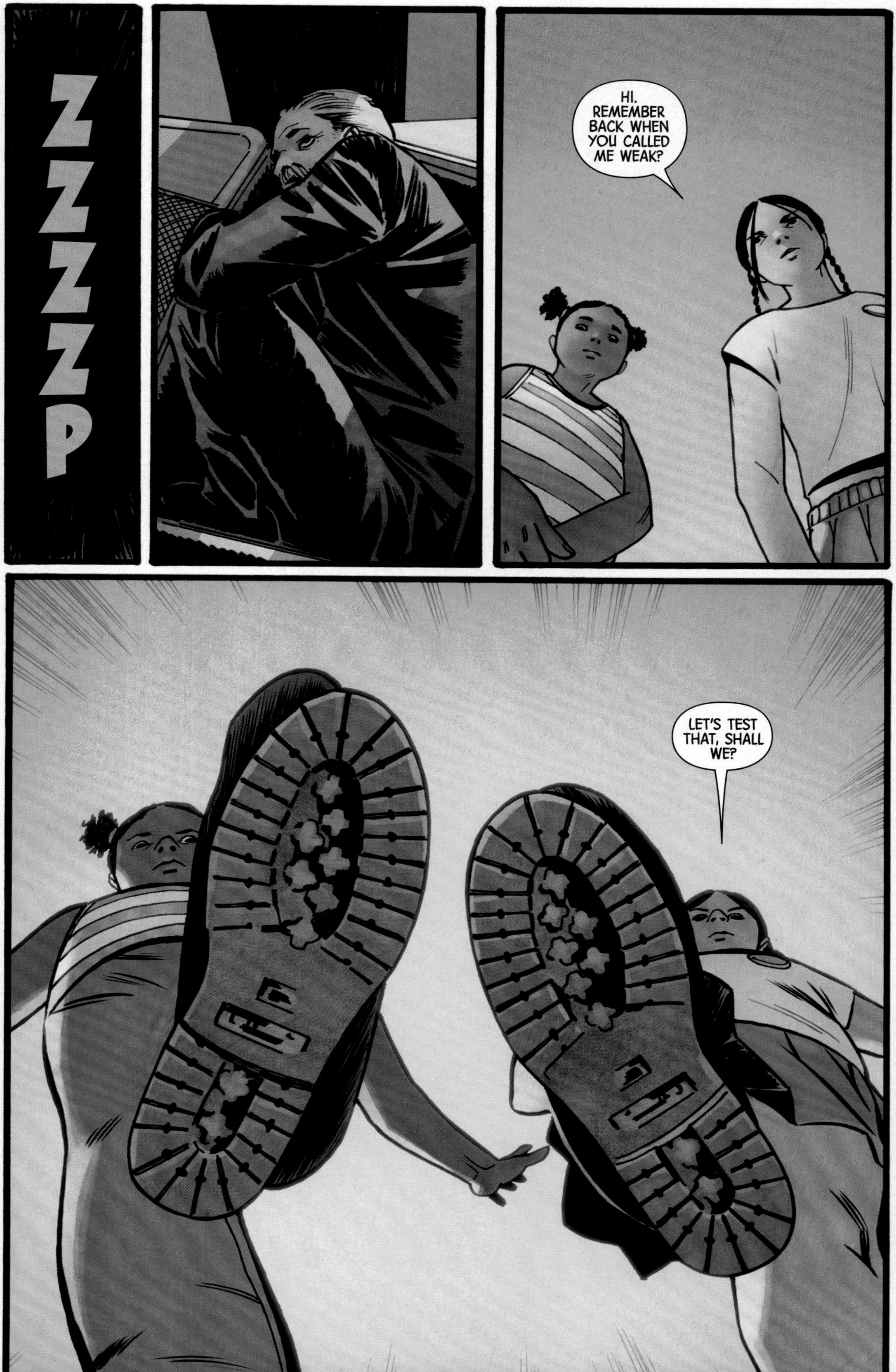
ZZZZP
HI. REMEMBER BACK WHEN YOU CALLED ME WEAK?
LET'S TEST THAT, SHALL WE?

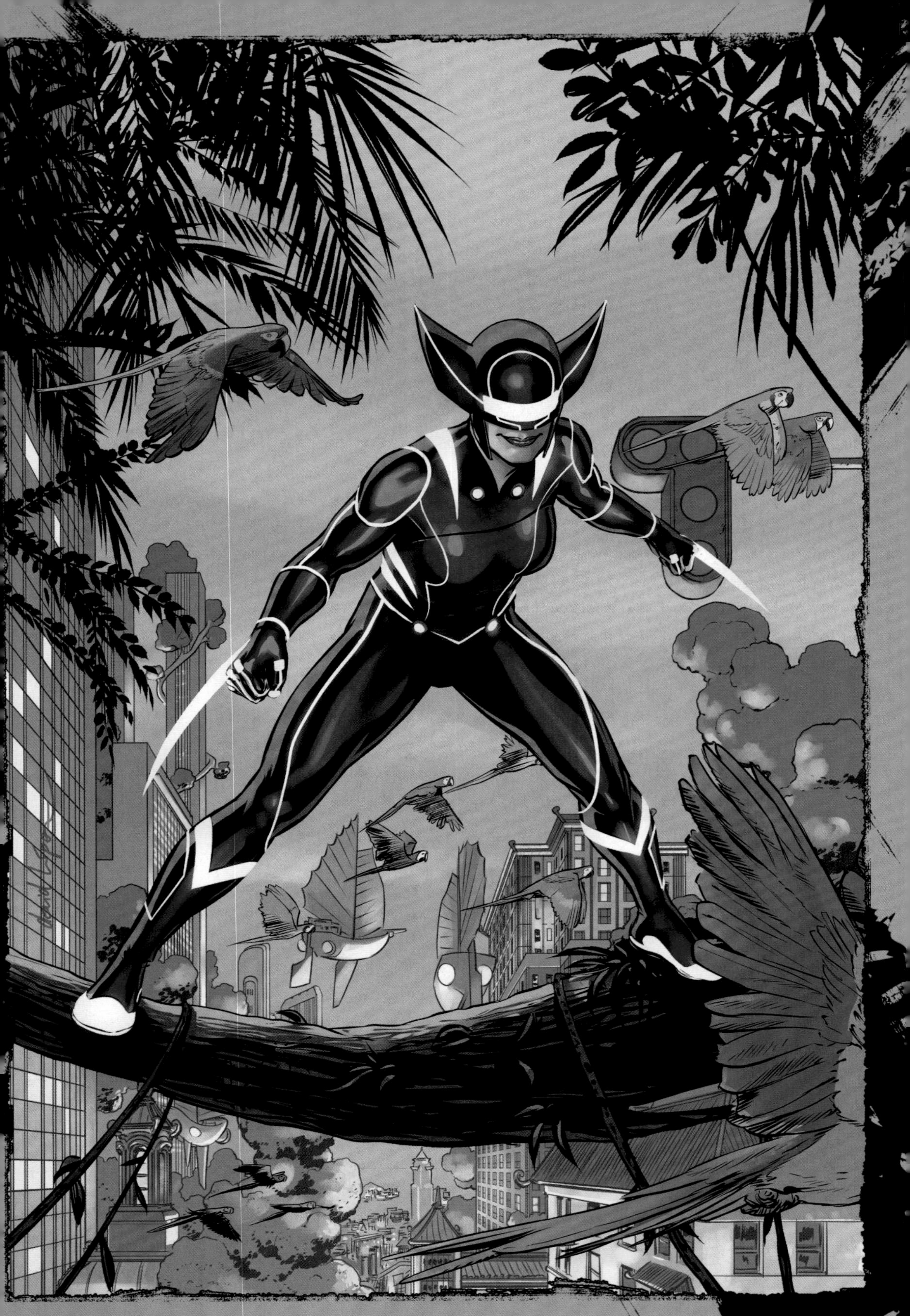

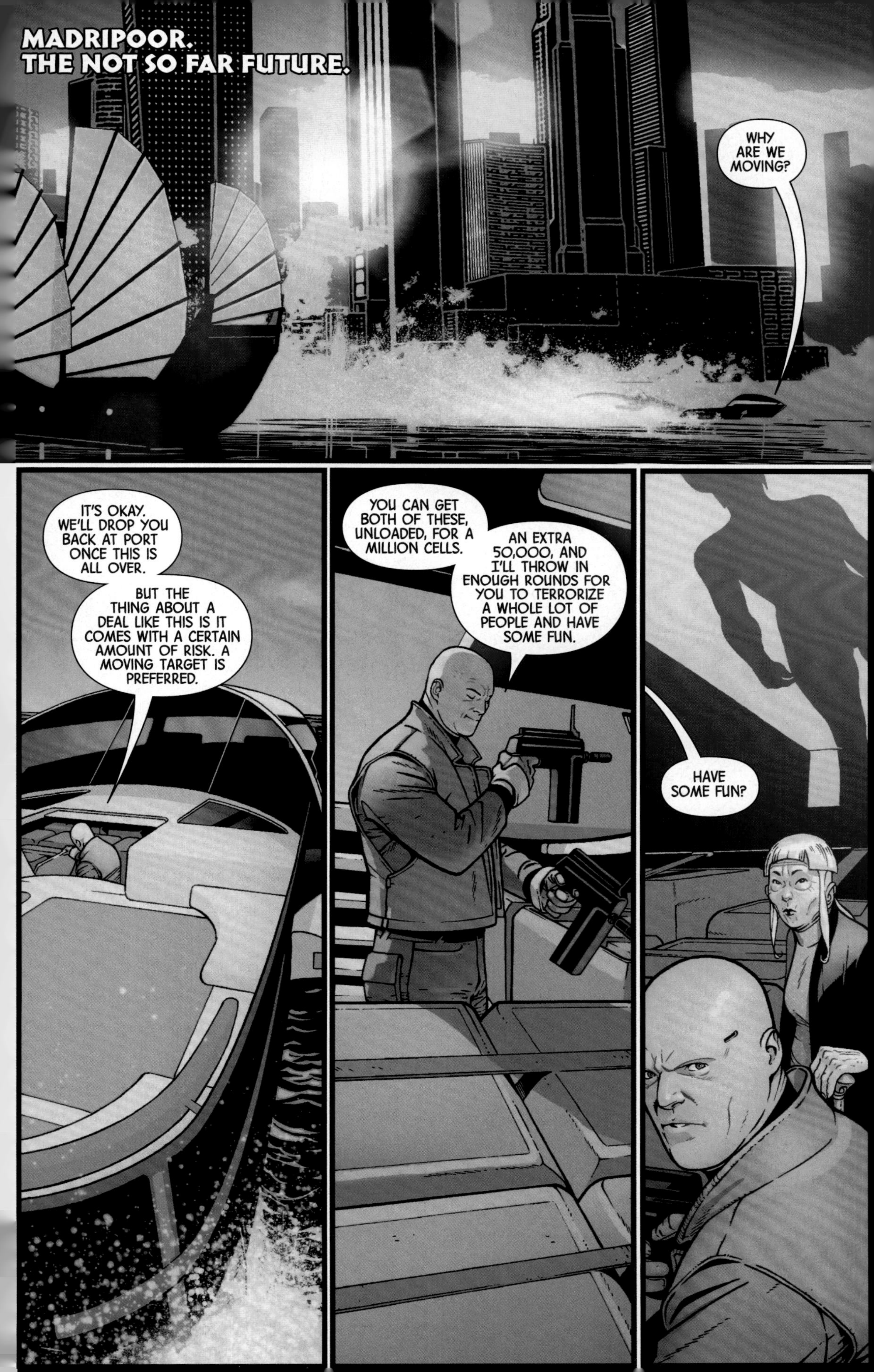
MADRIPOOR.
THE NOT SO FAR FUTURE.
WHY ARE WE MOVING?
IT'S OKAY. WE'LL DROP YOU BACK AT PORT ONCE THIS IS ALL OVER.
BUT THE THING ABOUT A DEAL LIKE THIS IS IT COMES WITH A CERTAIN AMOUNT OF RISK. A MOVING TARGET IS PREFERRED.
YOU CAN GET BOTH OF THESE, UNLOADED, FOR A MILLION CELLS.
AN EXTRA 50,000, AND I'LL THROW IN ENOUGH ROUNDS FOR YOU TO TERRORIZE A WHOLE LOT OF PEOPLE AND HAVE SOME FUN.
HAVE SOME FUN?

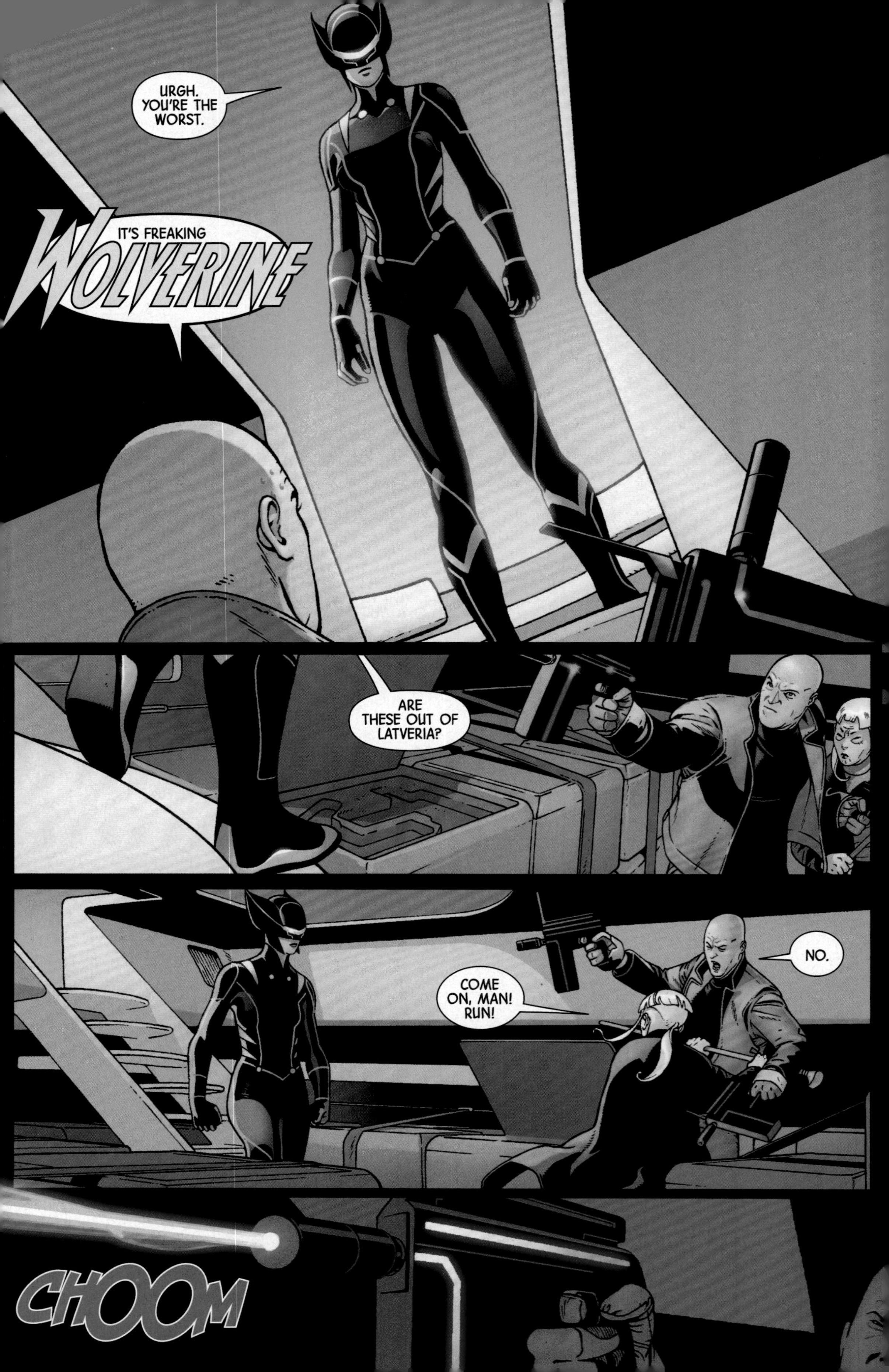
URGH. YOU'RE THE WORST.
IT'S FREAKING WOLVERINE
ARE THESE OUT OF LATVERIA?
NO.
COME ON, MAN! RUN!
CHOOM

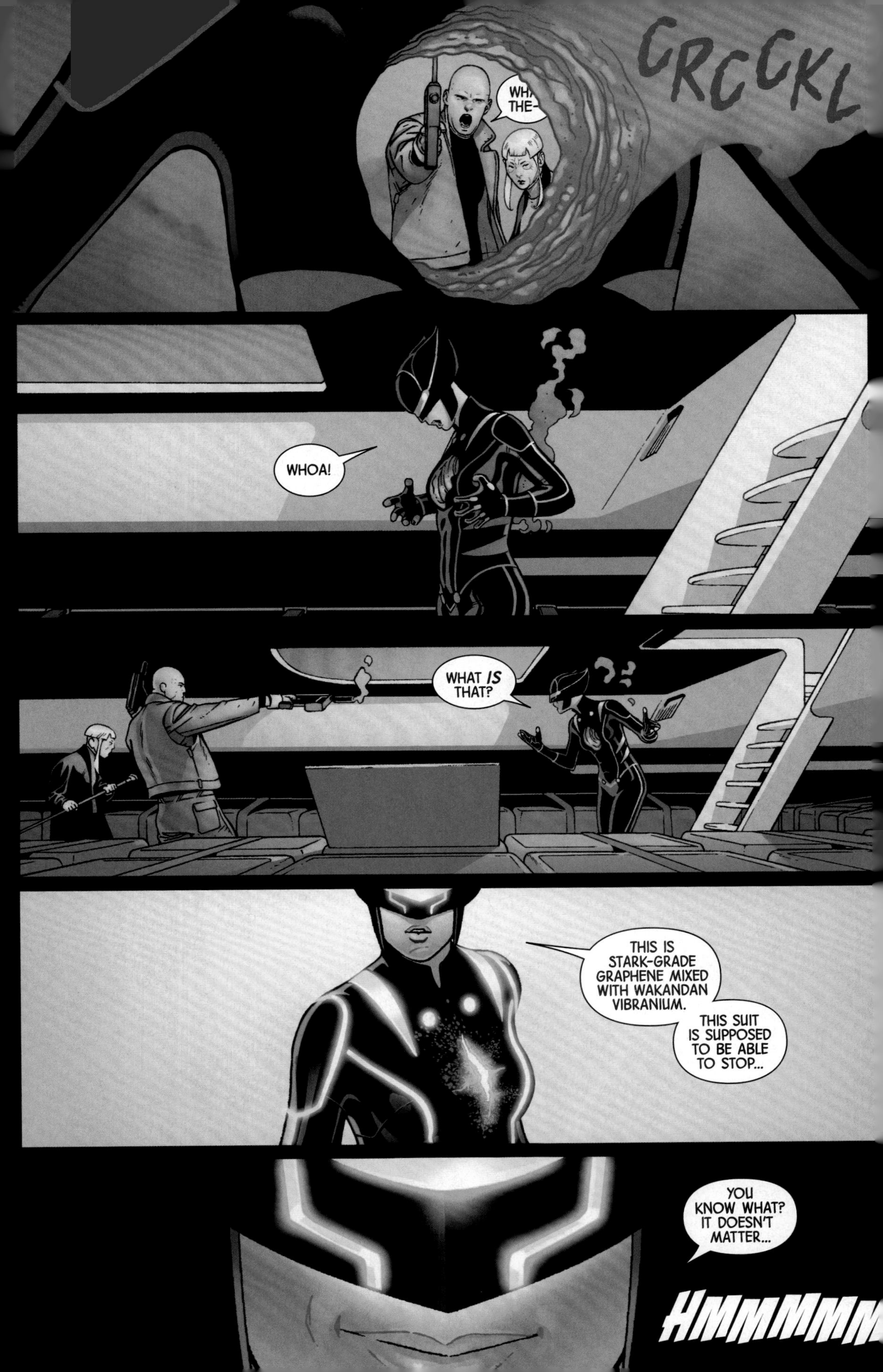
CRCCKL
WHA THE--
WHOA!
WHAT IS THAT?
THIS IS STARK-GRADE GRAPHENE MIXED WITH WAKANDAN VIBRANIUM.
THIS SUIT IS SUPPOSED TO BE ABLE TO STOP...
YOU KNOW WHAT? IT DOESN'T MATTER...
HMMMMM

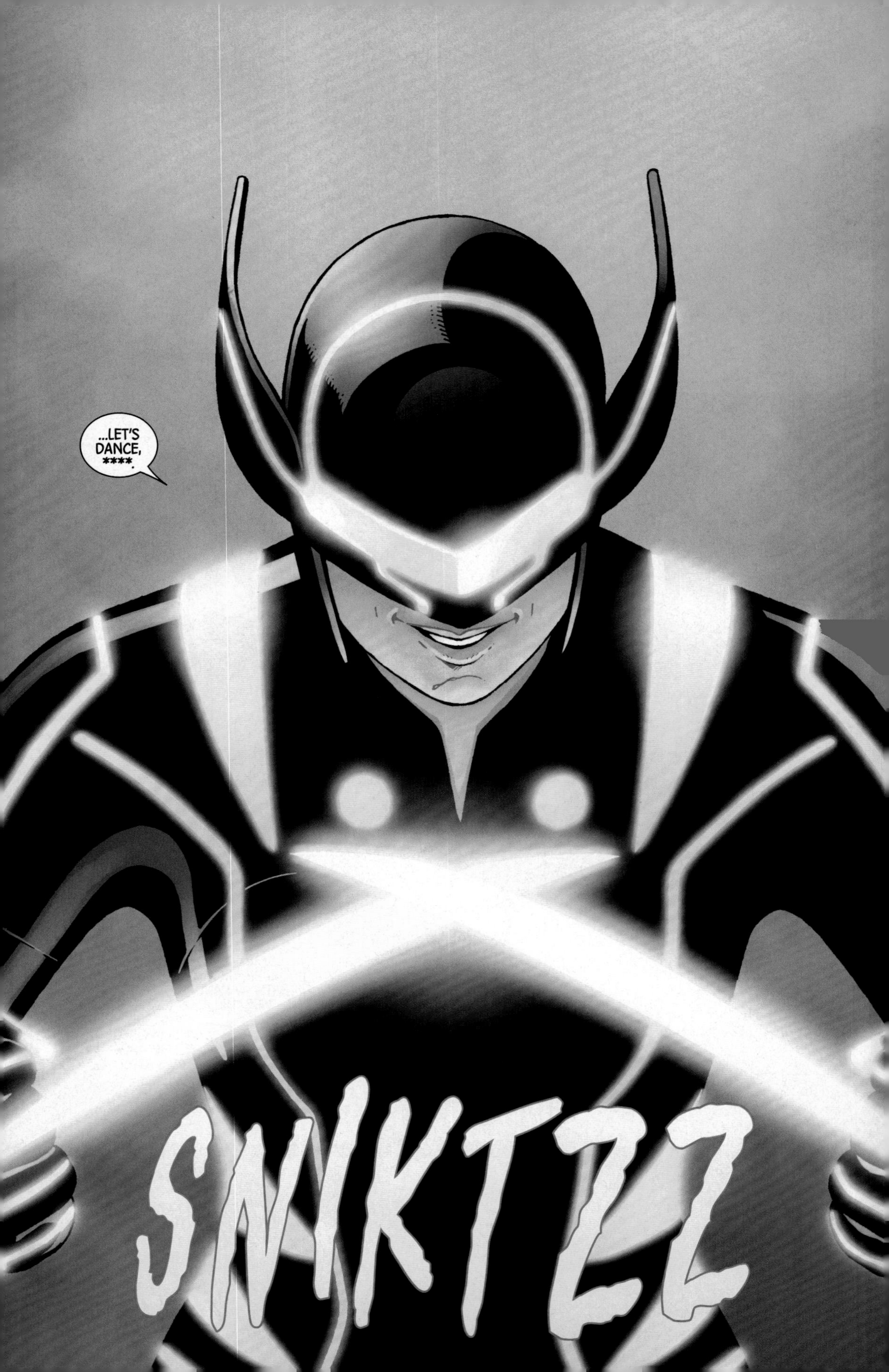
...LET'S DANCE, ****.
SNIKTZZ

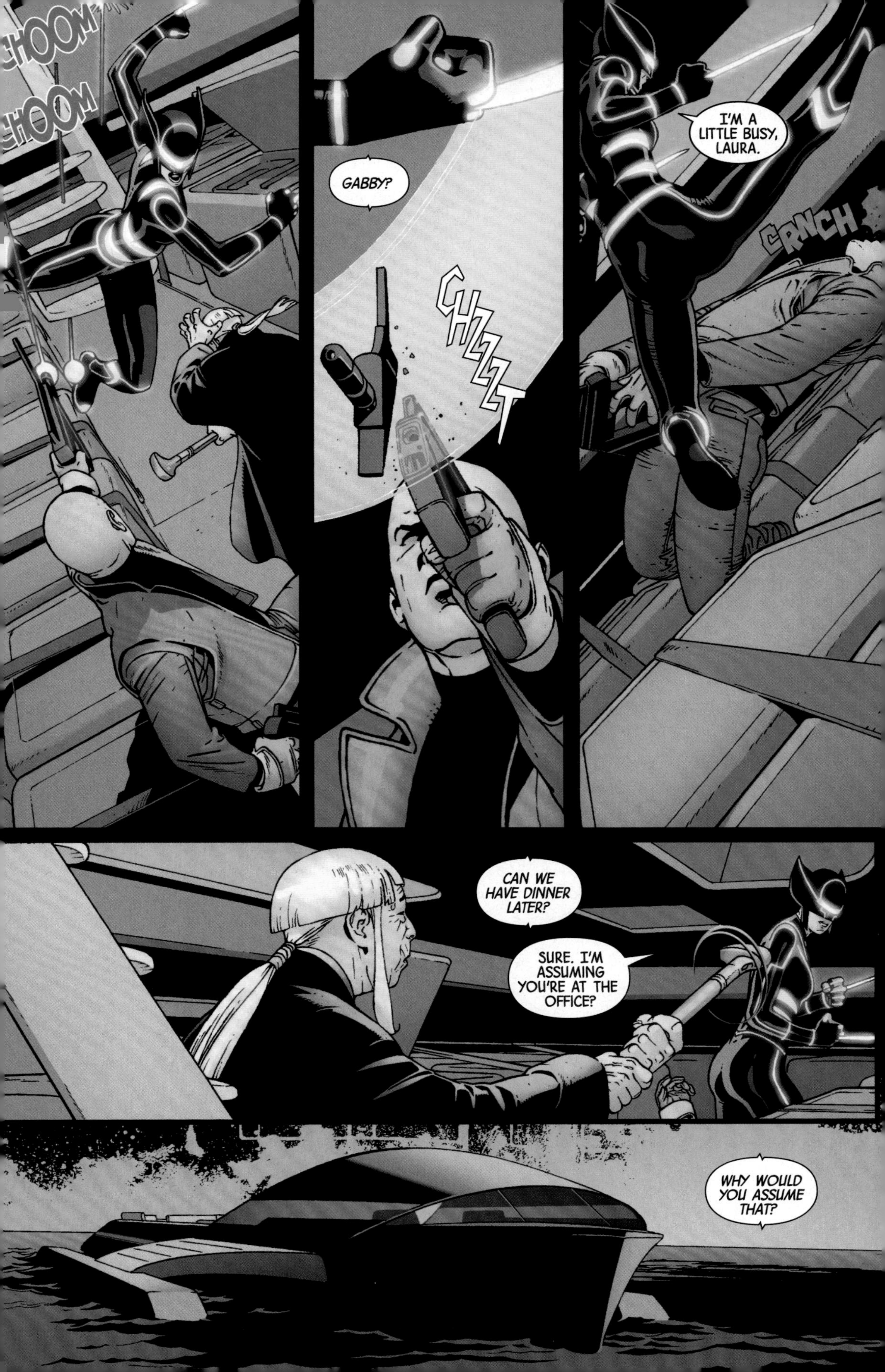
CHOOM
CHOOM
GABBY?
CHZZZT
I'M A LITTLE BUSY, LAURA.
CRNCH
CAN WE HAVE DINNER LATER?
SURE. I'M ASSUMING YOU'RE AT THE OFFICE?
WHY WOULD YOU ASSUME THAT?

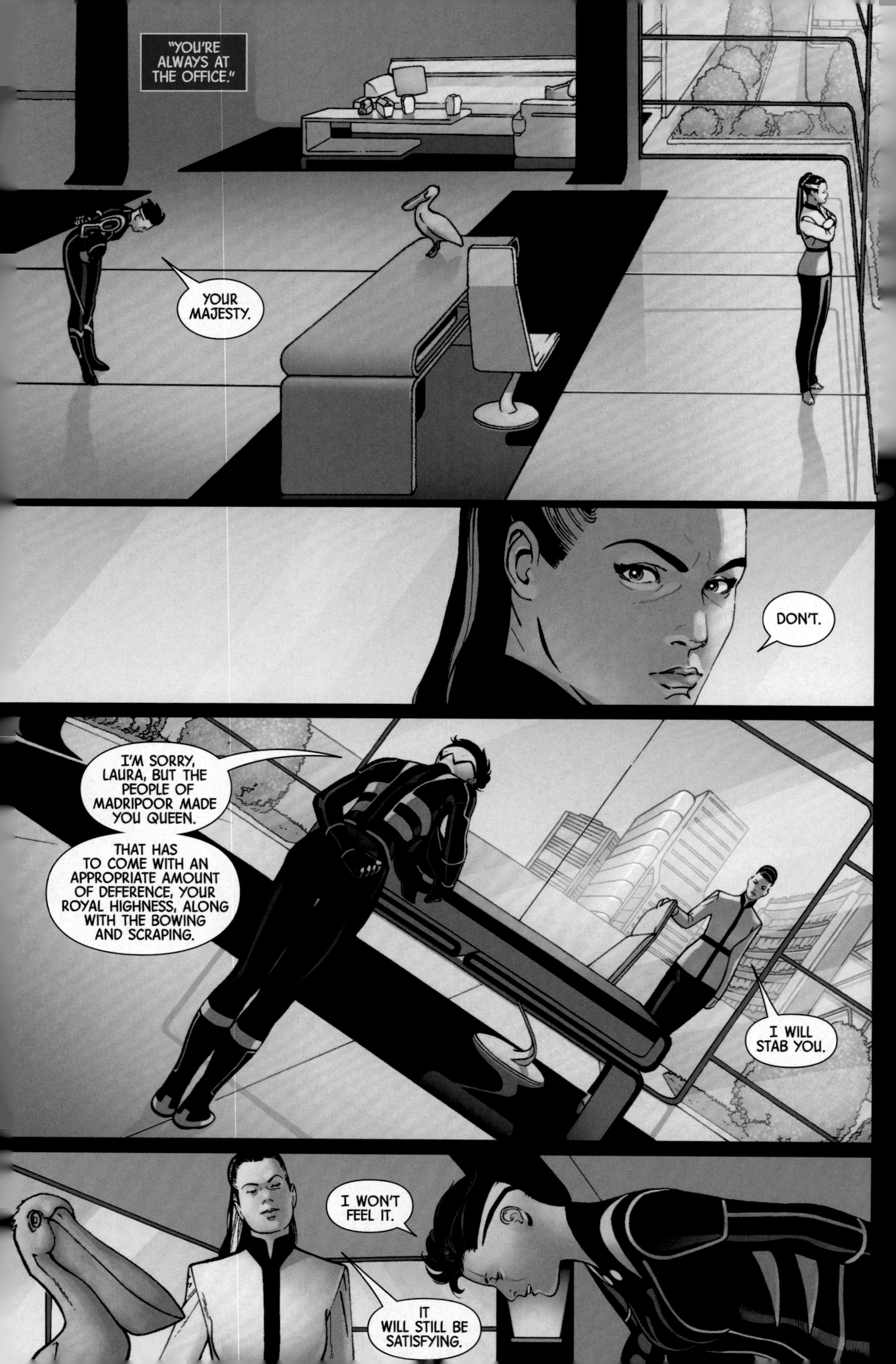
"YOU'RE ALWAYS AT THE OFFICE."
YOUR MAJESTY.
DON'T.
I'M SORRY, LAURA, BUT THE PEOPLE OF MADRIPOOR MADE YOU QUEEN.
THAT HAS TO COME WITH AN APPROPRIATE AMOUNT OF DEFERENCE, YOUR ROYAL HIGHNESS, ALONG WITH THE BOWING AND SCRAPING.
I WILL STAB YOU.
I WON'T FEEL IT.
IT WILL STILL BE SATISFYING.

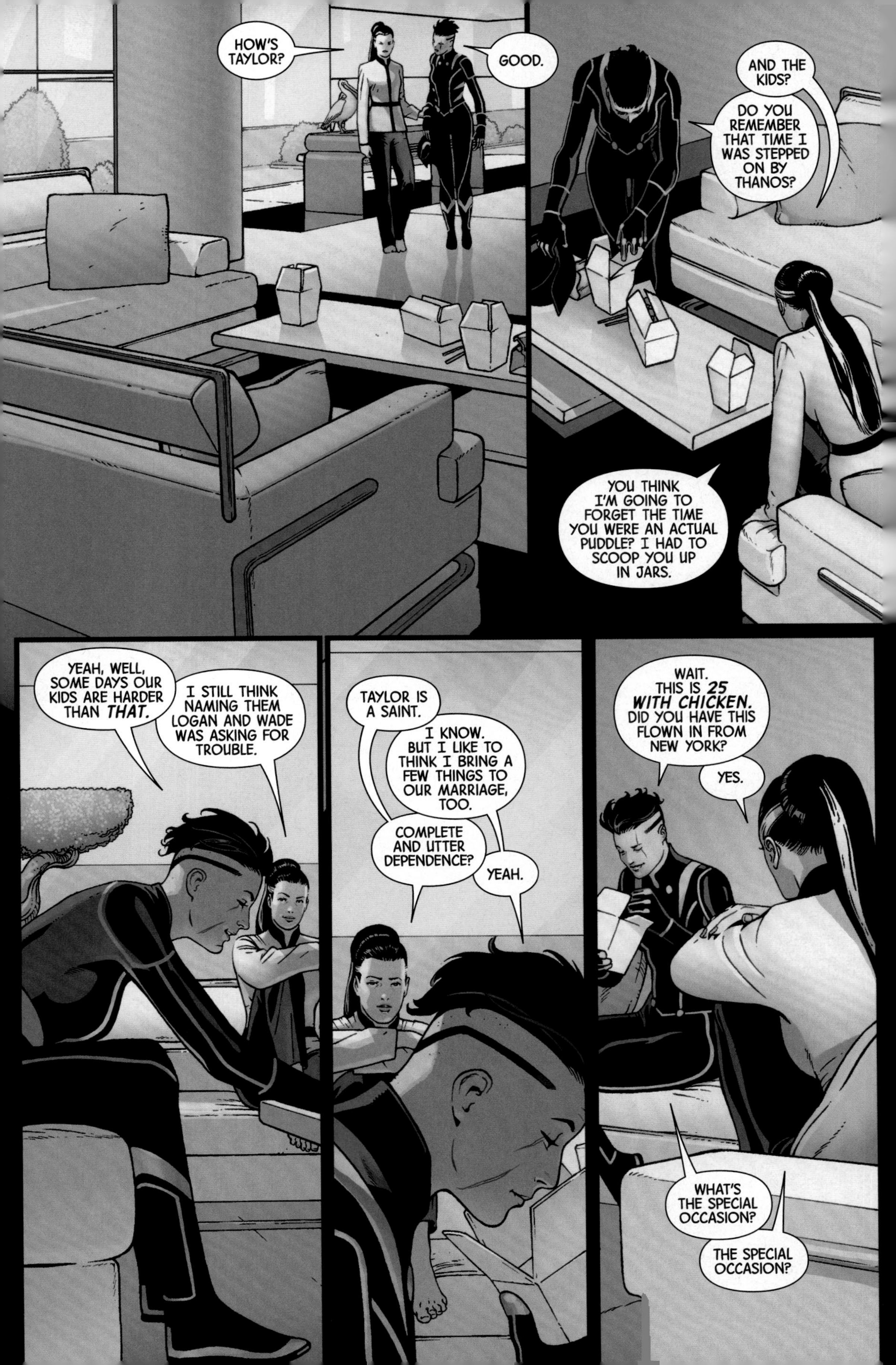
HOW'S TAYLOR?
GOOD.
AND THE KIDS?
DO YOU REMEMBER THAT TIME I WAS STEPPED ON BY THANOS?
YOU THINK I'M GOING TO FORGET THE TIME YOU WERE AN ACTUAL PUDDLE? I HAD TO SCOOP YOU UP IN JARS.
YEAH, WELL, SOME DAYS OUR KIDS ARE HARDER THAN *THAT.*
I STILL THINK NAMING THEM LOGAN AND WADE WAS ASKING FOR TROUBLE.
TAYLOR IS A SAINT.
I KNOW. BUT I LIKE TO THINK I BRING A FEW THINGS TO OUR MARRIAGE, TOO.
COMPLETE AND UTTER DEPENDENCE?
YEAH.
WAIT. THIS IS ***25 WITH CHICKEN.*** DID YOU HAVE THIS FLOWN IN FROM NEW YORK?
YES.
WHAT'S THE SPECIAL OCCASION?
THE SPECIAL OCCASION?

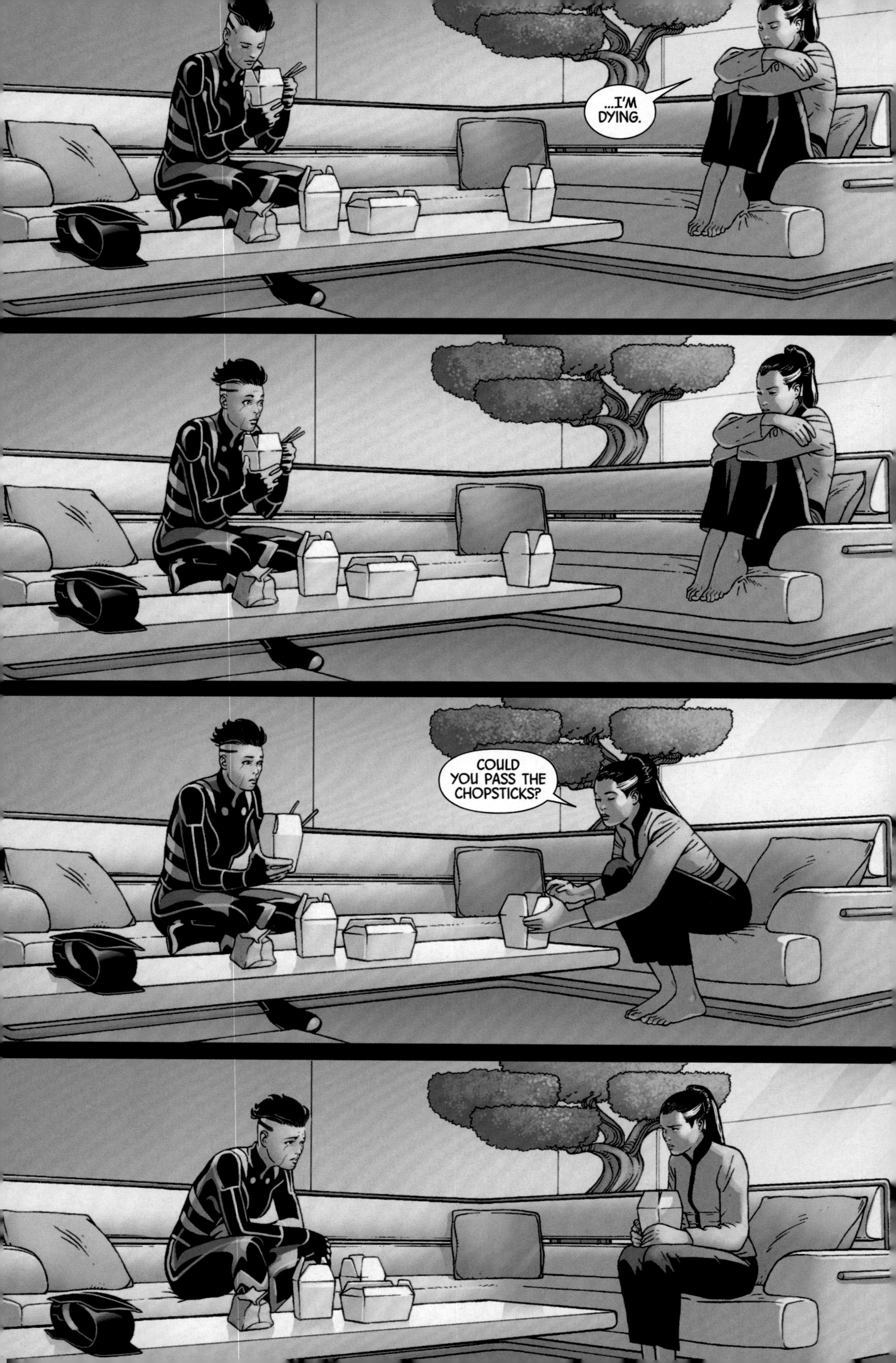
...I'M DYING.
COULD YOU PASS THE CHOPSTICKS?

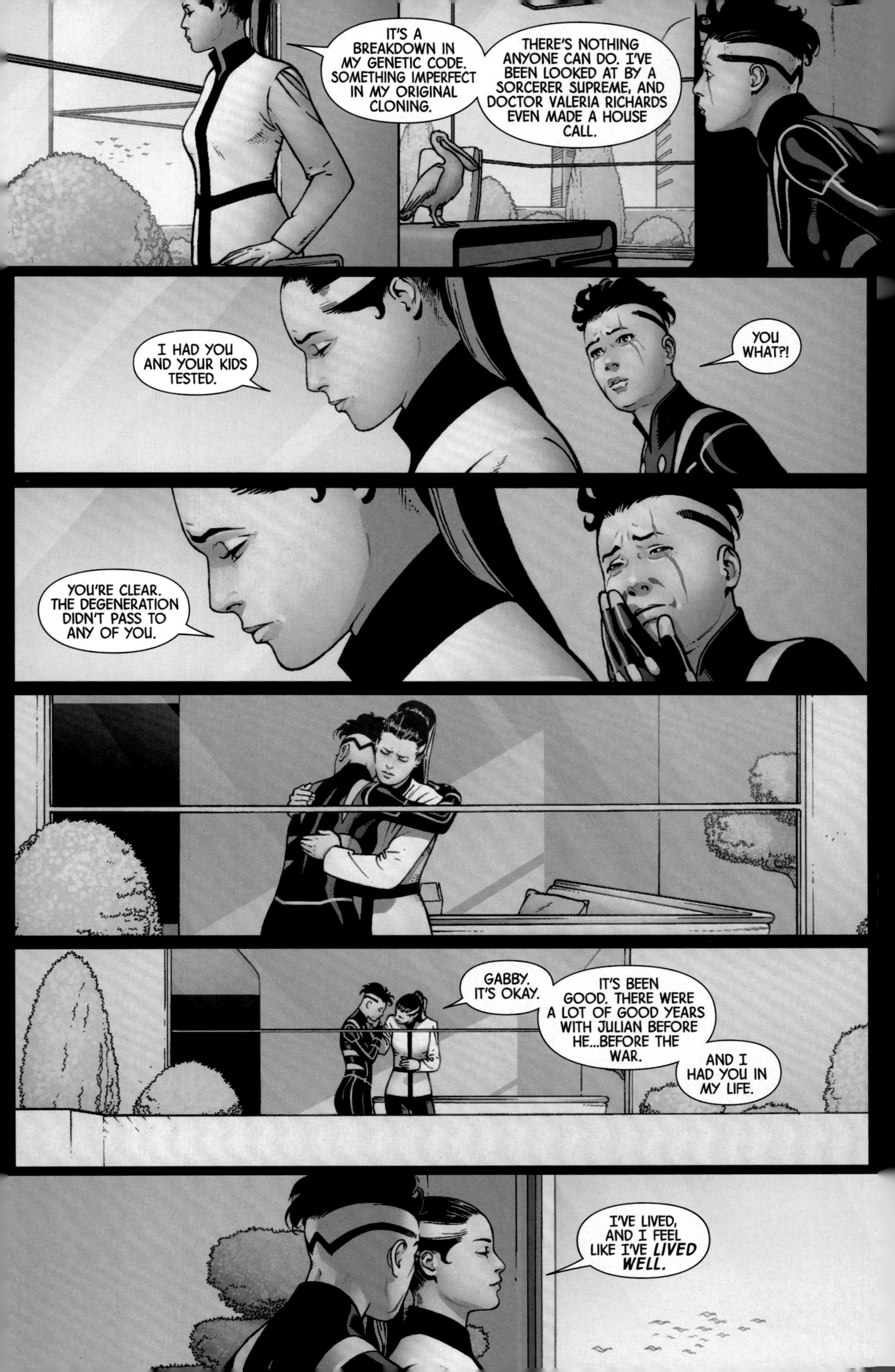
IT'S A BREAKDOWN IN MY GENETIC CODE. SOMETHING IMPERFECT IN MY ORIGINAL CLONING.
THERE'S NOTHING ANYONE CAN DO. I'VE BEEN LOOKED AT BY A SORCERER SUPREME, AND DOCTOR VALERIA RICHARDS EVEN MADE A HOUSE CALL.
I HAD YOU AND YOUR KIDS TESTED.
YOU WHAT?!
YOU'RE CLEAR. THE DEGENERATION DIDN'T PASS TO ANY OF YOU.
GABBY. IT'S OKAY.
IT'S BEEN GOOD. THERE WERE A LOT OF GOOD YEARS WITH JULIAN BEFORE HE...BEFORE THE WAR.
AND I HAD YOU IN MY LIFE.
I'VE LIVED, AND I FEEL LIKE I'VE LIVED WELL.

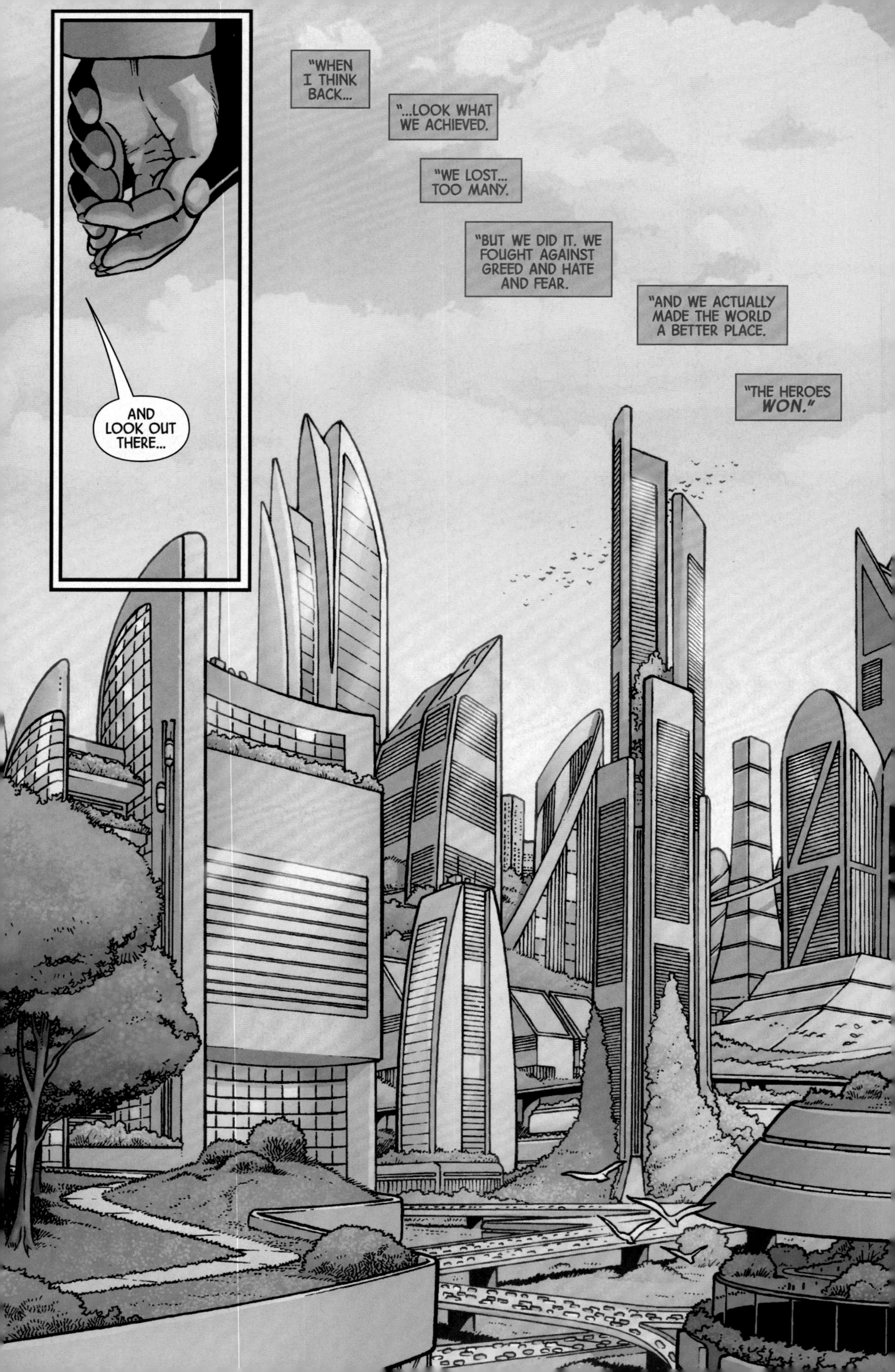
AND LOOK OUT THERE...
"WHEN I THINK BACK...
"...LOOK WHAT WE ACHIEVED.
"WE LOST... TOO MANY.
"BUT WE DID IT. WE FOUGHT AGAINST GREED AND HATE AND FEAR.
"AND WE ACTUALLY MADE THE WORLD A BETTER PLACE.
"THE HEROES WON."

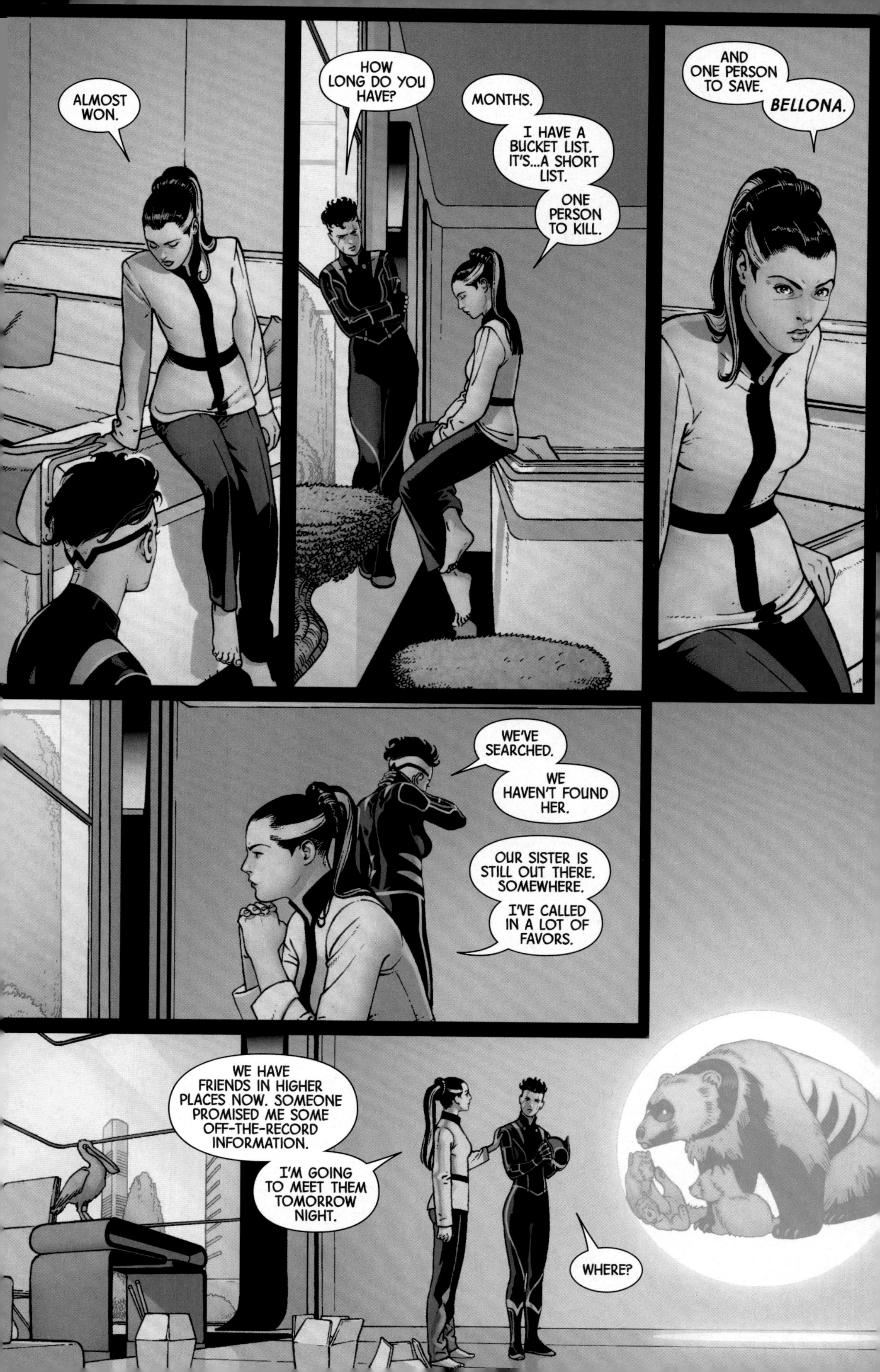

ALMOST WON.
HOW LONG DO YOU HAVE?
MONTHS.
I HAVE A BUCKET LIST. IT'S...A SHORT LIST.
ONE PERSON TO KILL.
AND ONE PERSON TO SAVE.
BELLONA.
WE'VE SEARCHED.
WE HAVEN'T FOUND HER.
OUR SISTER IS STILL OUT THERE. SOMEWHERE.
I'VE CALLED IN A LOT OF FAVORS.
WE HAVE FRIENDS IN HIGHER PLACES NOW. SOMEONE PROMISED ME SOME OFF-THE-RECORD INFORMATION.
I'M GOING TO MEET THEM TOMORROW NIGHT.
WHERE?

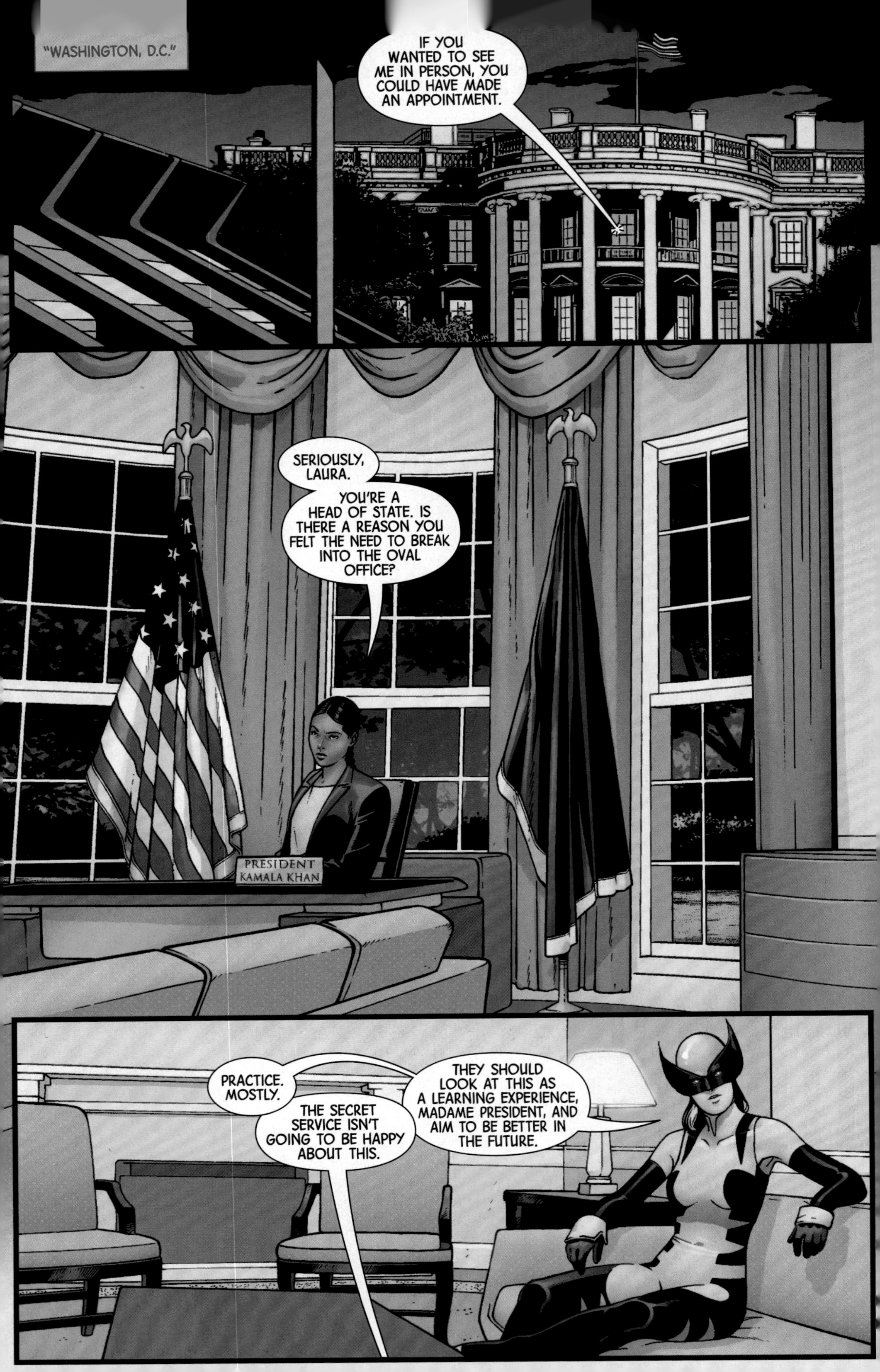
"WASHINGTON, D.C."
IF YOU WANTED TO SEE ME IN PERSON, YOU COULD HAVE MADE AN APPOINTMENT.
SERIOUSLY, LAURA.
YOU'RE A HEAD OF STATE. IS THERE A REASON YOU FELT THE NEED TO BREAK INTO THE OVAL OFFICE?
PRESIDENT KAMALA KHAN
PRACTICE. MOSTLY.
THEY SHOULD LOOK AT THIS AS A LEARNING EXPERIENCE, MADAME PRESIDENT, AND AIM TO BE BETTER IN THE FUTURE.
THE SECRET SERVICE ISN'T GOING TO BE HAPPY ABOUT THIS.

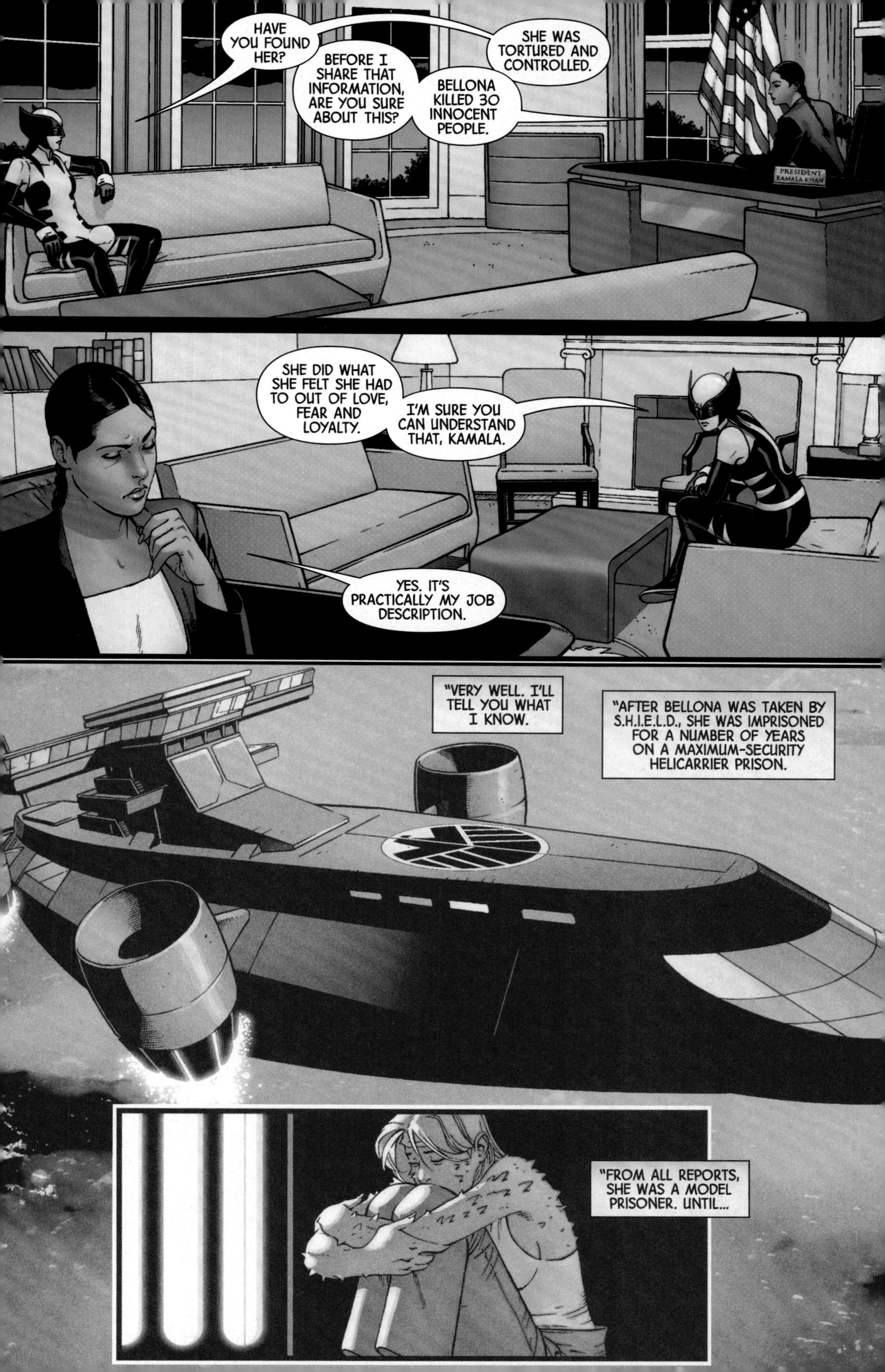
HAVE YOU FOUND HER?
BEFORE I SHARE THAT INFORMATION, ARE YOU SURE ABOUT THIS?
BELLONA KILLED 30 INNOCENT PEOPLE.
SHE WAS TORTURED AND CONTROLLED.
PRESIDENT KAMALA KHAN
SHE DID WHAT SHE FELT SHE HAD TO OUT OF LOVE, FEAR AND LOYALTY.
I'M SURE YOU CAN UNDERSTAND THAT, KAMALA.
YES. IT'S PRACTICALLY MY JOB DESCRIPTION.
"VERY WELL. I'LL TELL YOU WHAT I KNOW.
"AFTER BELLONA WAS TAKEN BY S.H.I.E.L.D., SHE WAS IMPRISONED FOR A NUMBER OF YEARS ON A MAXIMUM-SECURITY HELICARRIER PRISON.
"FROM ALL REPORTS, SHE WAS A MODEL PRISONER. UNTIL...

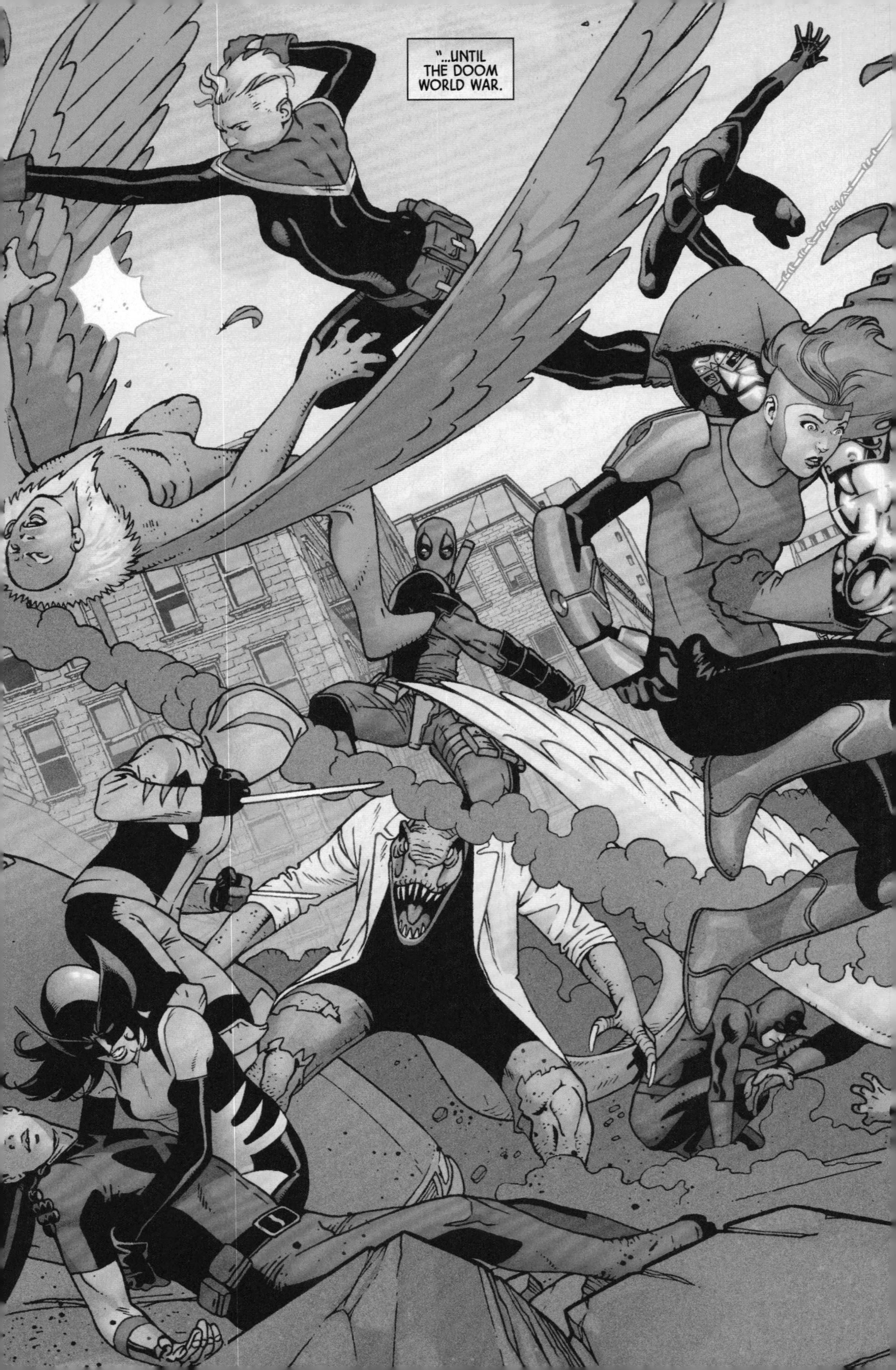
"...UNTIL THE DOOM WORLD WAR.

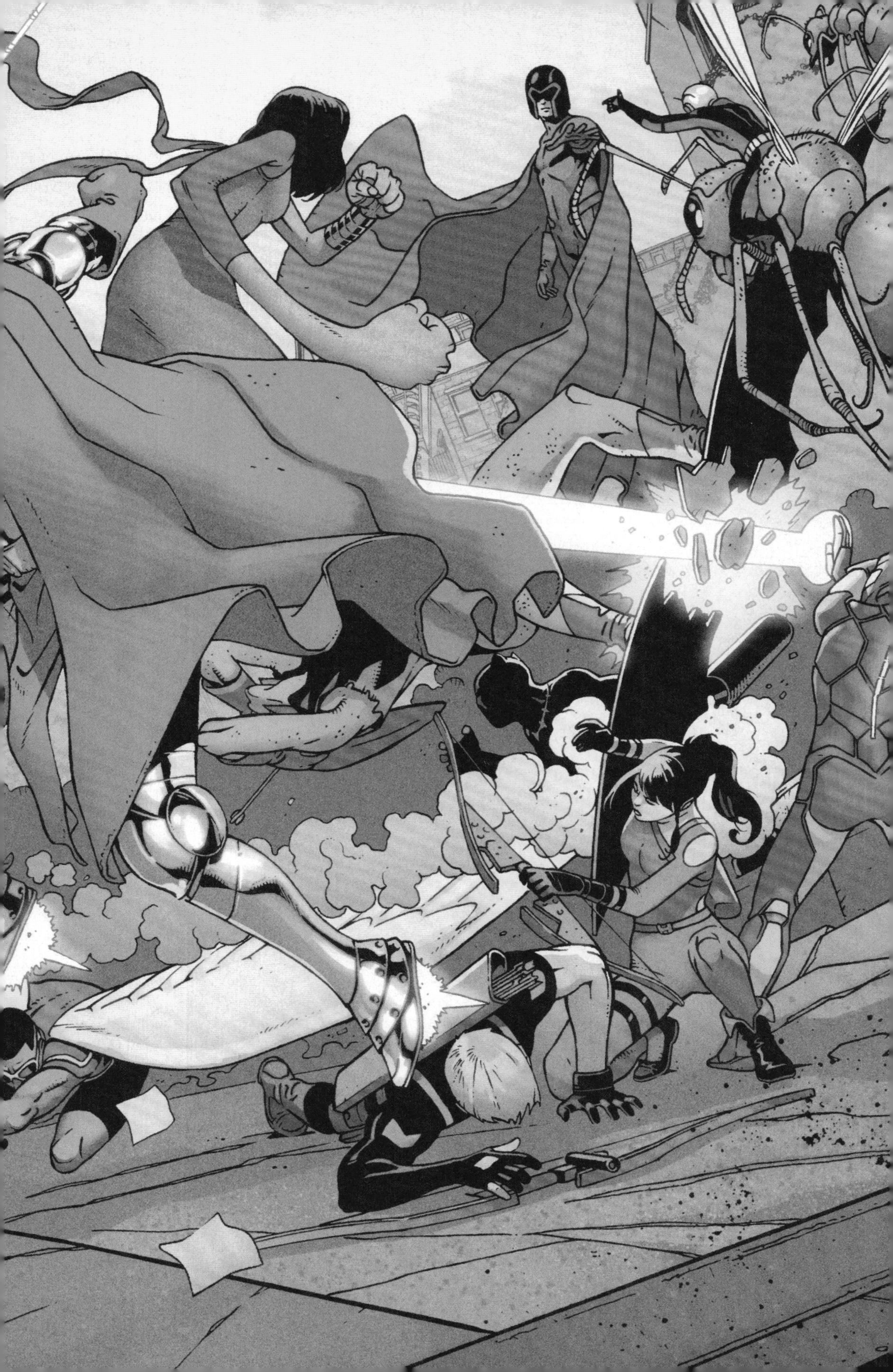

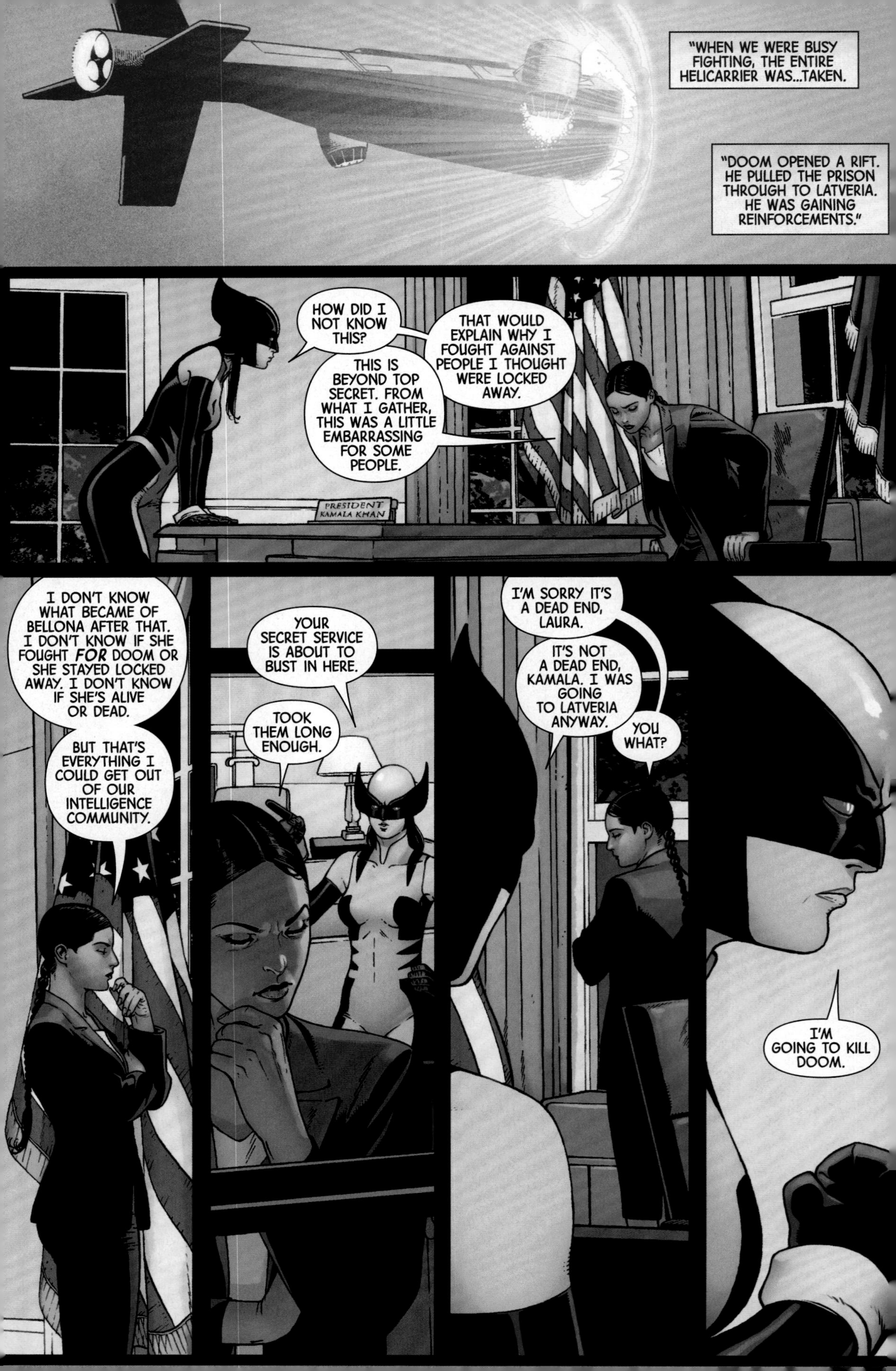
"WHEN WE WERE BUSY FIGHTING, THE ENTIRE HELICARRIER WAS...TAKEN.
"DOOM OPENED A RIFT. HE PULLED THE PRISON THROUGH TO LATVERIA. HE WAS GAINING REINFORCEMENTS."
HOW DID I NOT KNOW THIS?
THIS IS BEYOND TOP SECRET. FROM WHAT I GATHER, THIS WAS A LITTLE EMBARRASSING FOR SOME PEOPLE.
THAT WOULD EXPLAIN WHY I FOUGHT AGAINST PEOPLE I THOUGHT WERE LOCKED AWAY.
PRESIDENT KAMALA KHAN
I DON'T KNOW WHAT BECAME OF BELLONA AFTER THAT. I DON'T KNOW IF SHE FOUGHT *FOR* DOOM OR SHE STAYED LOCKED AWAY. I DON'T KNOW IF SHE'S ALIVE OR DEAD.
BUT THAT'S EVERYTHING I COULD GET OUT OF OUR INTELLIGENCE COMMUNITY.
YOUR SECRET SERVICE IS ABOUT TO BUST IN HERE.
TOOK THEM LONG ENOUGH.
I'M SORRY IT'S A DEAD END, LAURA.
IT'S NOT A DEAD END, KAMALA. I WAS GOING TO LATVERIA ANYWAY.
YOU WHAT?
I'M GOING TO KILL DOOM.

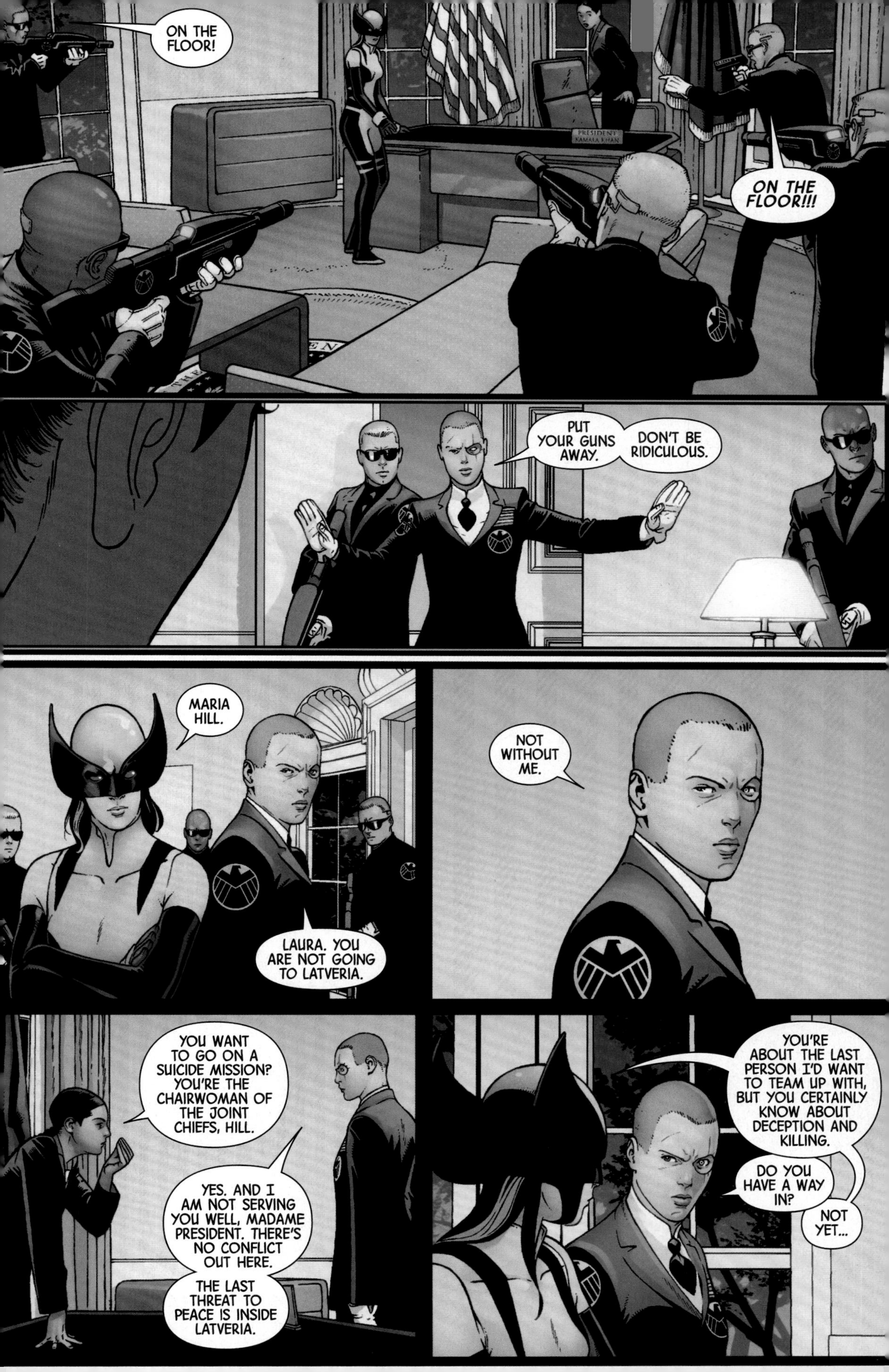
ON THE FLOOR!
PRESIDENT KAMALA KHAN
ON THE FLOOR!!!
PUT YOUR GUNS AWAY.
DON'T BE RIDICULOUS.
MARIA HILL.
LAURA. YOU ARE NOT GOING TO LATVERIA.
NOT WITHOUT ME.
YOU WANT TO GO ON A SUICIDE MISSION? YOU'RE THE CHAIRWOMAN OF THE JOINT CHIEFS, HILL.
YES. AND I AM NOT SERVING YOU WELL, MADAME PRESIDENT. THERE'S NO CONFLICT OUT HERE.
THE LAST THREAT TO PEACE IS INSIDE LATVERIA.
YOU'RE ABOUT THE LAST PERSON I'D WANT TO TEAM UP WITH, BUT YOU CERTAINLY KNOW ABOUT DECEPTION AND KILLING.
DO YOU HAVE A WAY IN?
NOT YET...

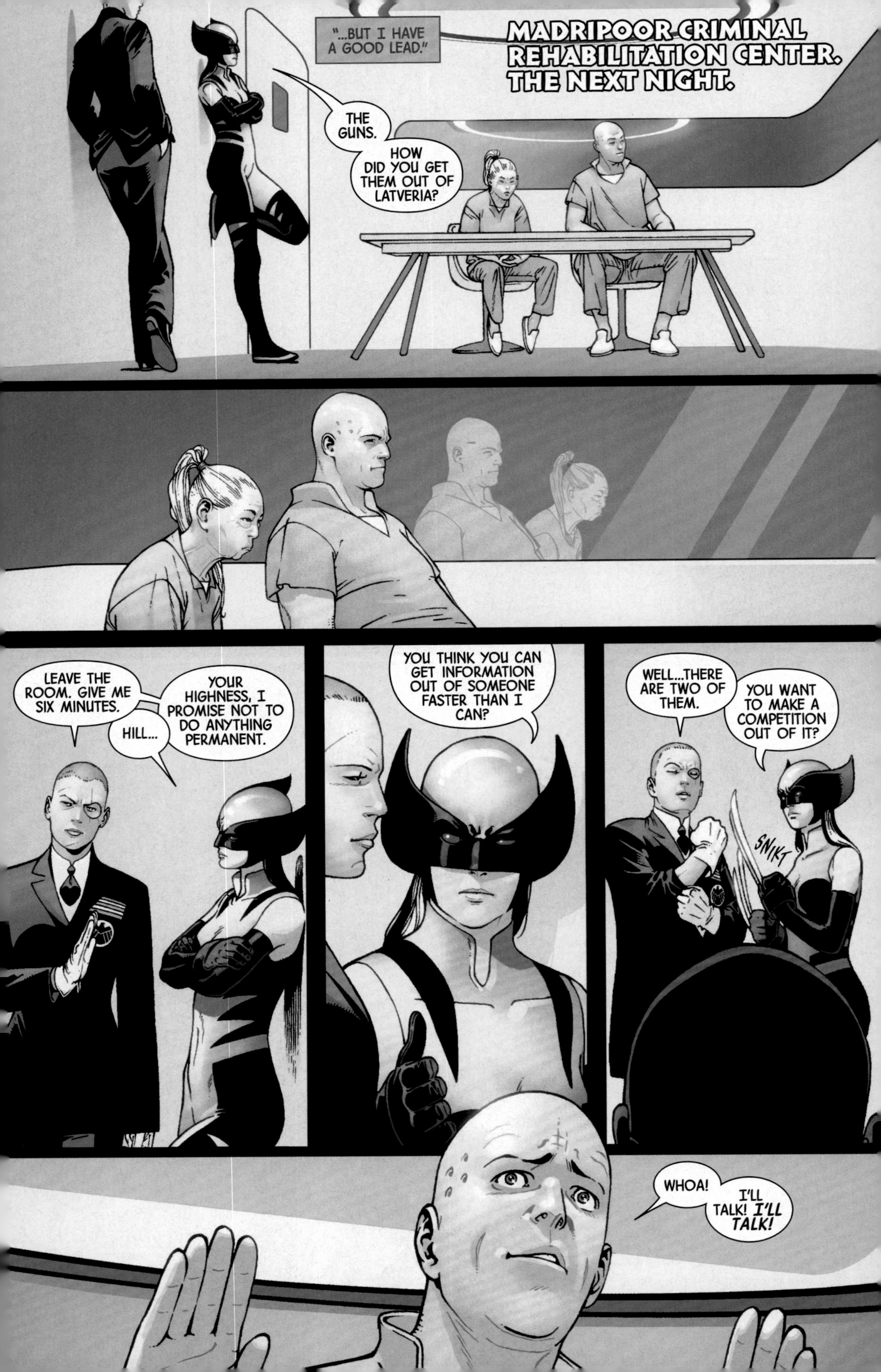
MADRIPOOR CRIMINAL REHABILITATION CENTER. THE NEXT NIGHT.
"...BUT I HAVE A GOOD LEAD."
THE GUNS.
HOW DID YOU GET THEM OUT OF LATVERIA?
LEAVE THE ROOM. GIVE ME SIX MINUTES.
HILL...
YOUR HIGHNESS, I PROMISE NOT TO DO ANYTHING PERMANENT.
YOU THINK YOU CAN GET INFORMATION OUT OF SOMEONE FASTER THAN I CAN?
WELL...THERE ARE TWO OF THEM.
YOU WANT TO MAKE A COMPETITION OUT OF IT?
SNIKT
WHOA!
I'LL TALK! *I'LL TALK!*

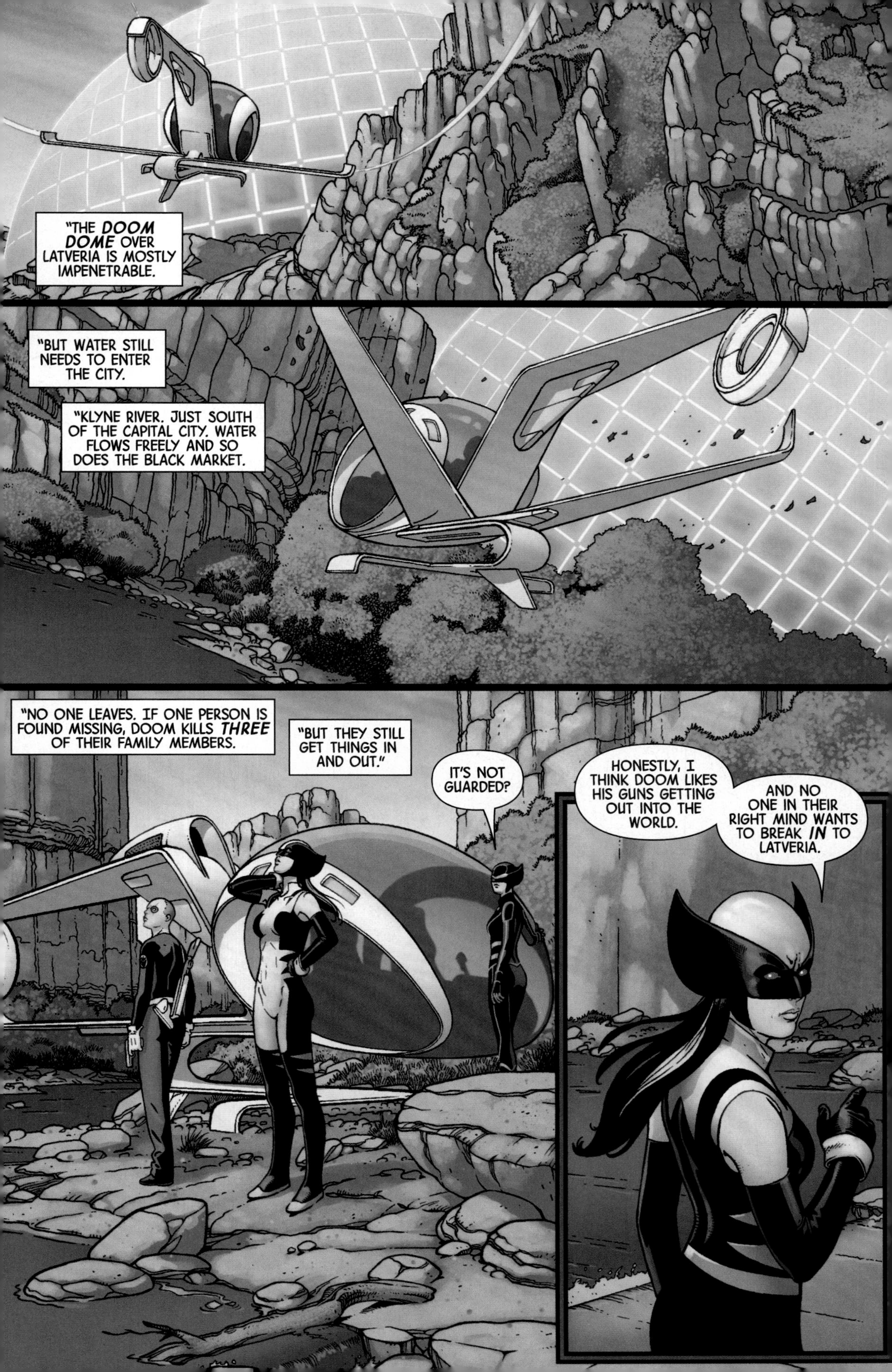
"THE DOOM DOME OVER LATVERIA IS MOSTLY IMPENETRABLE.
"BUT WATER STILL NEEDS TO ENTER THE CITY.
"KLYNE RIVER. JUST SOUTH OF THE CAPITAL CITY. WATER FLOWS FREELY AND SO DOES THE BLACK MARKET.
"NO ONE LEAVES. IF ONE PERSON IS FOUND MISSING, DOOM KILLS THREE OF THEIR FAMILY MEMBERS.
"BUT THEY STILL GET THINGS IN AND OUT."
IT'S NOT GUARDED?
HONESTLY, I THINK DOOM LIKES HIS GUNS GETTING OUT INTO THE WORLD.
AND NO ONE IN THEIR RIGHT MIND WANTS TO BREAK IN TO LATVERIA.

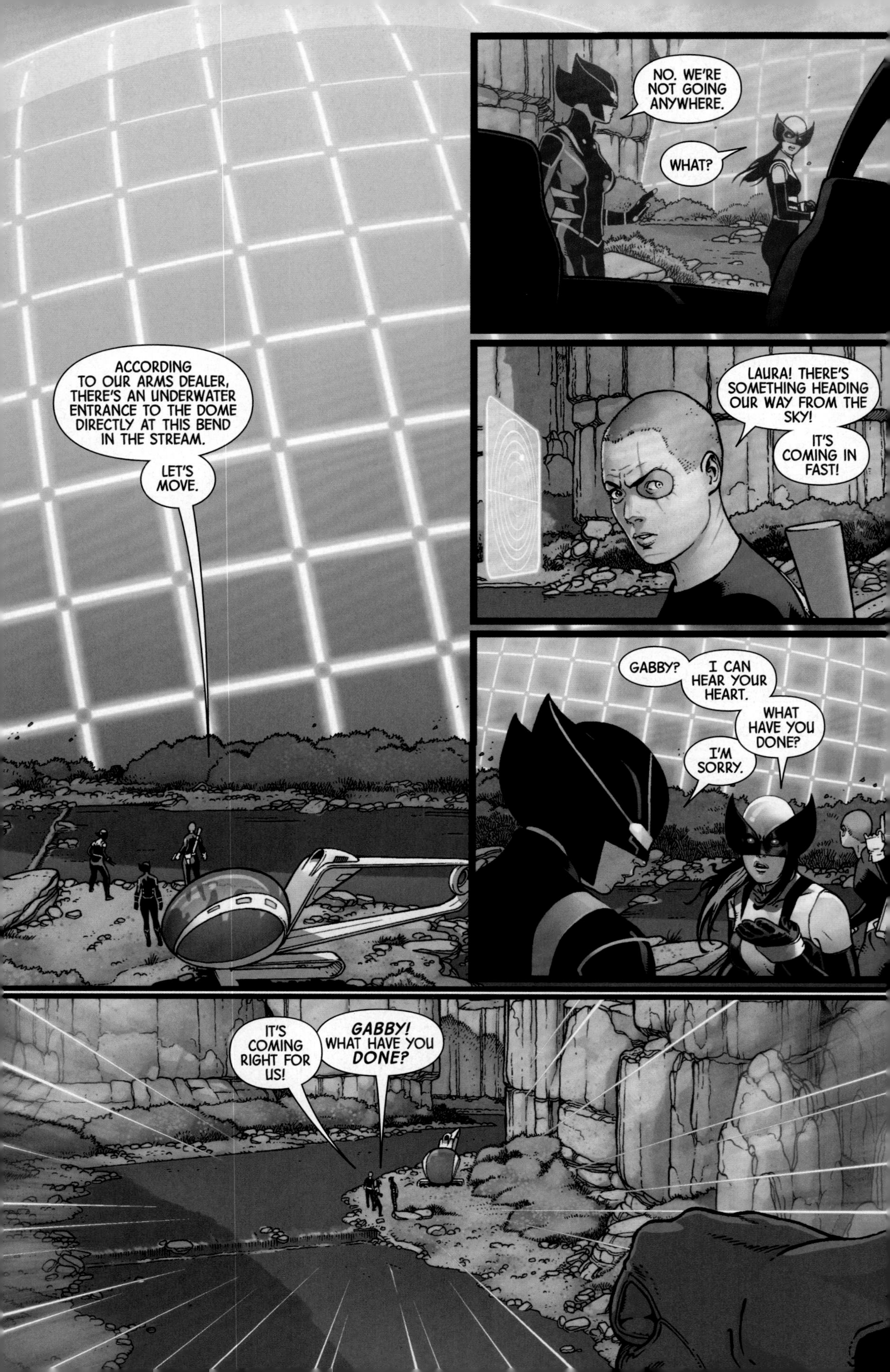

ACCORDING TO OUR ARMS DEALER, THERE'S AN UNDERWATER ENTRANCE TO THE DOME DIRECTLY AT THIS BEND IN THE STREAM.
LET'S MOVE.
NO. WE'RE NOT GOING ANYWHERE.
WHAT?
LAURA! THERE'S SOMETHING HEADING OUR WAY FROM THE SKY!
IT'S COMING IN FAST!
GABBY?
I CAN HEAR YOUR HEART.
WHAT HAVE YOU DONE?
I'M SORRY.
IT'S COMING RIGHT FOR US!
GABBY! WHAT HAVE YOU DONE?

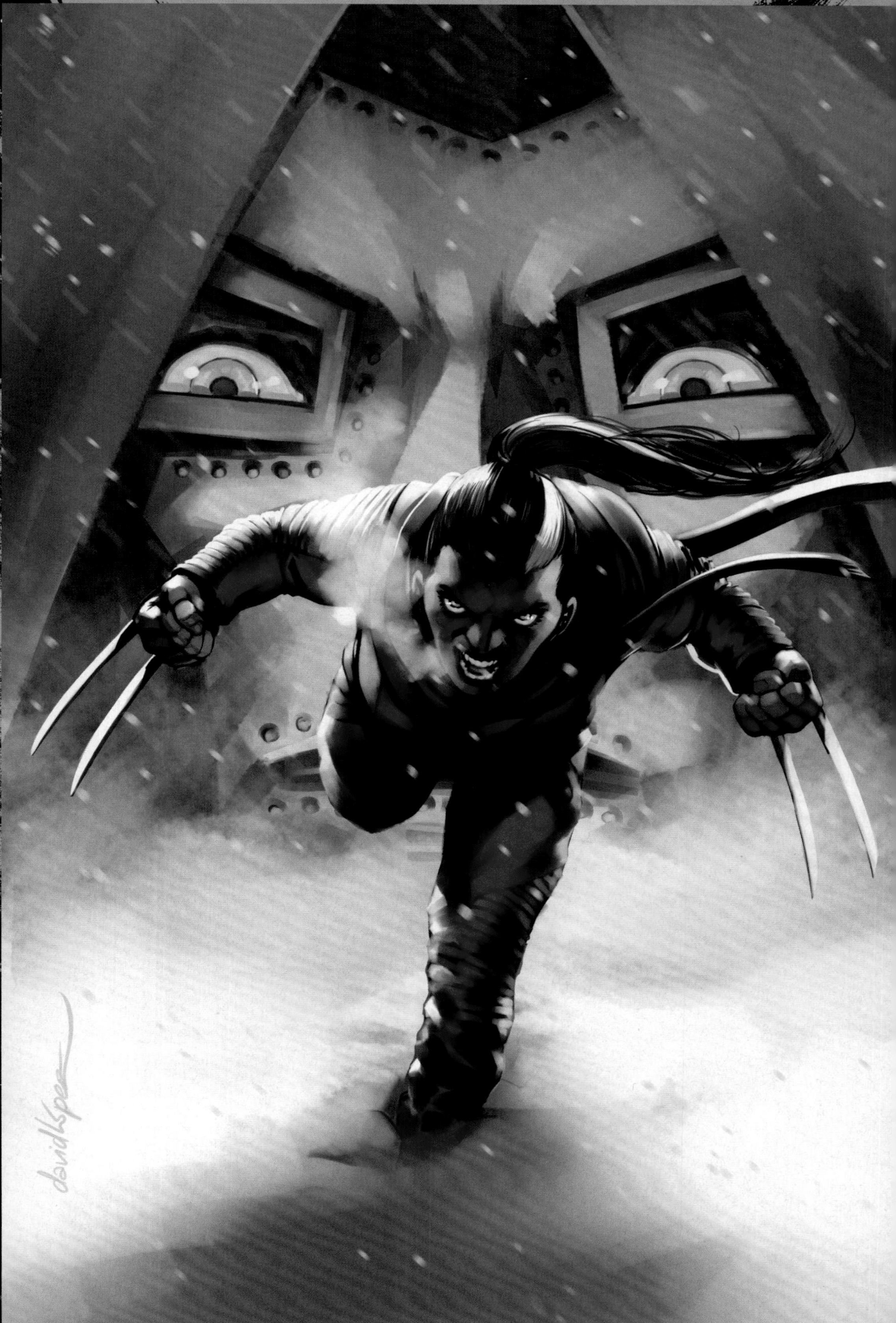

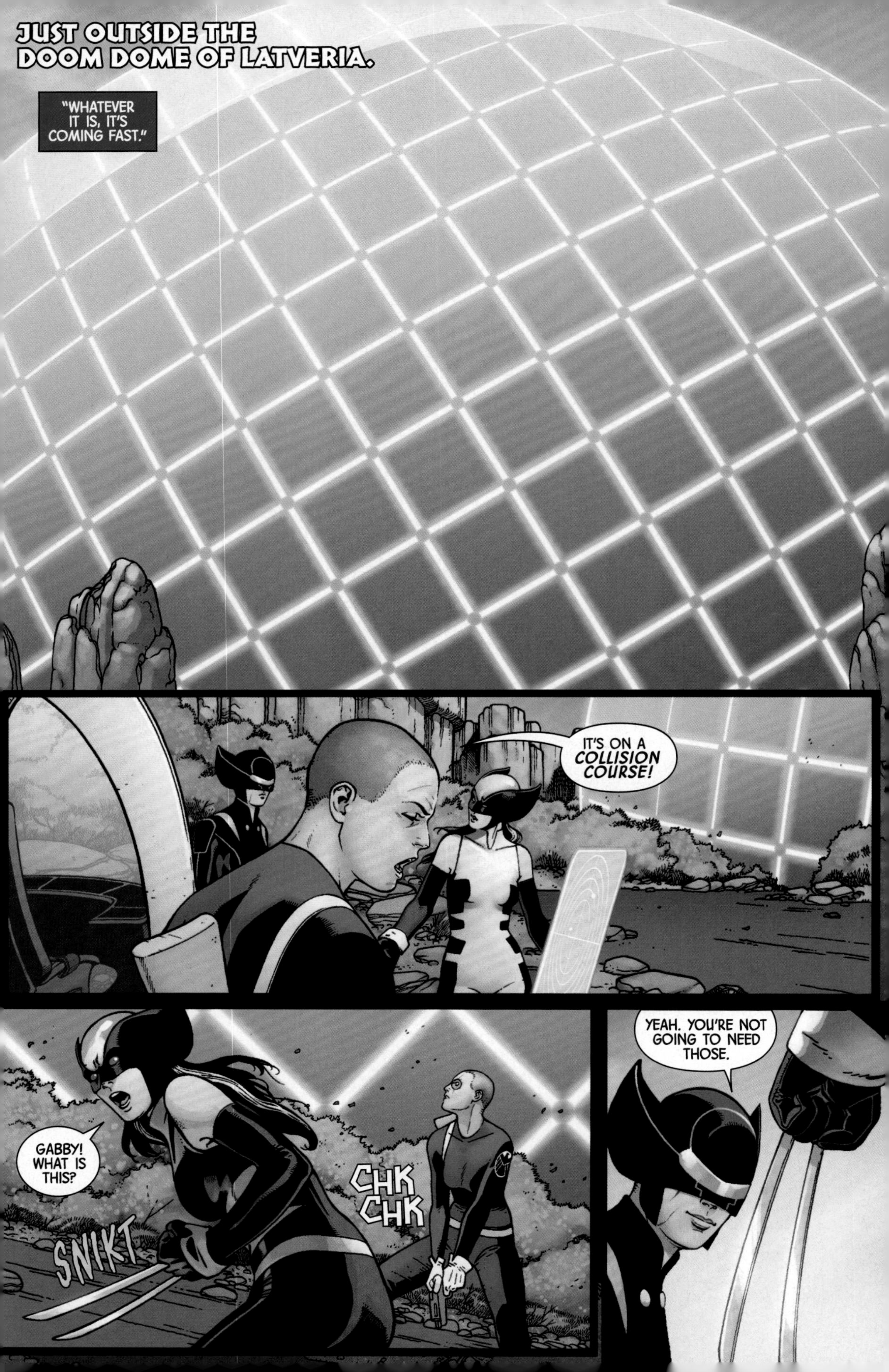
JUST OUTSIDE THE DOOM DOME OF LATVERIA.
"WHATEVER IT IS, IT'S COMING FAST."
IT'S ON A COLLISION COURSE!
GABBY! WHAT IS THIS?
SNIKT
CHK CHK
YEAH. YOU'RE NOT GOING TO NEED THOSE.

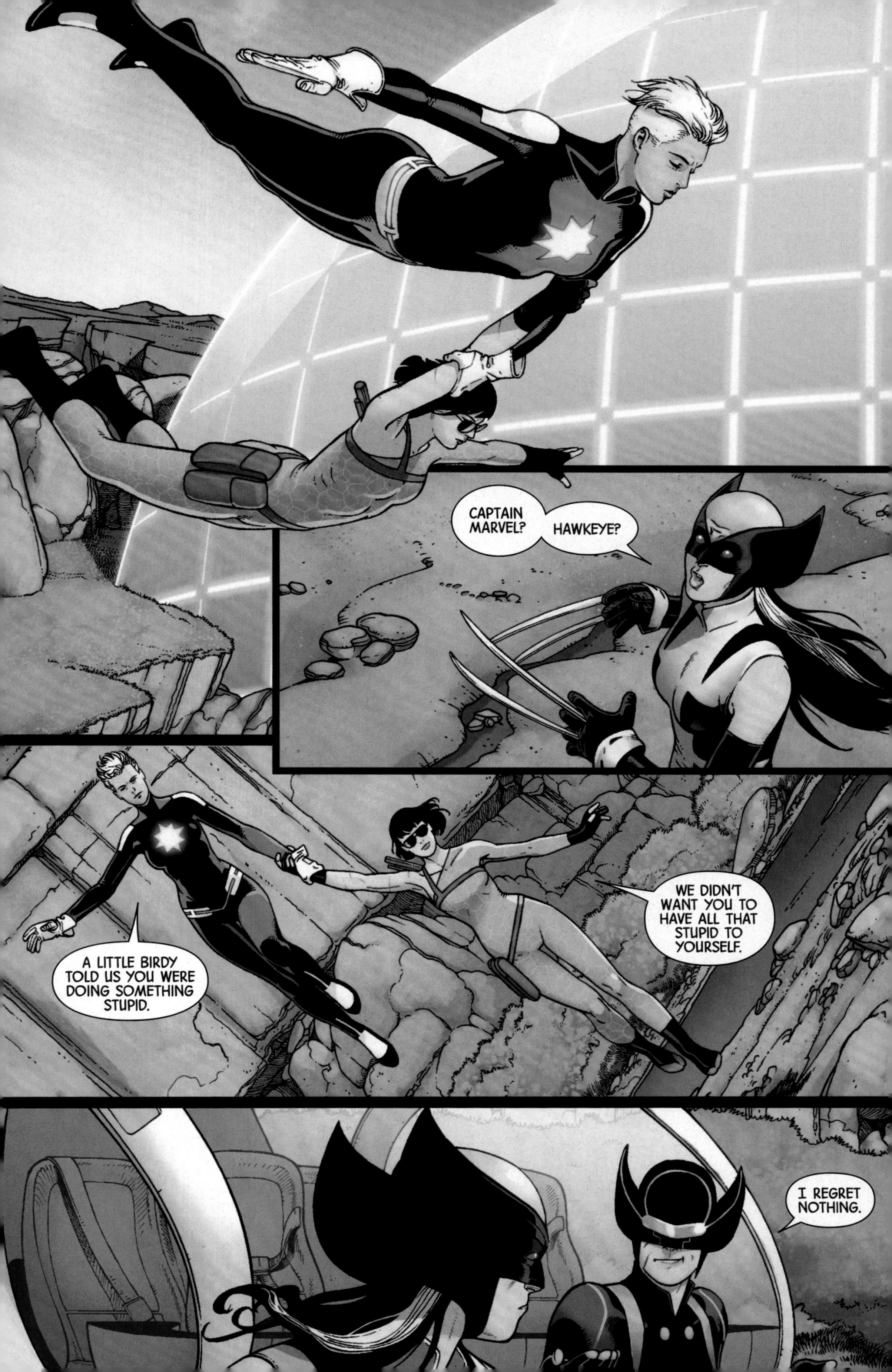
CAPTAIN MARVEL?
HAWKEYE?
A LITTLE BIRDY TOLD US YOU WERE DOING SOMETHING STUPID.
WE DIDN'T WANT YOU TO HAVE ALL THAT STUPID TO YOURSELF.
I REGRET NOTHING.

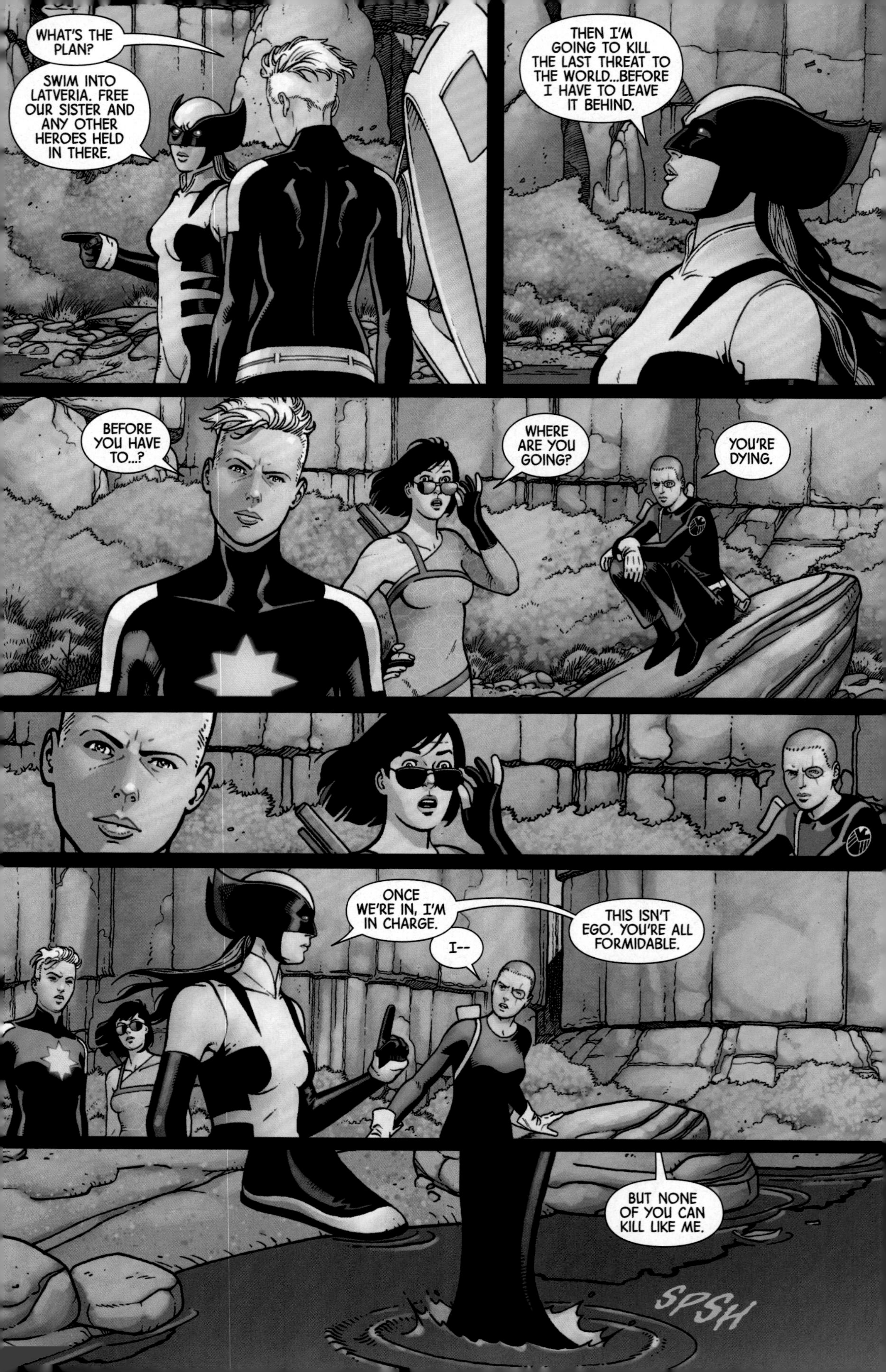
WHAT'S THE PLAN?
SWIM INTO LATVERIA. FREE OUR SISTER AND ANY OTHER HEROES HELD IN THERE.
THEN I'M GOING TO KILL THE LAST THREAT TO THE WORLD...BEFORE I HAVE TO LEAVE IT BEHIND.
BEFORE YOU HAVE TO...?
WHERE ARE YOU GOING?
YOU'RE DYING.
ONCE WE'RE IN, I'M IN CHARGE.
I--
THIS ISN'T EGO. YOU'RE ALL FORMIDABLE.
BUT NONE OF YOU CAN KILL LIKE ME.
SPSH

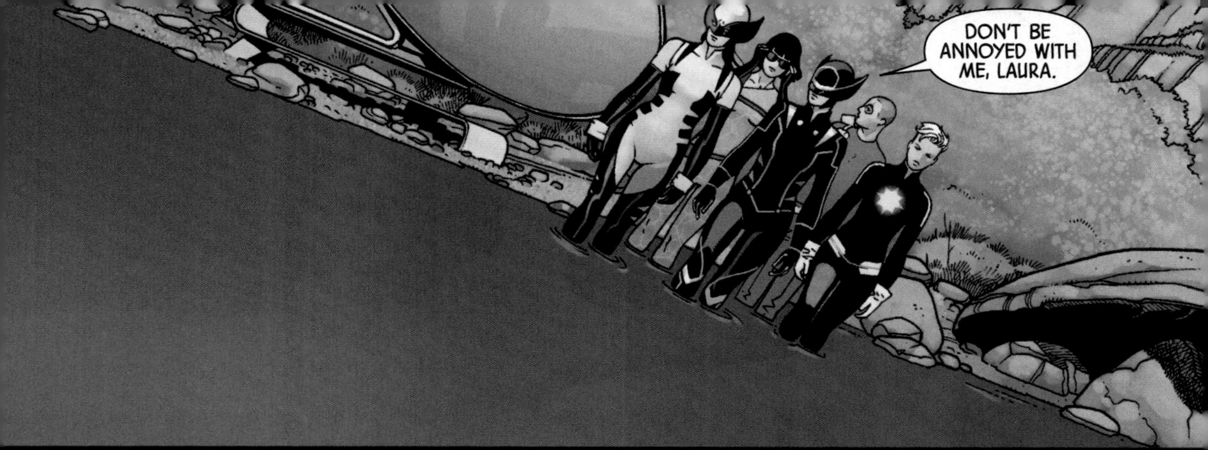
DON'T BE ANNOYED WITH ME, LAURA.

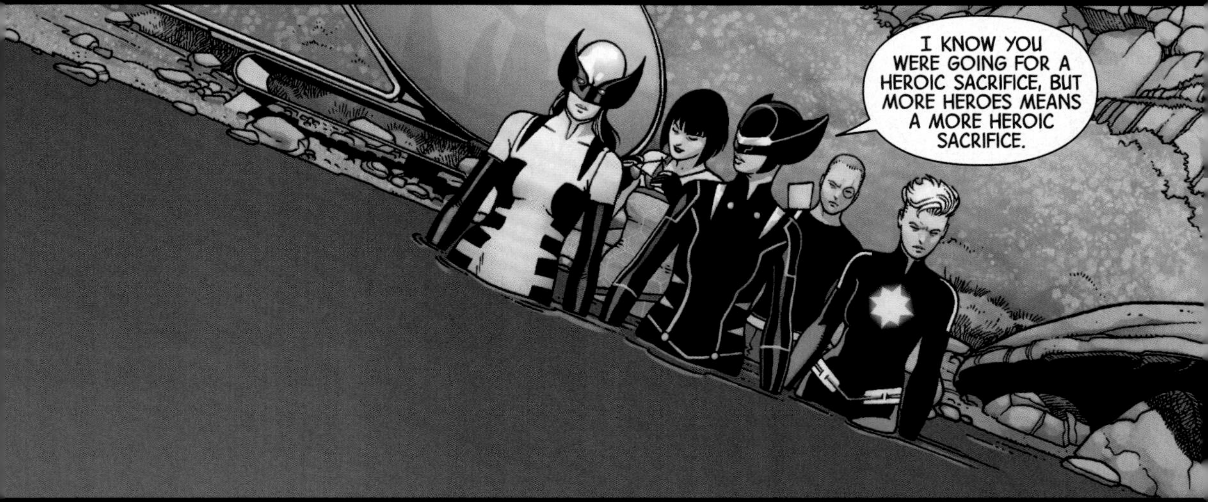
I KNOW YOU WERE GOING FOR A HEROIC SACRIFICE, BUT MORE HEROES MEANS A MORE HEROIC SACRIFICE.

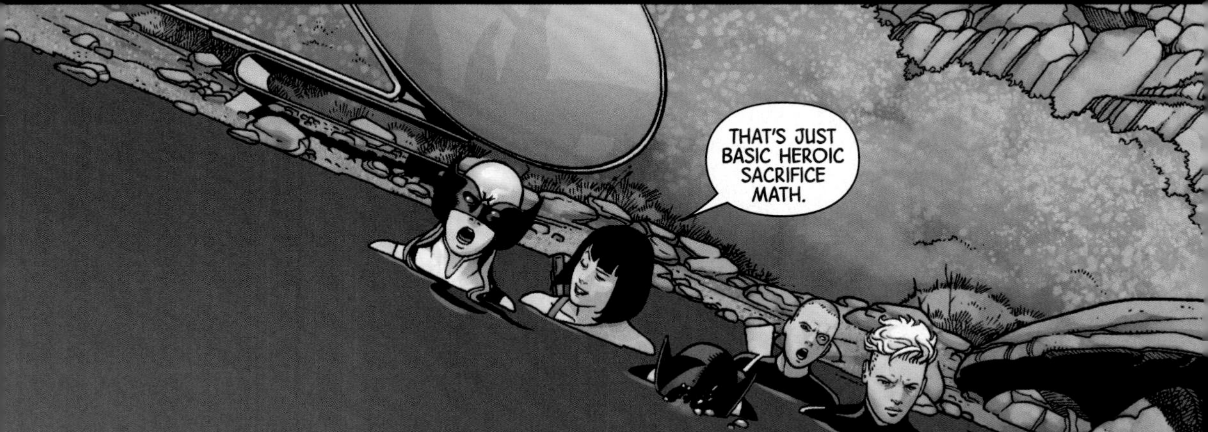
THAT'S JUST BASIC HEROIC SACRIFICE MATH.

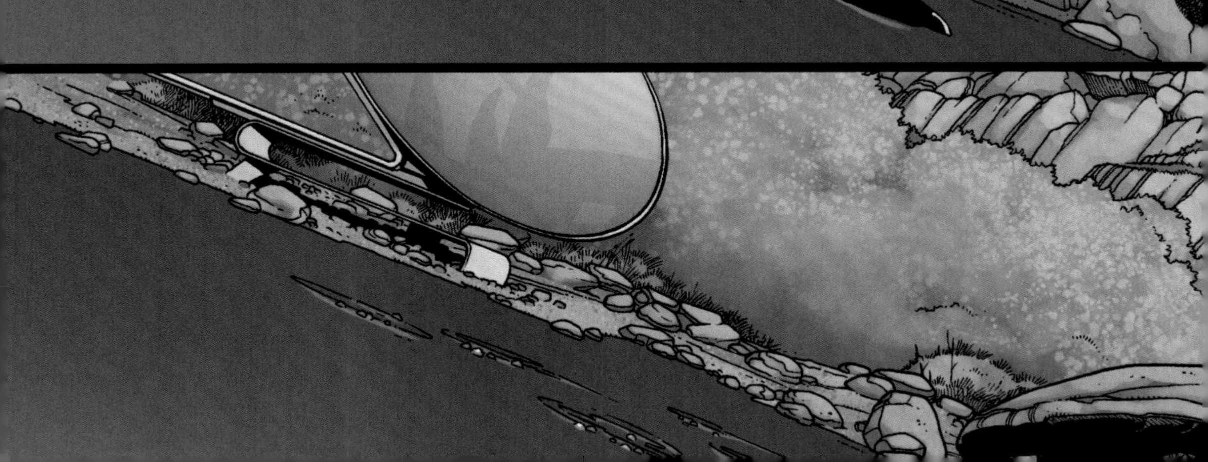

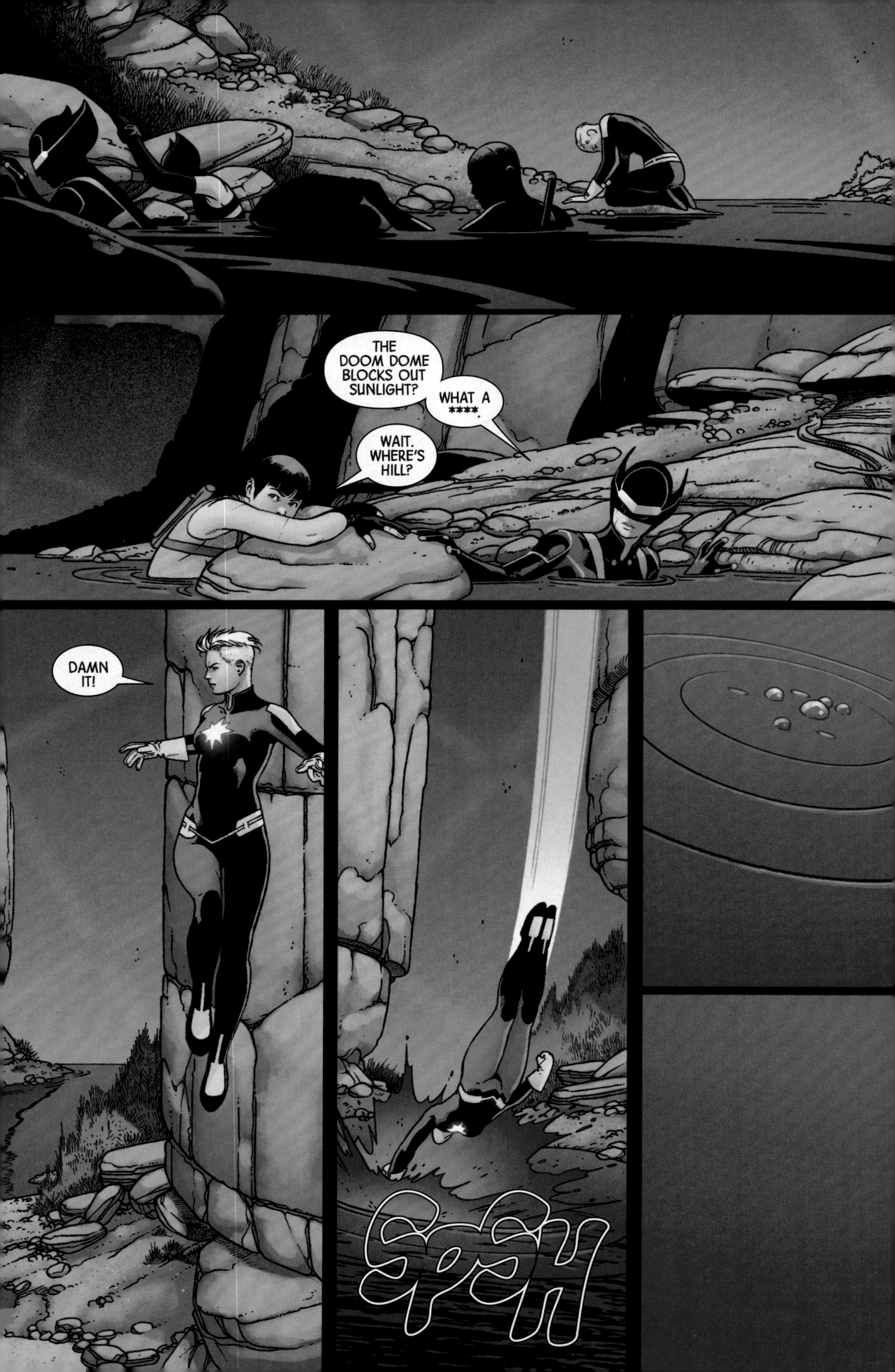
THE DOOM DOME BLOCKS OUT SUNLIGHT?
WHAT A ****.
WAIT. WHERE'S HILL?
DAMN IT!
SPSH

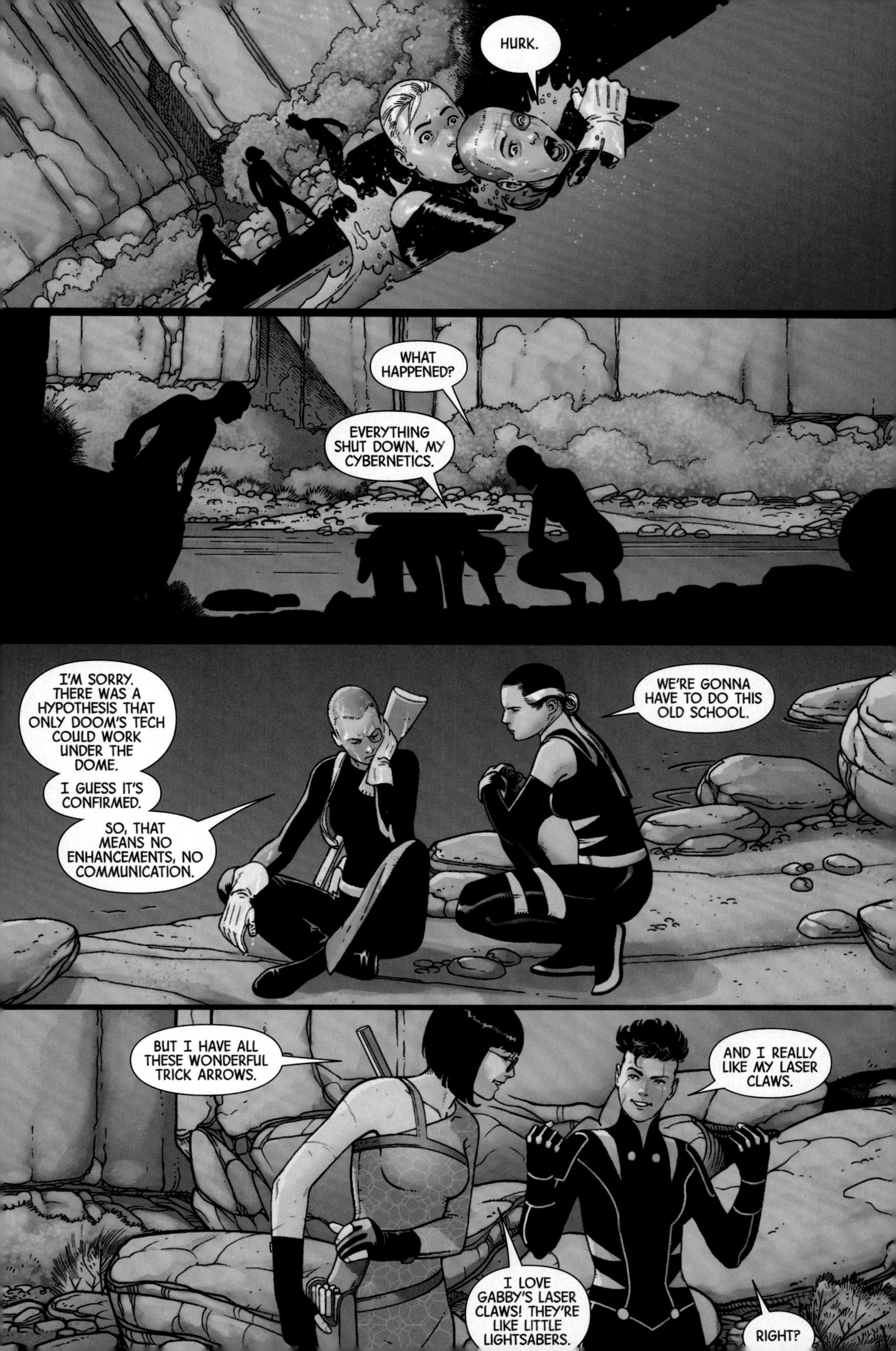
HURK.
WHAT HAPPENED?
EVERYTHING SHUT DOWN. MY CYBERNETICS.
I'M SORRY. THERE WAS A HYPOTHESIS THAT ONLY DOOM'S TECH COULD WORK UNDER THE DOME.
I GUESS IT'S CONFIRMED.
SO, THAT MEANS NO ENHANCEMENTS, NO COMMUNICATION.
WE'RE GONNA HAVE TO DO THIS OLD SCHOOL.
BUT I HAVE ALL THESE WONDERFUL TRICK ARROWS.
AND I REALLY LIKE MY LASER CLAWS.
I LOVE GABBY'S LASER CLAWS! THEY'RE LIKE LITTLE LIGHTSABERS.
RIGHT?

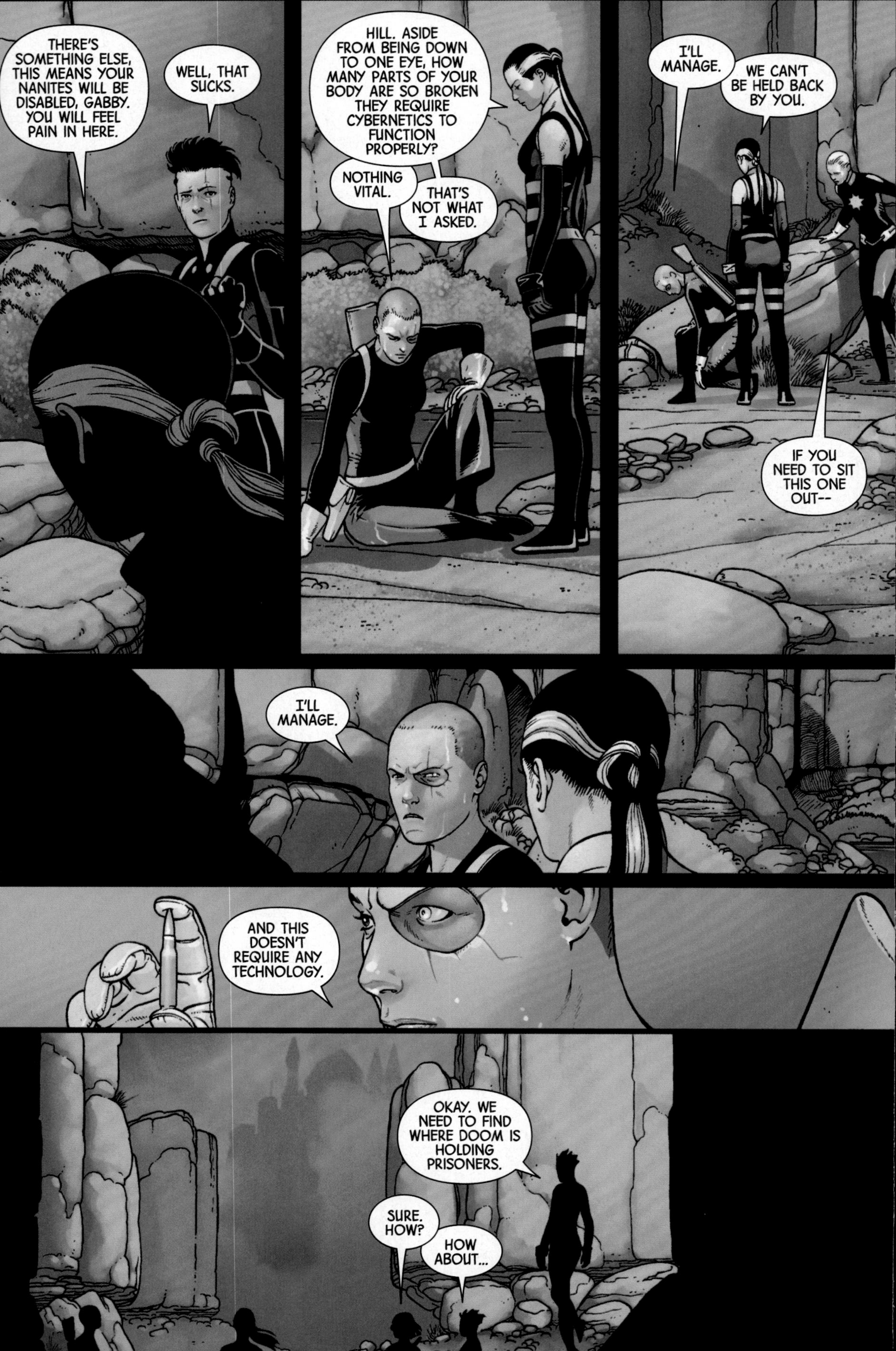
THERE'S SOMETHING ELSE, THIS MEANS YOUR NANITES WILL BE DISABLED, GABBY. YOU WILL FEEL PAIN IN HERE.
WELL, THAT SUCKS.
HILL. ASIDE FROM BEING DOWN TO ONE EYE, HOW MANY PARTS OF YOUR BODY ARE SO BROKEN THEY REQUIRE CYBERNETICS TO FUNCTION PROPERLY?
NOTHING VITAL.
THAT'S NOT WHAT I ASKED.
I'LL MANAGE.
WE CAN'T BE HELD BACK BY YOU.
IF YOU NEED TO SIT THIS ONE OUT--
I'LL MANAGE.
AND THIS DOESN'T REQUIRE ANY TECHNOLOGY.
OKAY. WE NEED TO FIND WHERE DOOM IS HOLDING PRISONERS.
SURE. HOW?
HOW ABOUT...

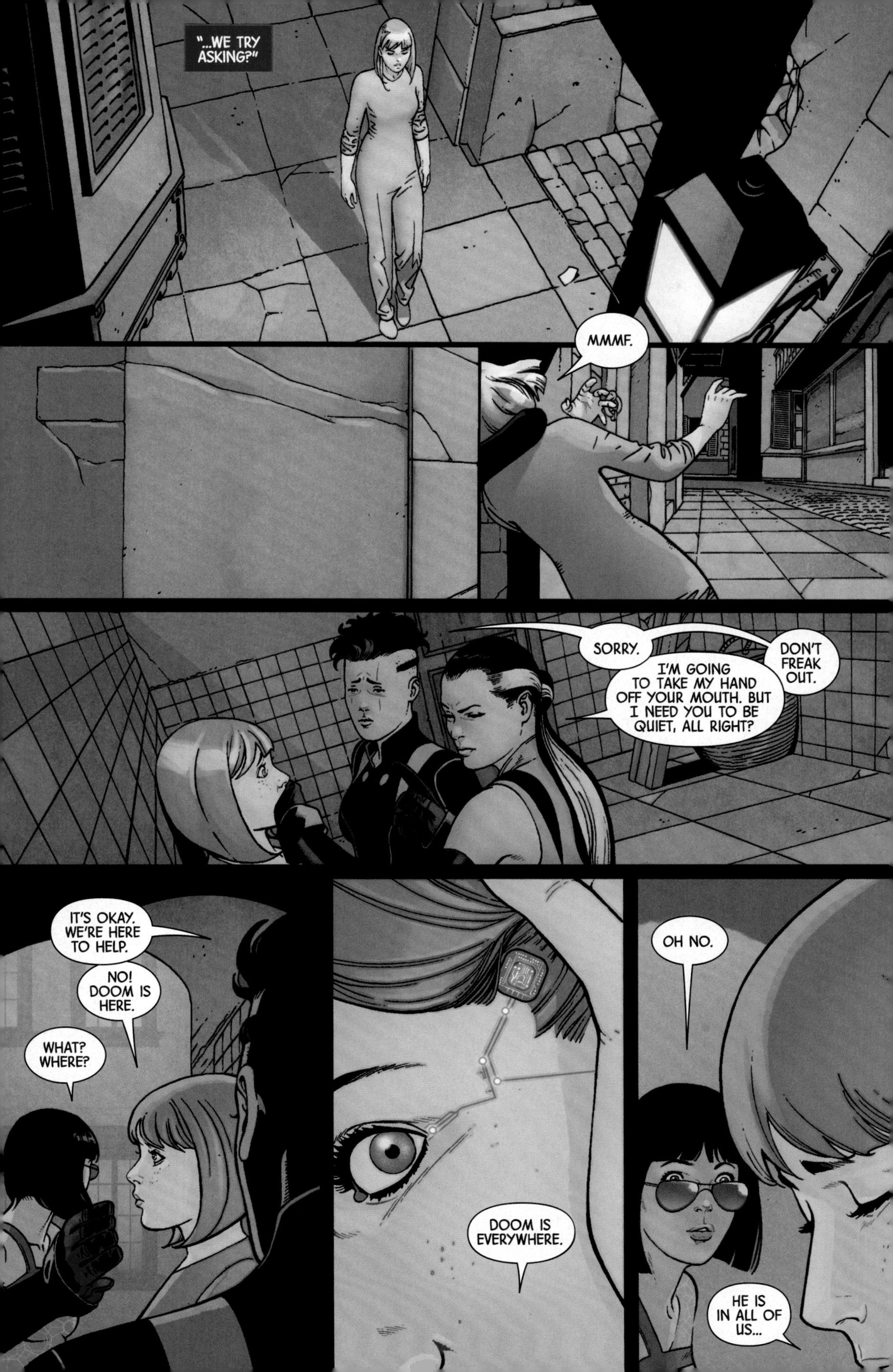
"...WE TRY ASKING?"
MMMF.
SORRY.
DON'T FREAK OUT.
I'M GOING TO TAKE MY HAND OFF YOUR MOUTH. BUT I NEED YOU TO BE QUIET, ALL RIGHT?
IT'S OKAY. WE'RE HERE TO HELP.
NO! DOOM IS HERE.
WHAT? WHERE?
DOOM IS EVERYWHERE.
OH NO.
HE IS IN ALL OF US...

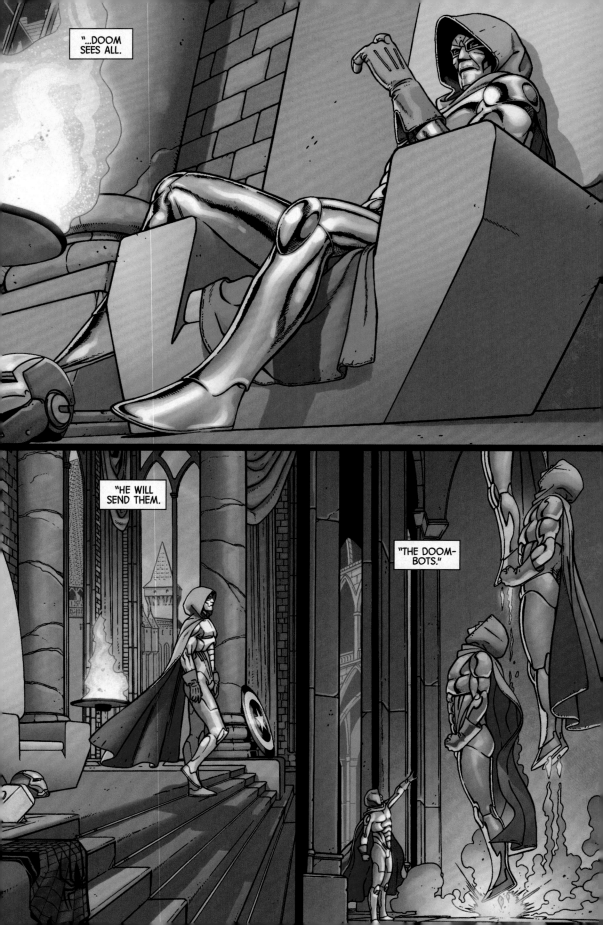

"...DOOM SEES ALL.

"HE WILL SEND THEM.

"THE DOOM-BOTS."

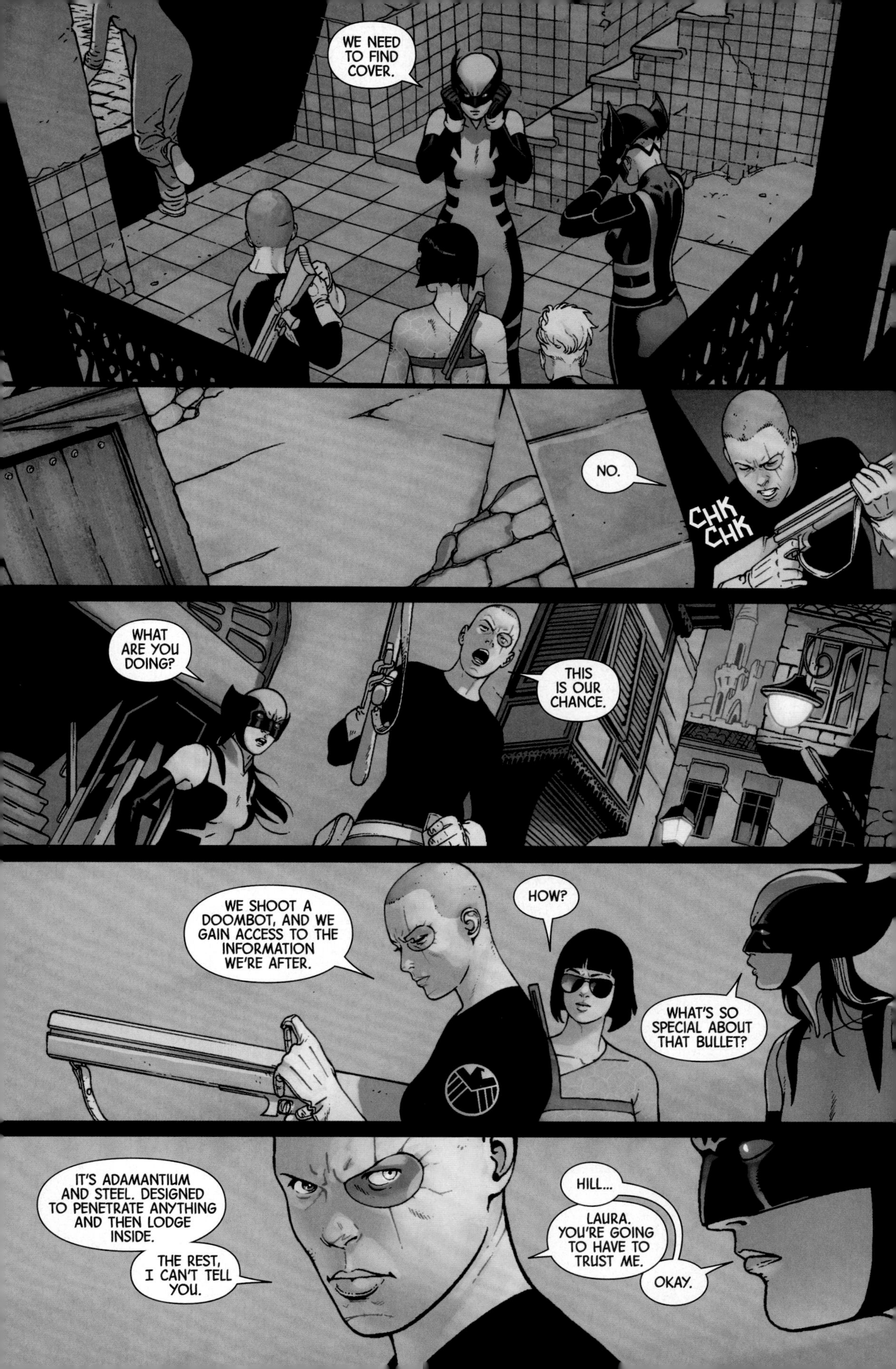
WE NEED TO FIND COVER.
NO.
CHK CHK
WHAT ARE YOU DOING?
THIS IS OUR CHANCE.
WE SHOOT A DOOMBOT, AND WE GAIN ACCESS TO THE INFORMATION WE'RE AFTER.
HOW?
WHAT'S SO SPECIAL ABOUT THAT BULLET?
IT'S ADAMANTIUM AND STEEL. DESIGNED TO PENETRATE ANYTHING AND THEN LODGE INSIDE.
THE REST, I CAN'T TELL YOU.
HILL...
LAURA. YOU'RE GOING TO HAVE TO TRUST ME.
OKAY.

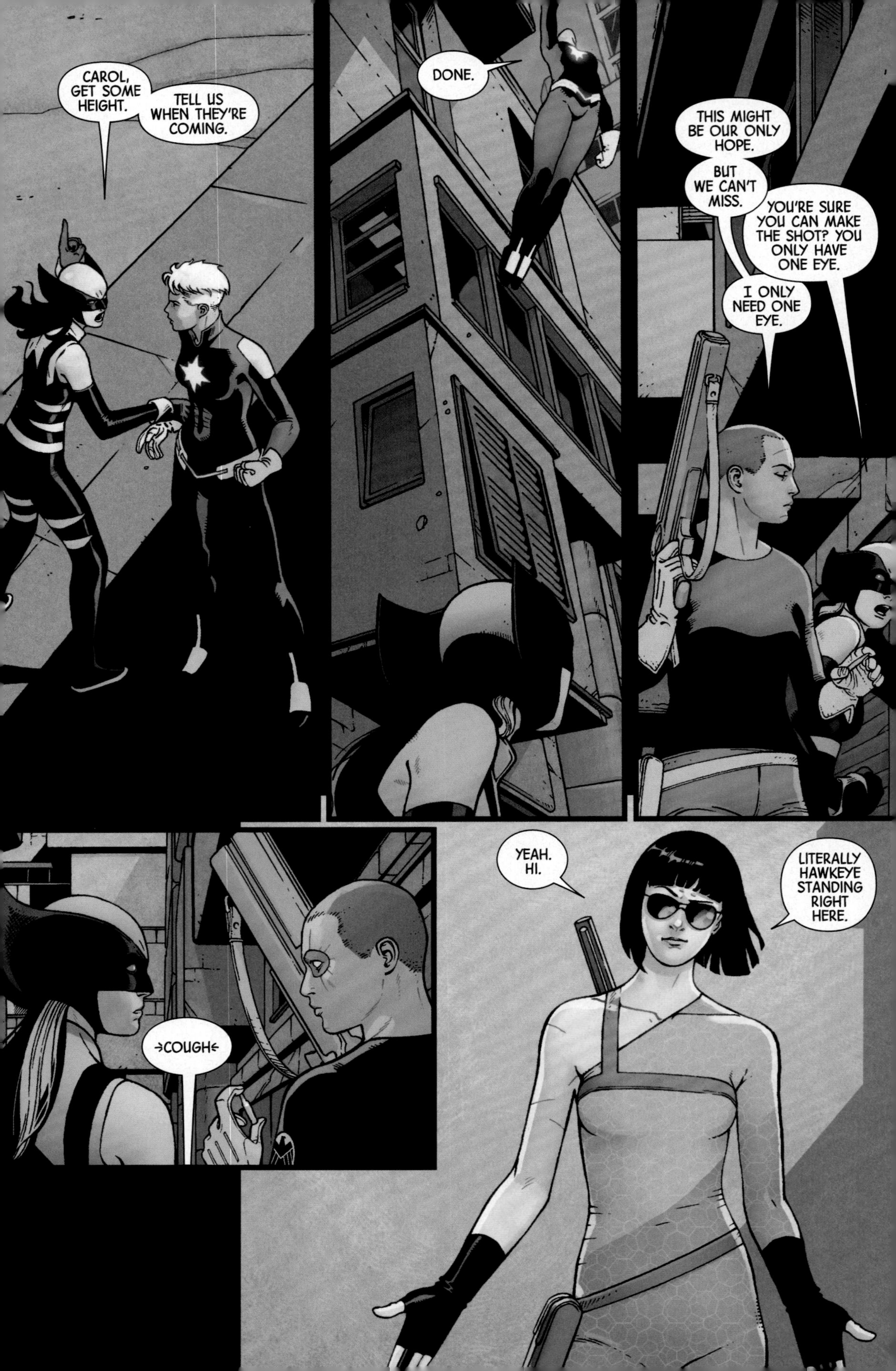
CAROL, GET SOME HEIGHT.
TELL US WHEN THEY'RE COMING.
DONE.
THIS MIGHT BE OUR ONLY HOPE.
BUT WE CAN'T MISS.
YOU'RE SURE YOU CAN MAKE THE SHOT? YOU ONLY HAVE ONE EYE.
I ONLY NEED ONE EYE.
›COUGH‹
YEAH. HI.
LITERALLY HAWKEYE STANDING RIGHT HERE.

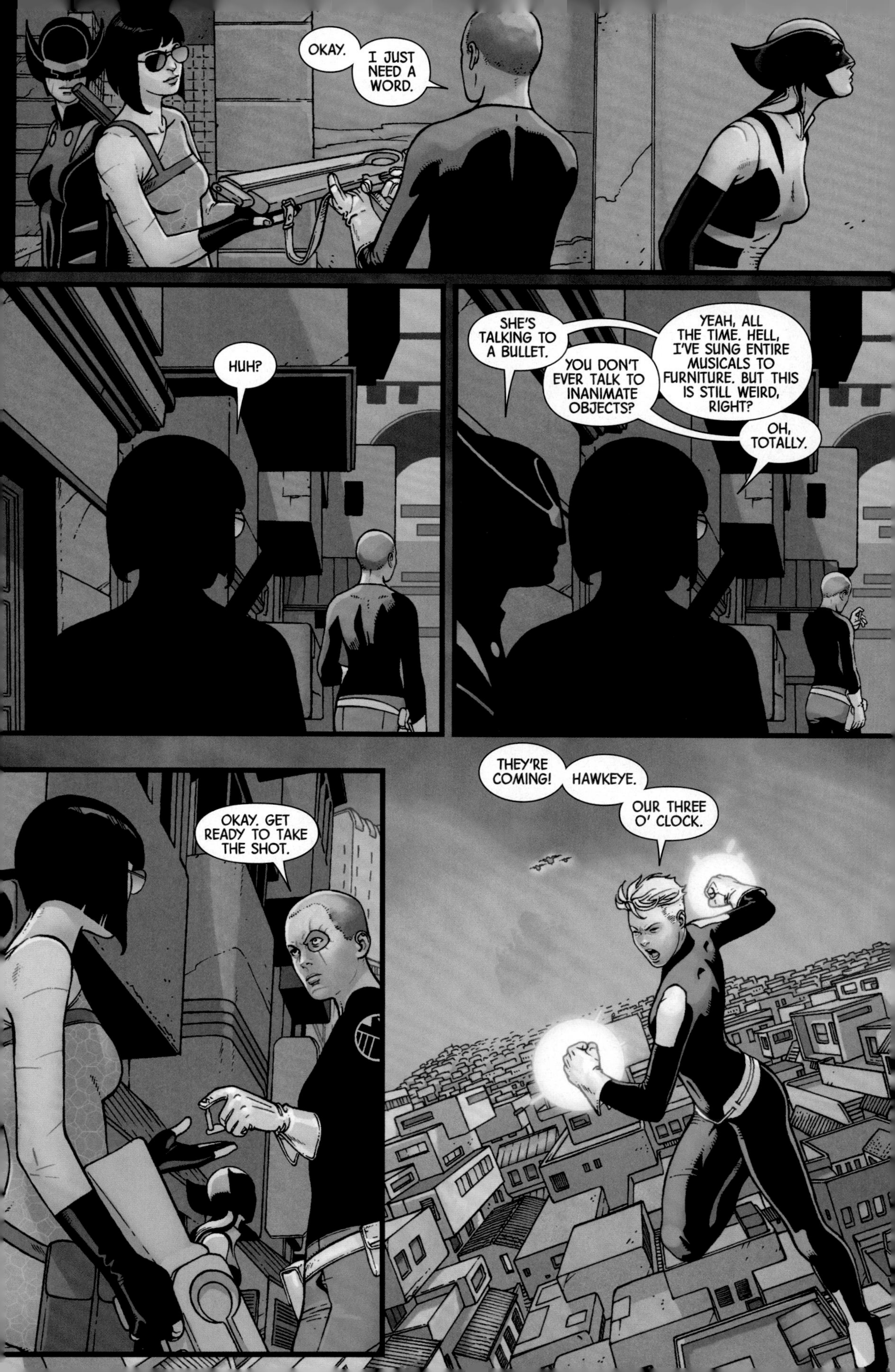

OKAY.
I JUST NEED A WORD.
HUH?
SHE'S TALKING TO A BULLET.
YOU DON'T EVER TALK TO INANIMATE OBJECTS?
YEAH, ALL THE TIME. HELL, I'VE SUNG ENTIRE MUSICALS TO FURNITURE. BUT THIS IS STILL WEIRD, RIGHT?
OH, TOTALLY.
OKAY. GET READY TO TAKE THE SHOT.
THEY'RE COMING!
HAWKEYE.
OUR THREE O' CLOCK.

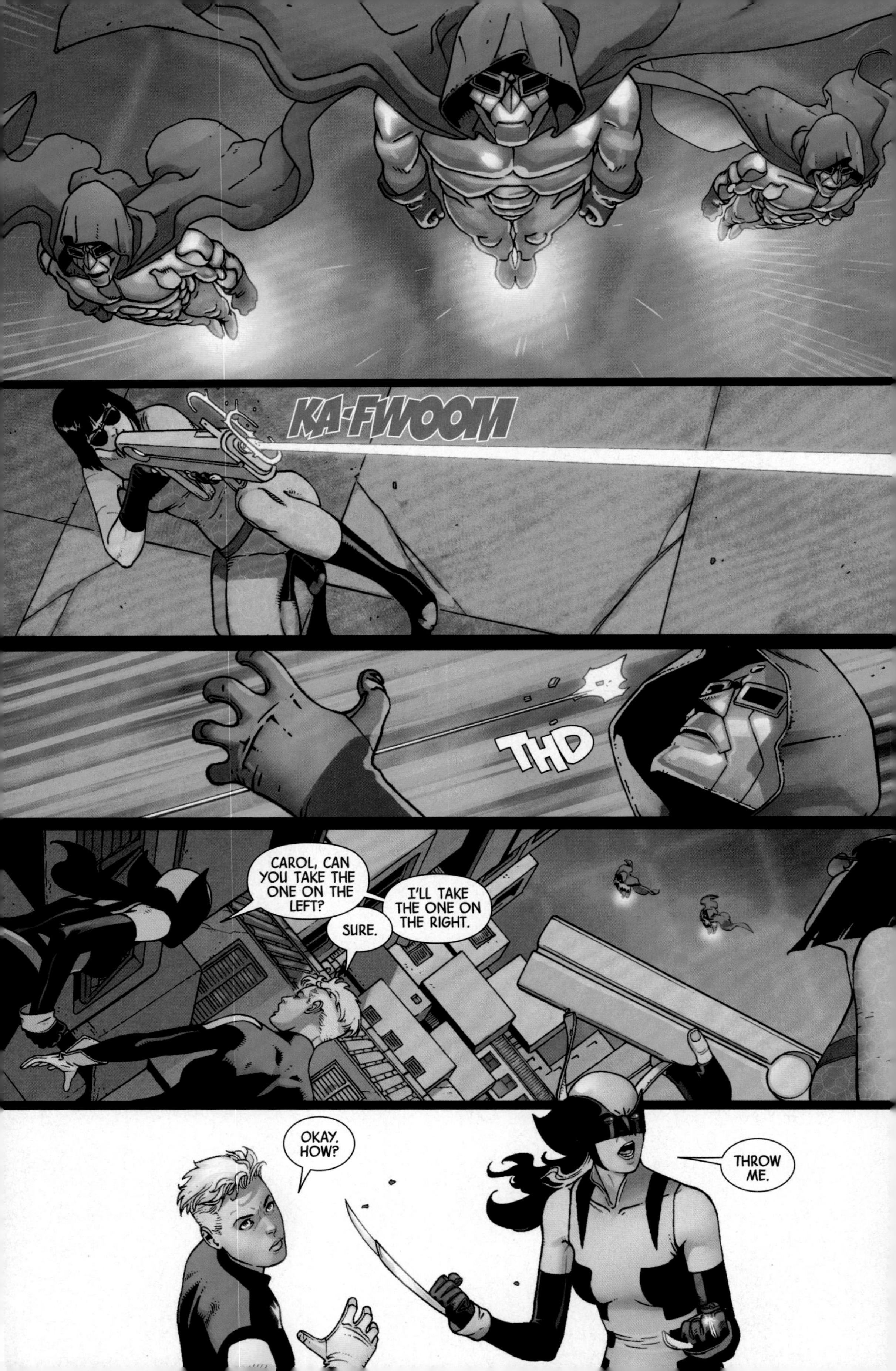
KA-FWOOM
THD
CAROL, CAN YOU TAKE THE ONE ON THE LEFT?
I'LL TAKE THE ONE ON THE RIGHT.
SURE.
OKAY. HOW?
THROW ME.

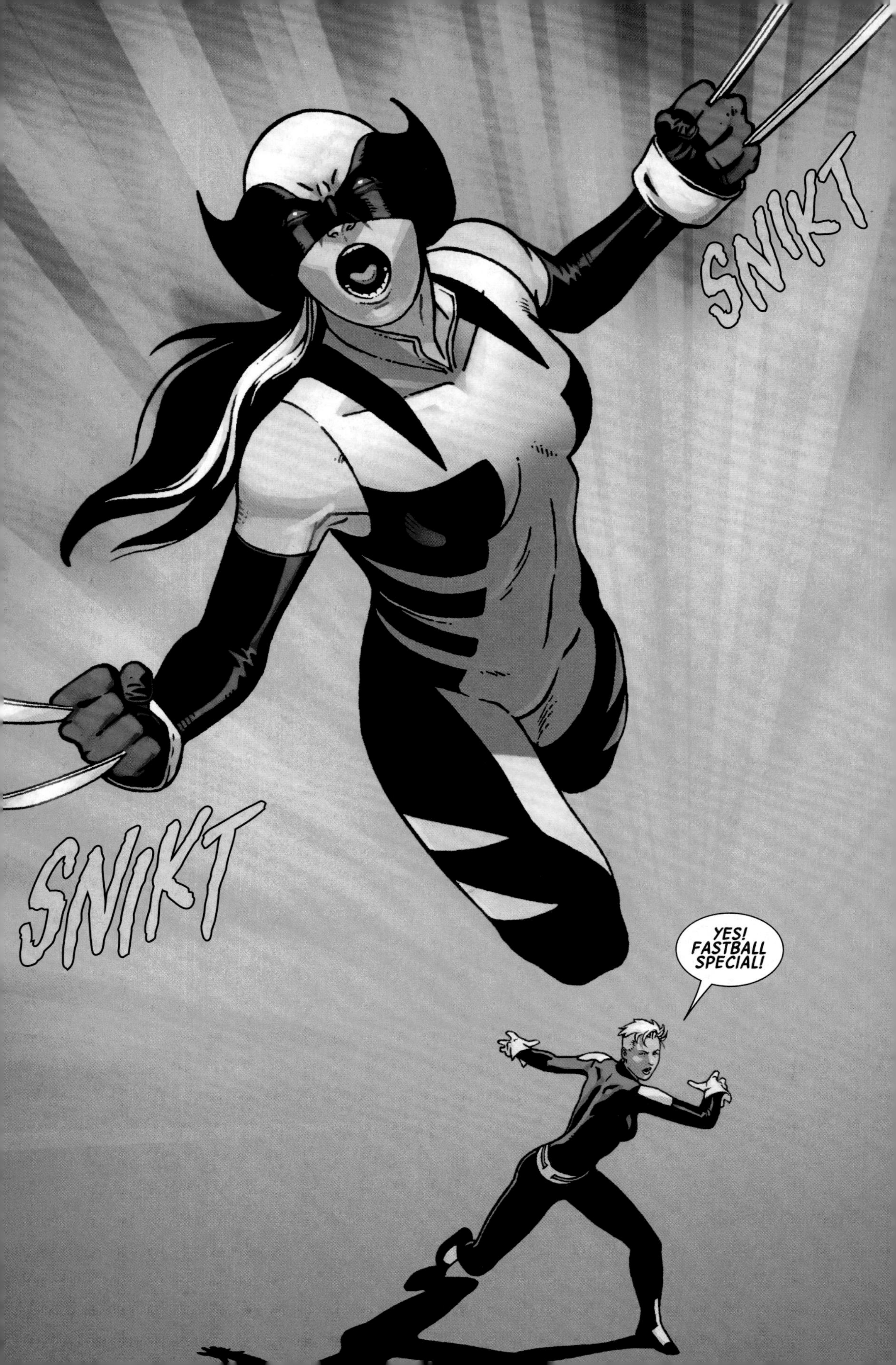
SNIKT
SNIKT
YES! FASTBALL SPECIAL!

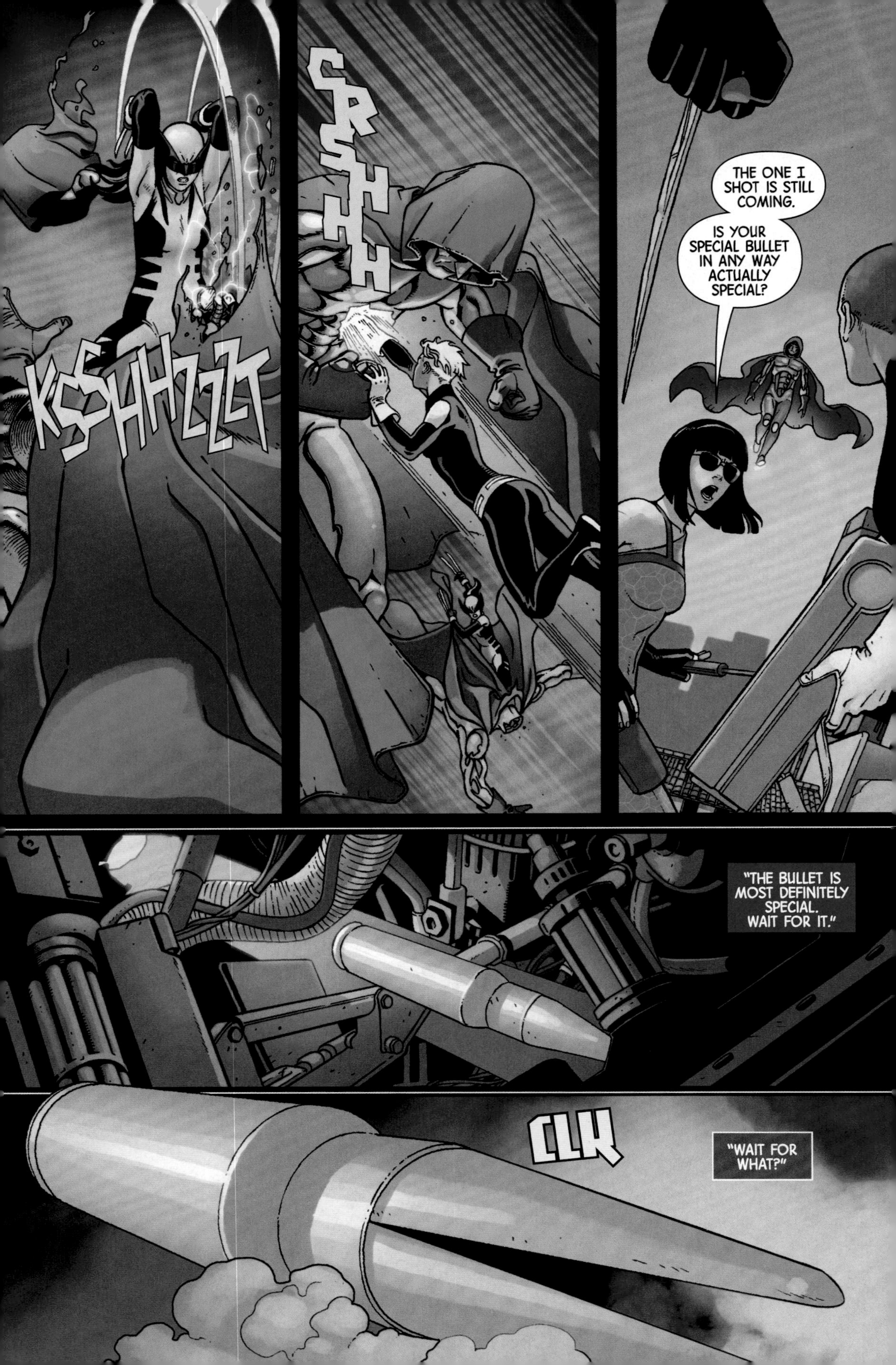
KSHHZZZT
CRSHHH
THE ONE I SHOT IS STILL COMING.
IS YOUR SPECIAL BULLET IN ANY WAY ACTUALLY SPECIAL?
"THE BULLET IS MOST DEFINITELY SPECIAL. WAIT FOR IT."
CLK
"WAIT FOR WHAT?"

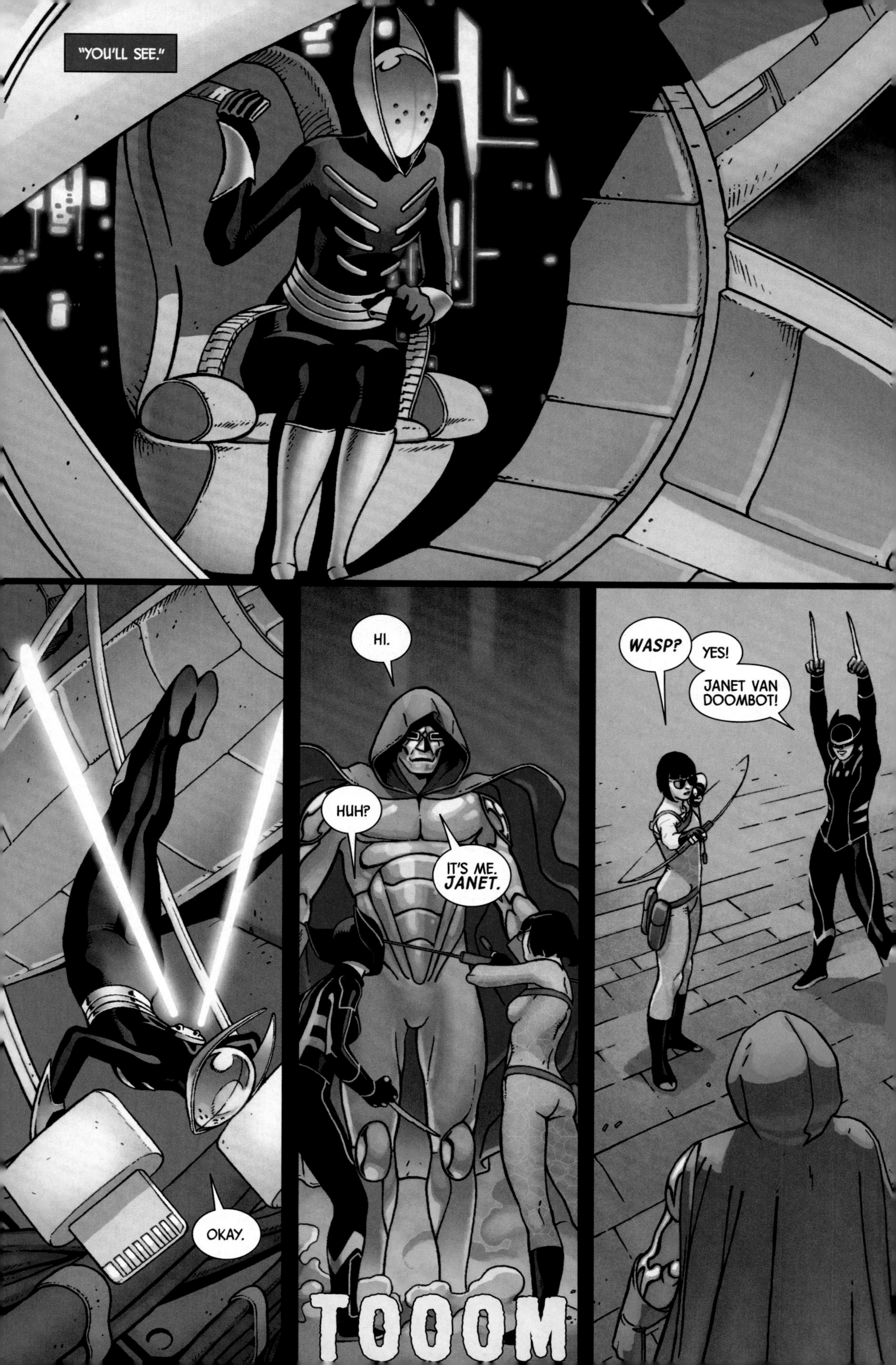
"YOU'LL SEE."
OKAY.
HI.
HUH?
IT'S ME. JANET.
TOOOM
WASP?
YES!
JANET VAN DOOMBOT!

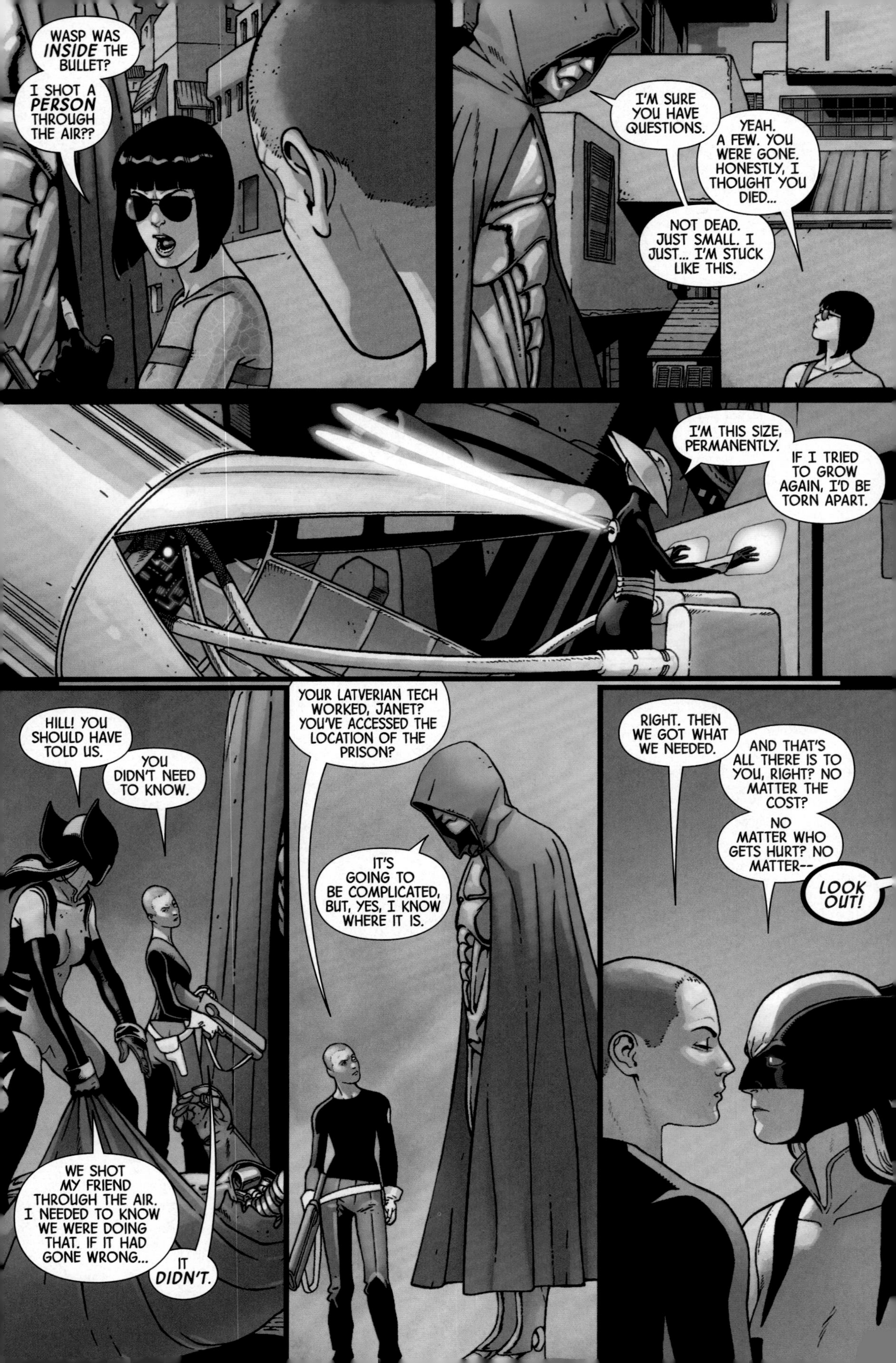
WASP WAS *INSIDE* THE BULLET?
I SHOT A *PERSON* THROUGH THE AIR??
I'M SURE YOU HAVE QUESTIONS.
YEAH. A FEW. YOU WERE GONE. HONESTLY, I THOUGHT YOU DIED...
NOT DEAD. JUST SMALL. I JUST... I'M STUCK LIKE THIS.
I'M THIS SIZE, PERMANENTLY.
IF I TRIED TO GROW AGAIN, I'D BE TORN APART.
HILL! YOU SHOULD HAVE TOLD US.
YOU DIDN'T NEED TO KNOW.
WE SHOT MY FRIEND THROUGH THE AIR. I NEEDED TO KNOW WE WERE DOING THAT. IF IT HAD GONE WRONG...
IT *DIDN'T*.
YOUR LATVERIAN TECH WORKED, JANET? YOU'VE ACCESSED THE LOCATION OF THE PRISON?
IT'S GOING TO BE COMPLICATED, BUT, YES, I KNOW WHERE IT IS.
RIGHT. THEN WE GOT WHAT WE NEEDED.
AND THAT'S ALL THERE IS TO YOU, RIGHT? NO MATTER THE COST?
NO MATTER WHO GETS HURT? NO MATTER--
LOOK OUT!

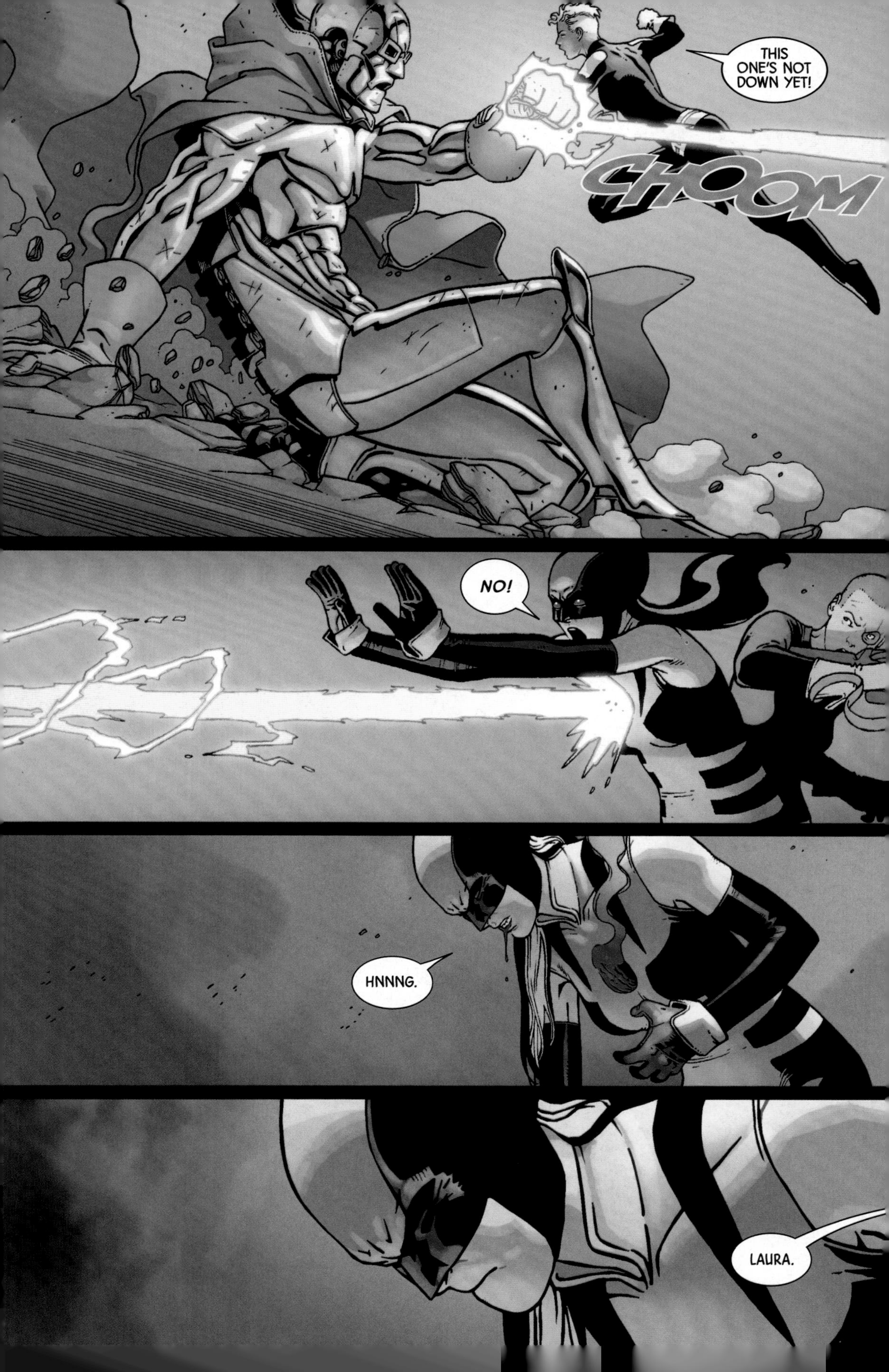
THIS ONE'S NOT DOWN YET!
CHOOM
NO!
HNNNG.
LAURA.

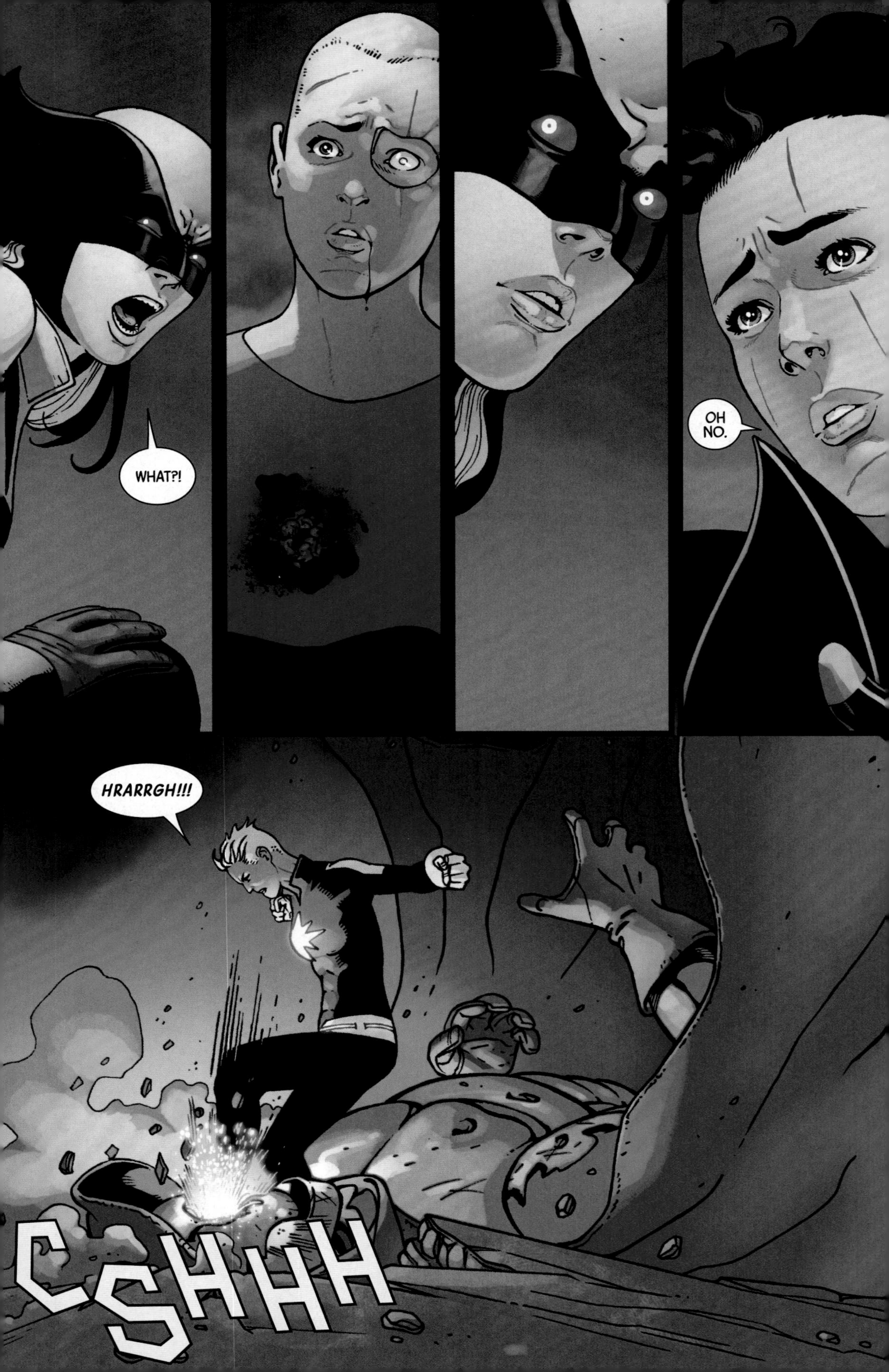
WHAT?!
OH NO.
HRARRGH!!!
CSHHH

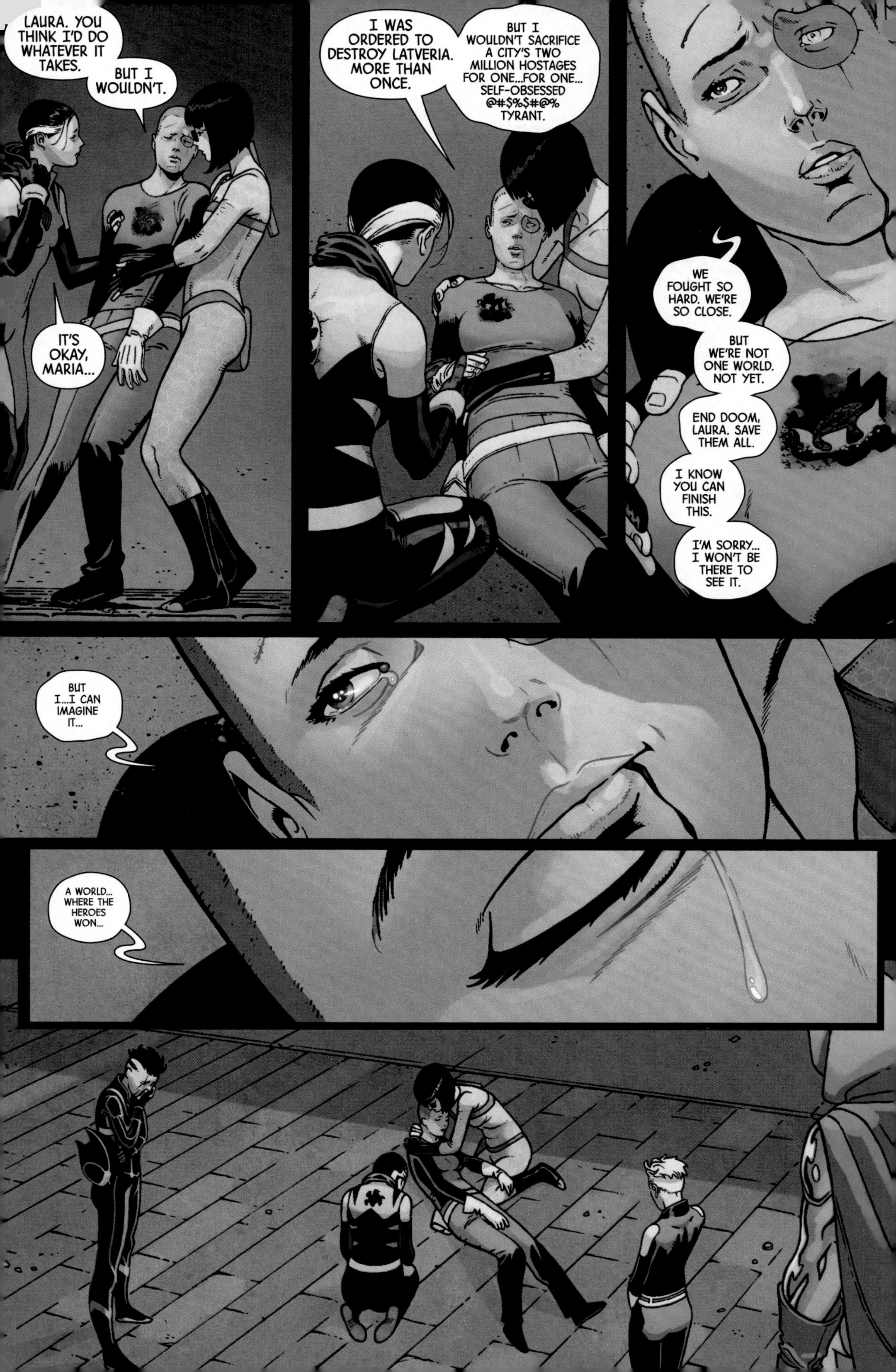
LAURA. YOU THINK I'D DO WHATEVER IT TAKES.
BUT I WOULDN'T.
IT'S OKAY, MARIA...
I WAS ORDERED TO DESTROY LATVERIA. MORE THAN ONCE.
BUT I WOULDN'T SACRIFICE A CITY'S TWO MILLION HOSTAGES FOR ONE...FOR ONE... SELF-OBSESSED @#$%$#@% TYRANT.
WE FOUGHT SO HARD. WE'RE SO CLOSE.
BUT WE'RE NOT ONE WORLD. NOT YET.
END DOOM, LAURA. SAVE THEM ALL.
I KNOW YOU CAN FINISH THIS.
I'M SORRY... I WON'T BE THERE TO SEE IT.
BUT I...I CAN IMAGINE IT...
A WORLD... WHERE THE HEROES WON...

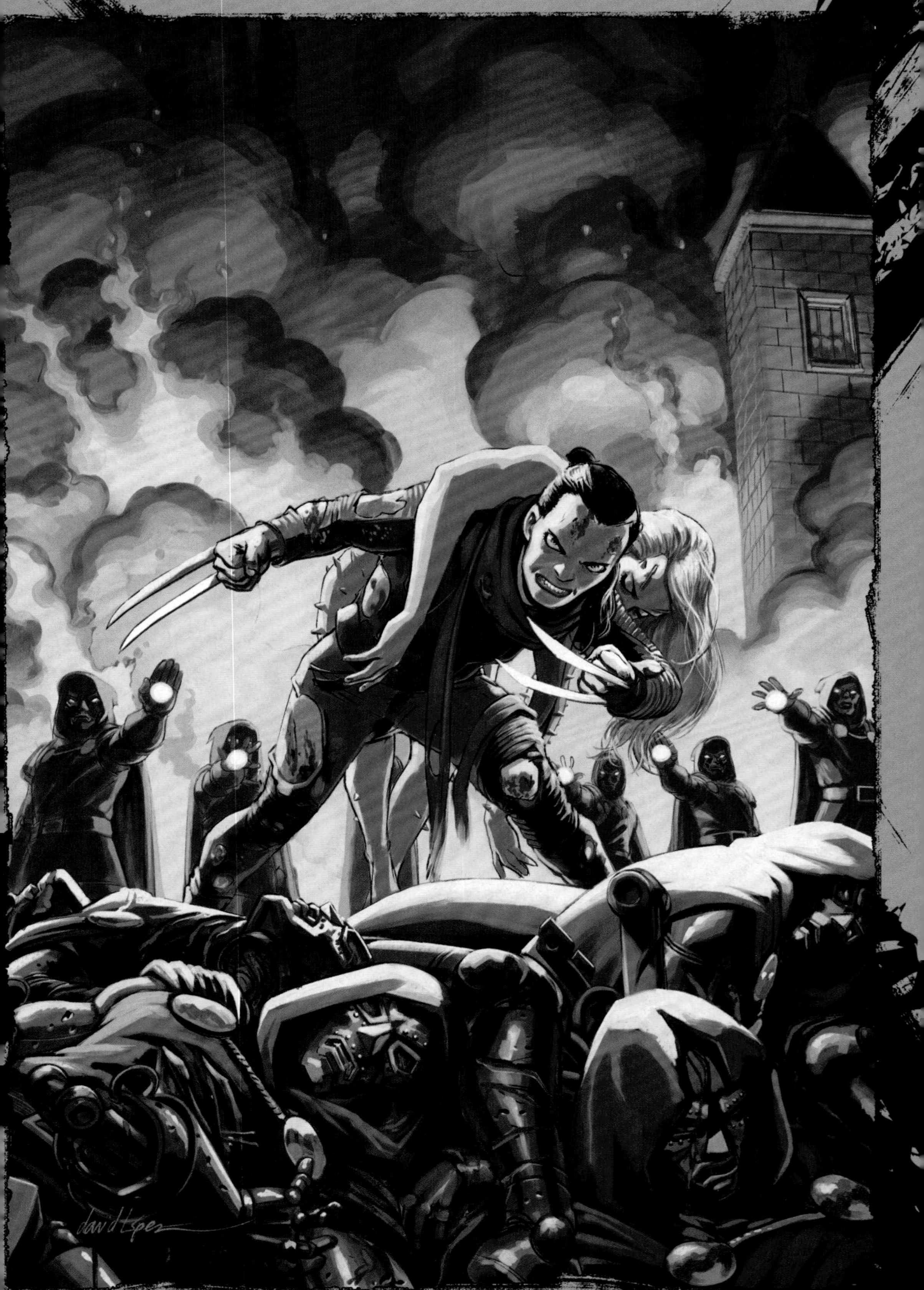

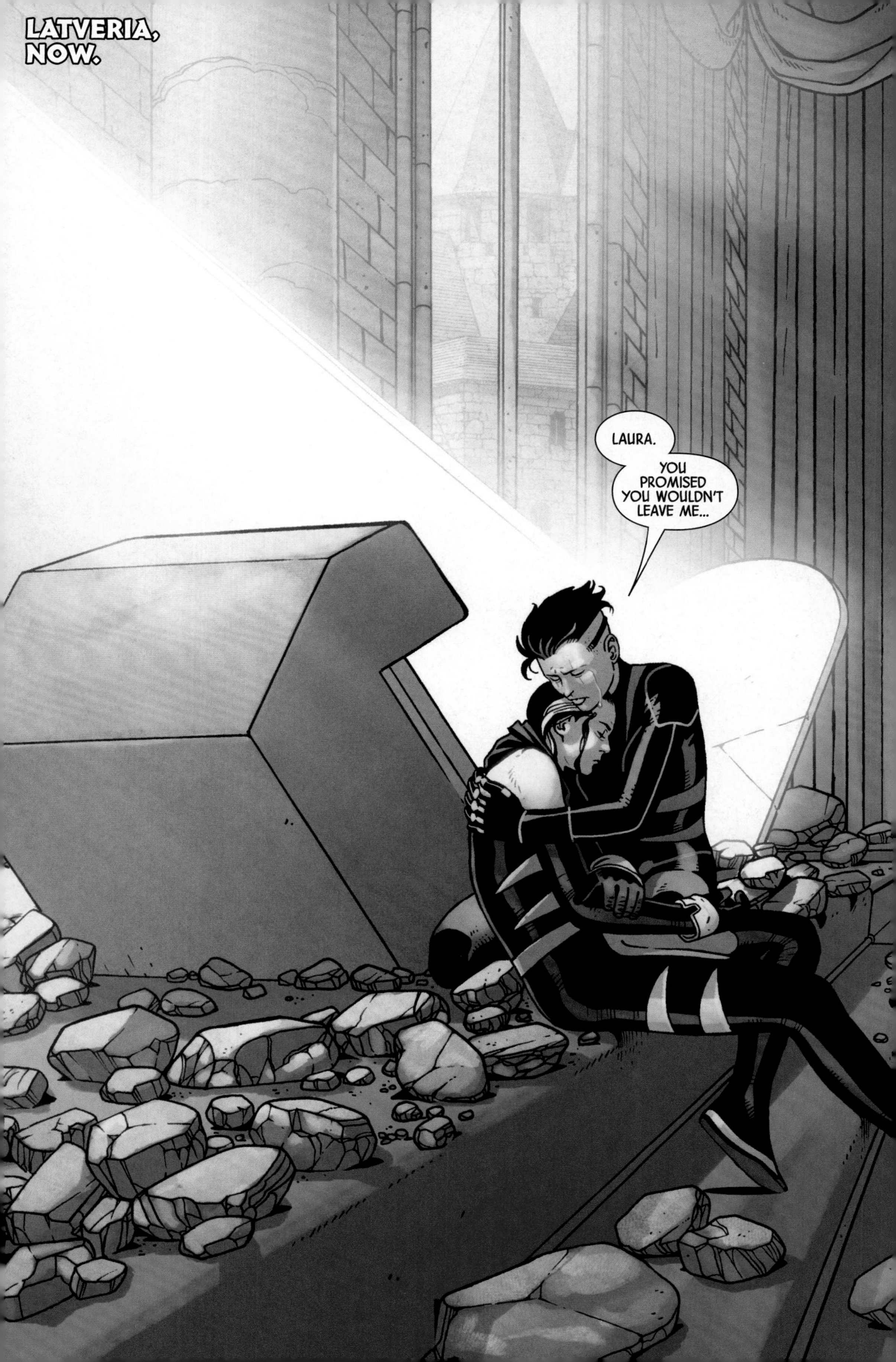
LATVERIA, NOW.
LAURA.
YOU PROMISED YOU WOULDN'T LEAVE ME...

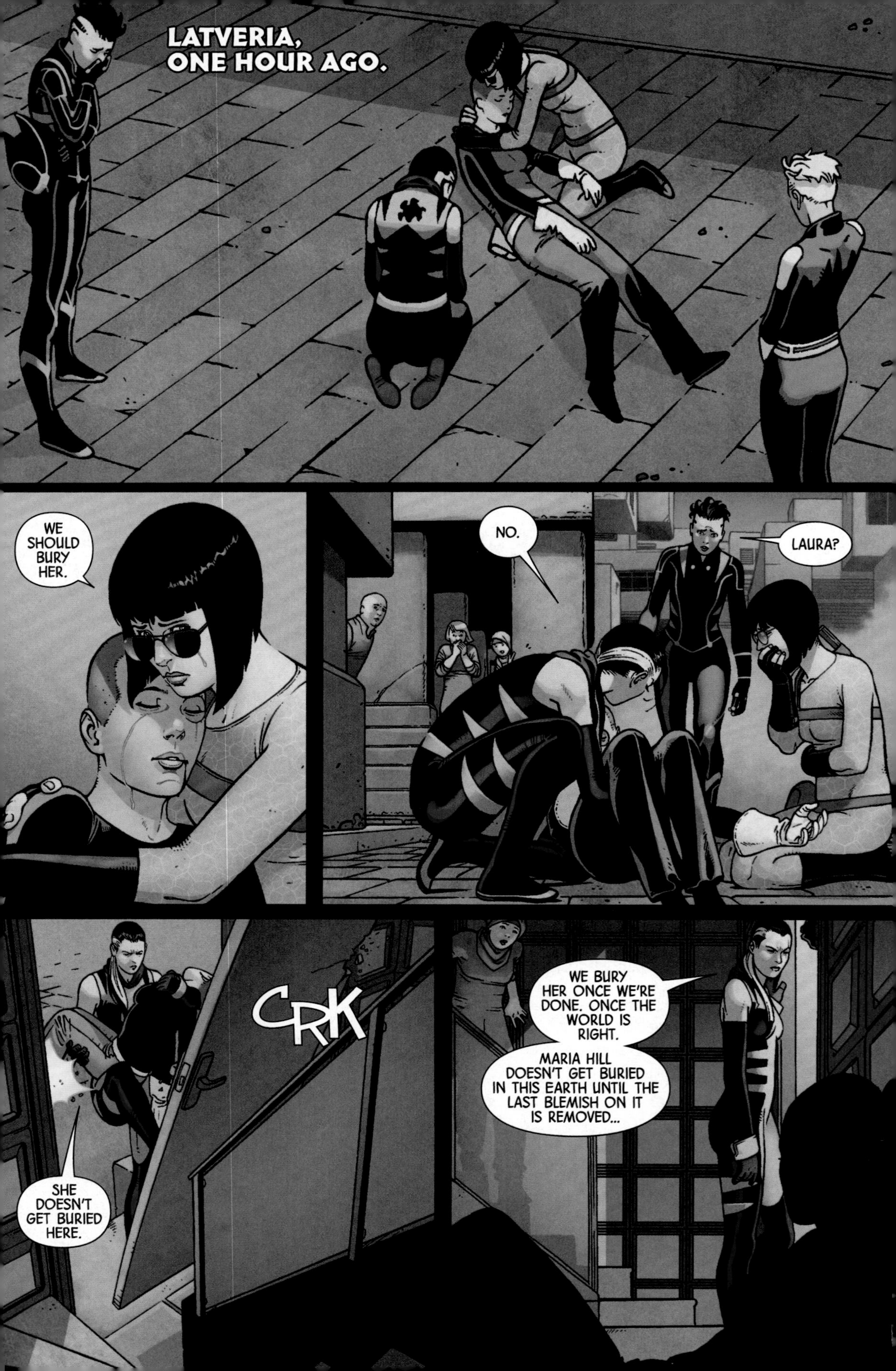

LATVERIA, ONE HOUR AGO.
WE SHOULD BURY HER.
NO.
LAURA?
CRK
SHE DOESN'T GET BURIED HERE.
WE BURY HER ONCE WE'RE DONE. ONCE THE WORLD IS RIGHT.
MARIA HILL DOESN'T GET BURIED IN THIS EARTH UNTIL THE LAST BLEMISH ON IT IS REMOVED...

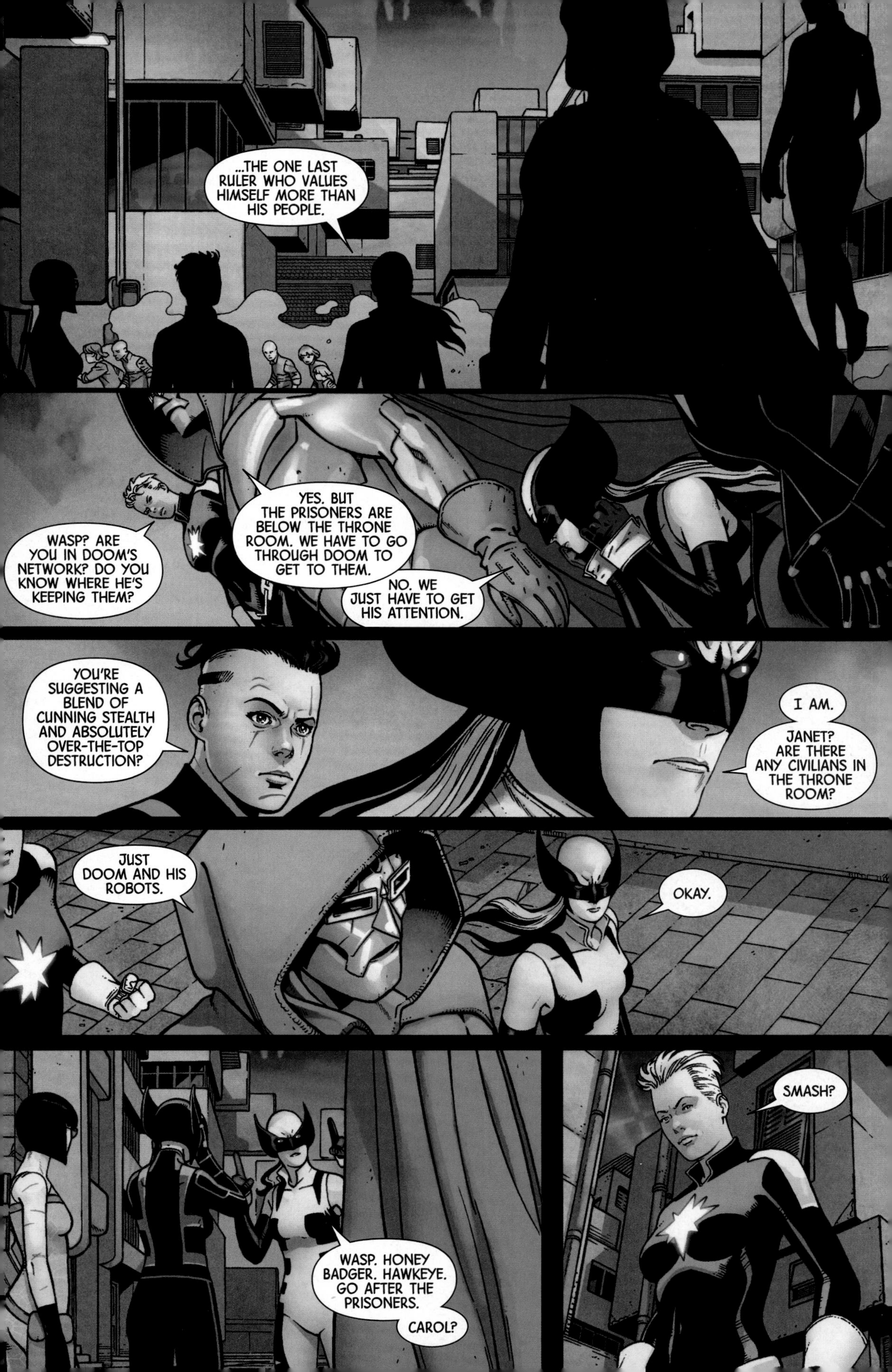
...THE ONE LAST RULER WHO VALUES HIMSELF MORE THAN HIS PEOPLE.
WASP? ARE YOU IN DOOM'S NETWORK? DO YOU KNOW WHERE HE'S KEEPING THEM?
YES. BUT THE PRISONERS ARE BELOW THE THRONE ROOM. WE HAVE TO GO THROUGH DOOM TO GET TO THEM.
NO. WE JUST HAVE TO GET HIS ATTENTION.
YOU'RE SUGGESTING A BLEND OF CUNNING STEALTH AND ABSOLUTELY OVER-THE-TOP DESTRUCTION?
I AM.
JANET? ARE THERE ANY CIVILIANS IN THE THRONE ROOM?
JUST DOOM AND HIS ROBOTS.
OKAY.
WASP. HONEY BADGER. HAWKEYE. GO AFTER THE PRISONERS.
CAROL?
SMASH?

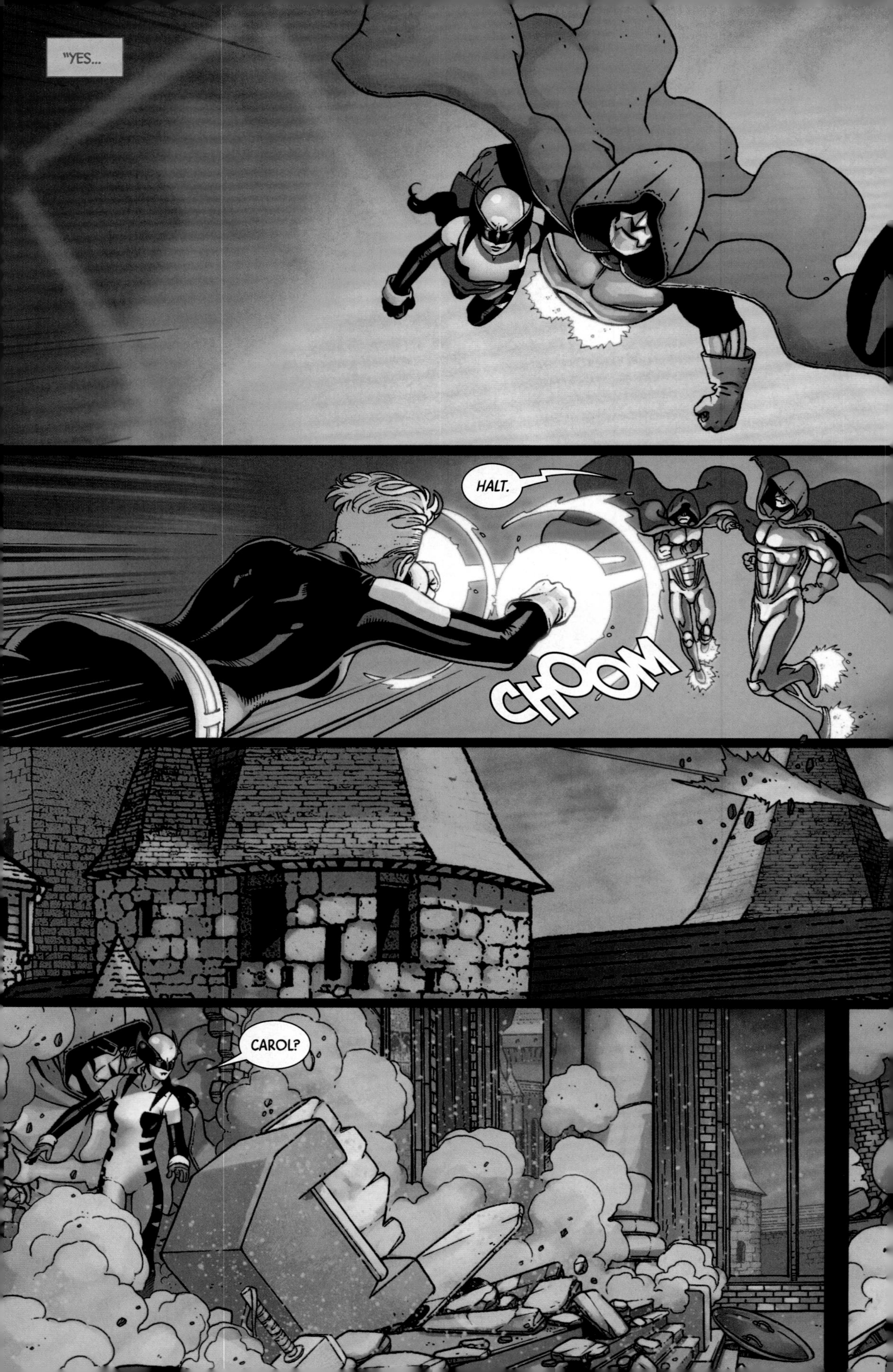
"YES...
HALT.
CHOOM
CAROL?

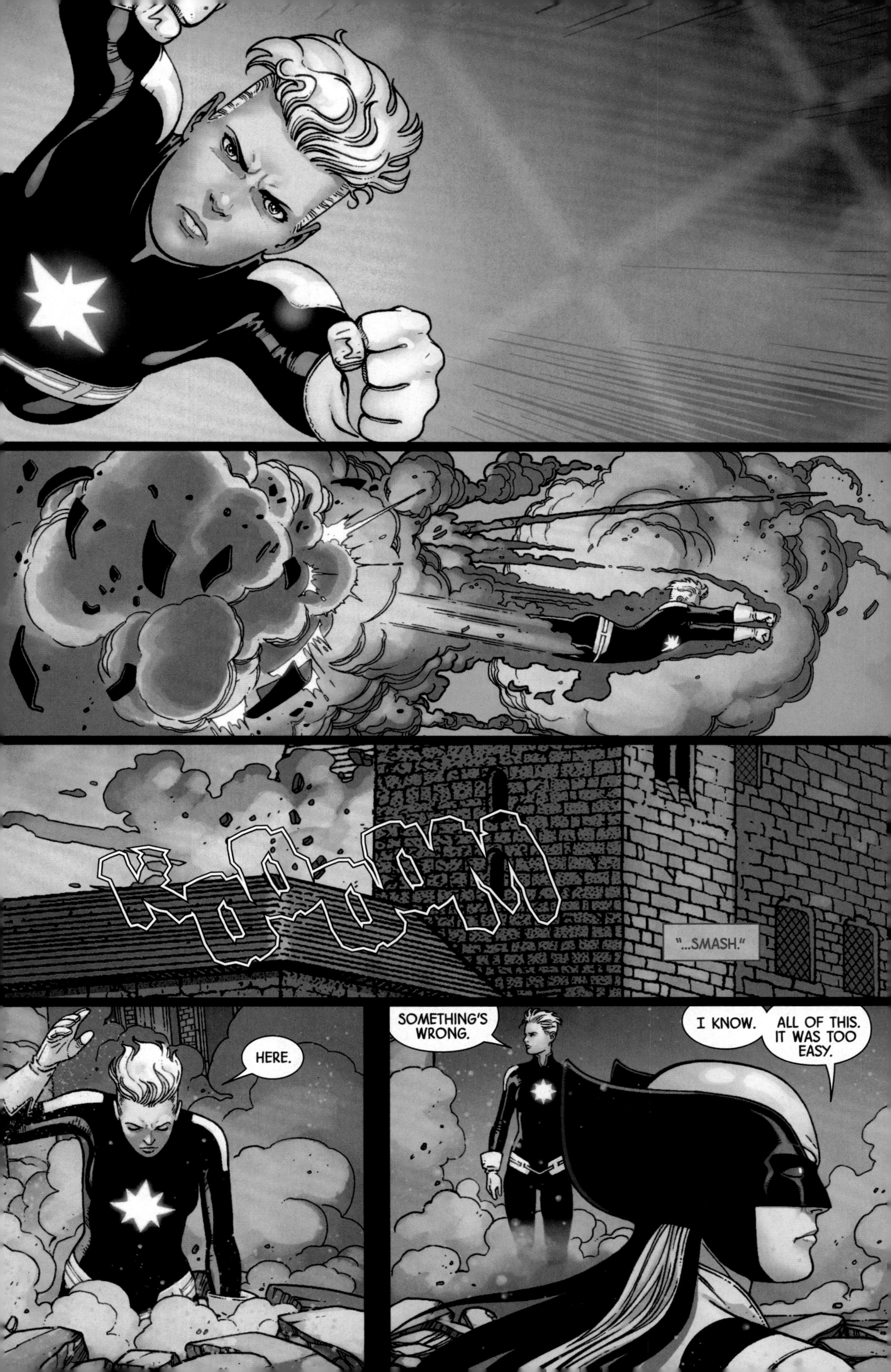
KRA-KOOM
"...SMASH."
HERE.
SOMETHING'S WRONG.
I KNOW.
ALL OF THIS. IT WAS TOO EASY.

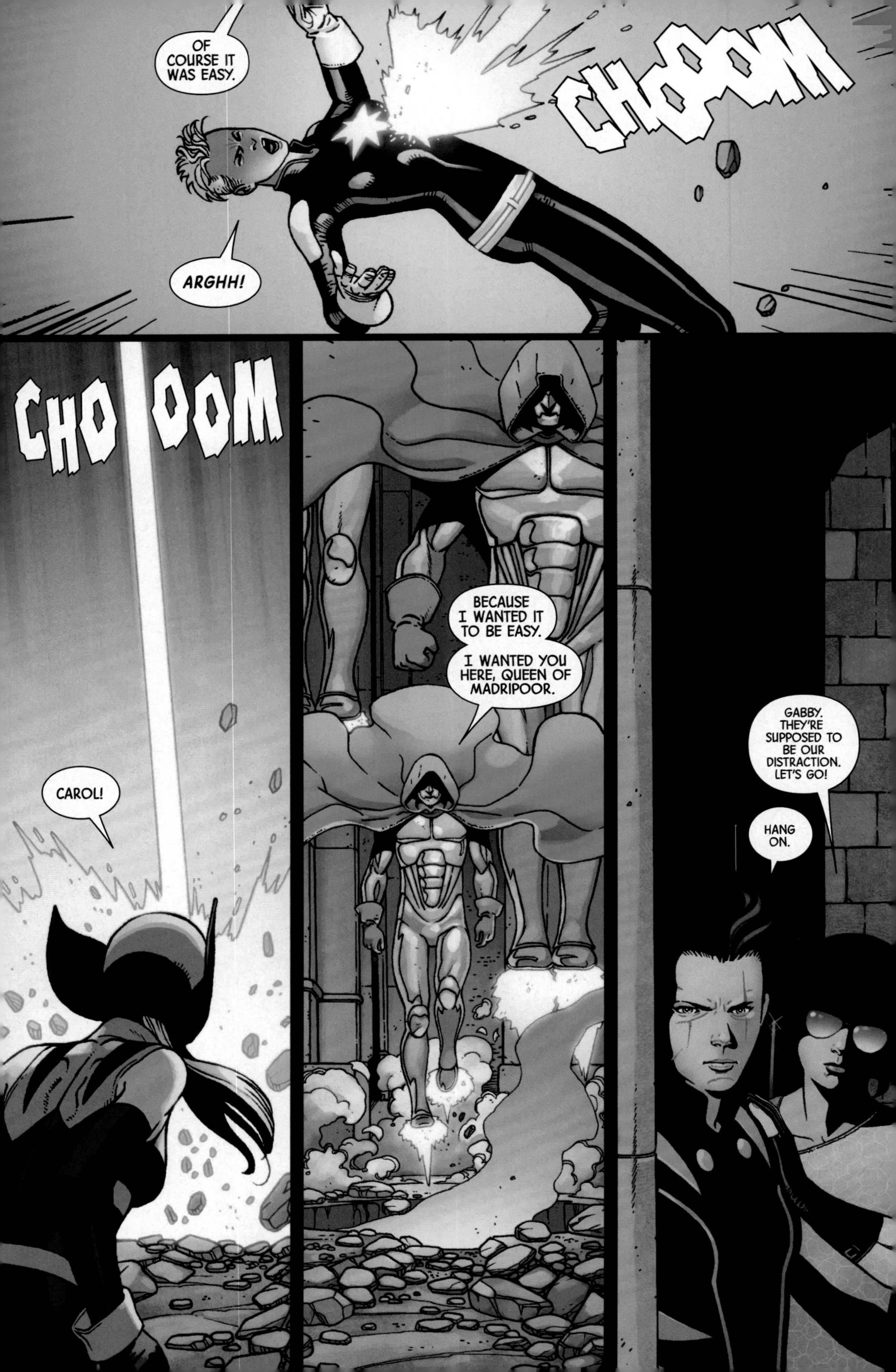
OF COURSE IT WAS EASY.
CHOOOM
ARGHH!
CHOOOM
BECAUSE I WANTED IT TO BE EASY.
I WANTED YOU HERE, QUEEN OF MADRIPOOR.
CAROL!
GABBY. THEY'RE SUPPOSED TO BE OUR DISTRACTION. LET'S GO!
HANG ON.

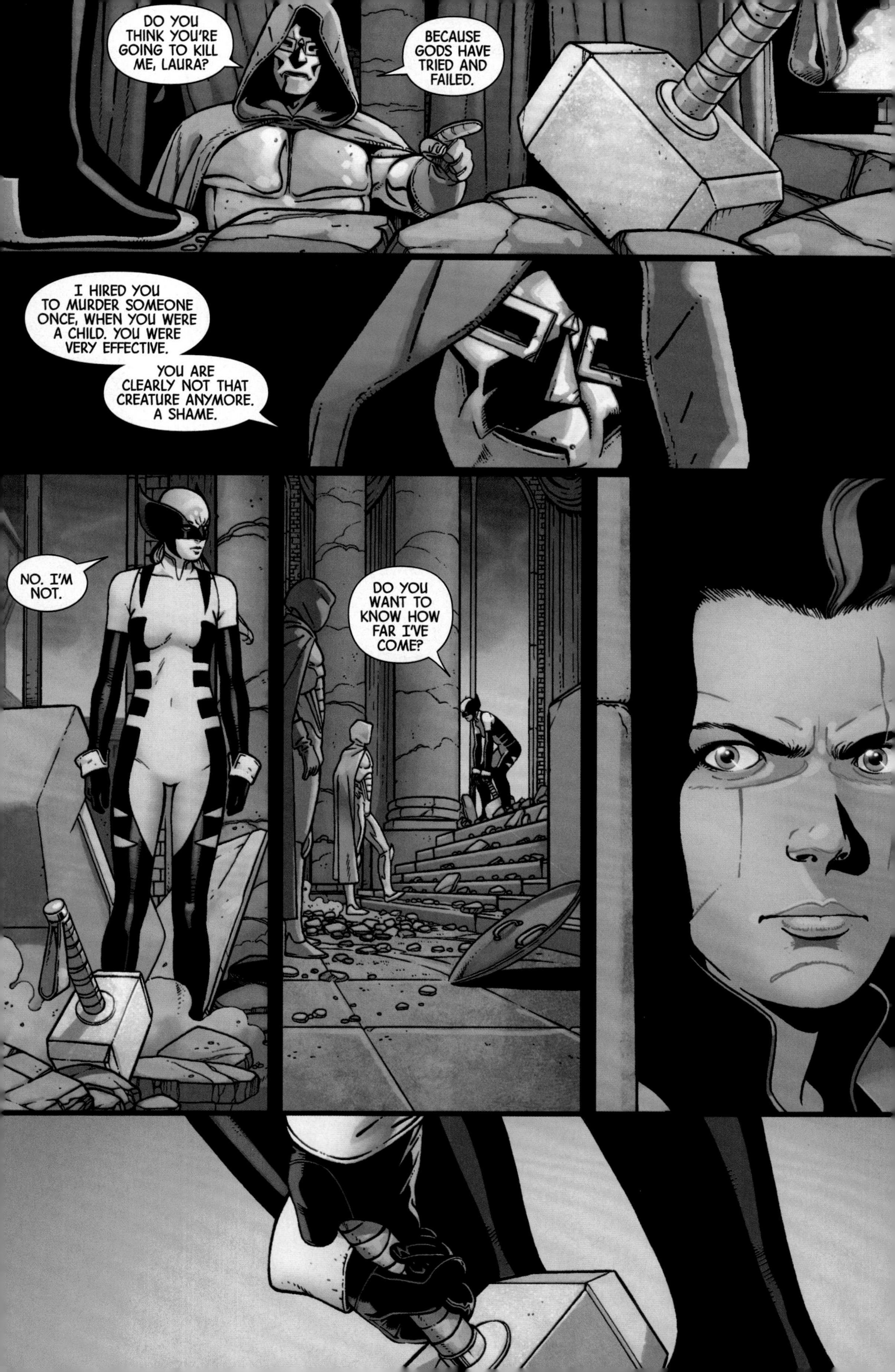
DO YOU THINK YOU'RE GOING TO KILL ME, LAURA?
BECAUSE GODS HAVE TRIED AND FAILED.
I HIRED YOU TO MURDER SOMEONE ONCE, WHEN YOU WERE A CHILD. YOU WERE VERY EFFECTIVE.
YOU ARE CLEARLY NOT THAT CREATURE ANYMORE. A SHAME.
NO. I'M NOT.
DO YOU WANT TO KNOW HOW FAR I'VE COME?

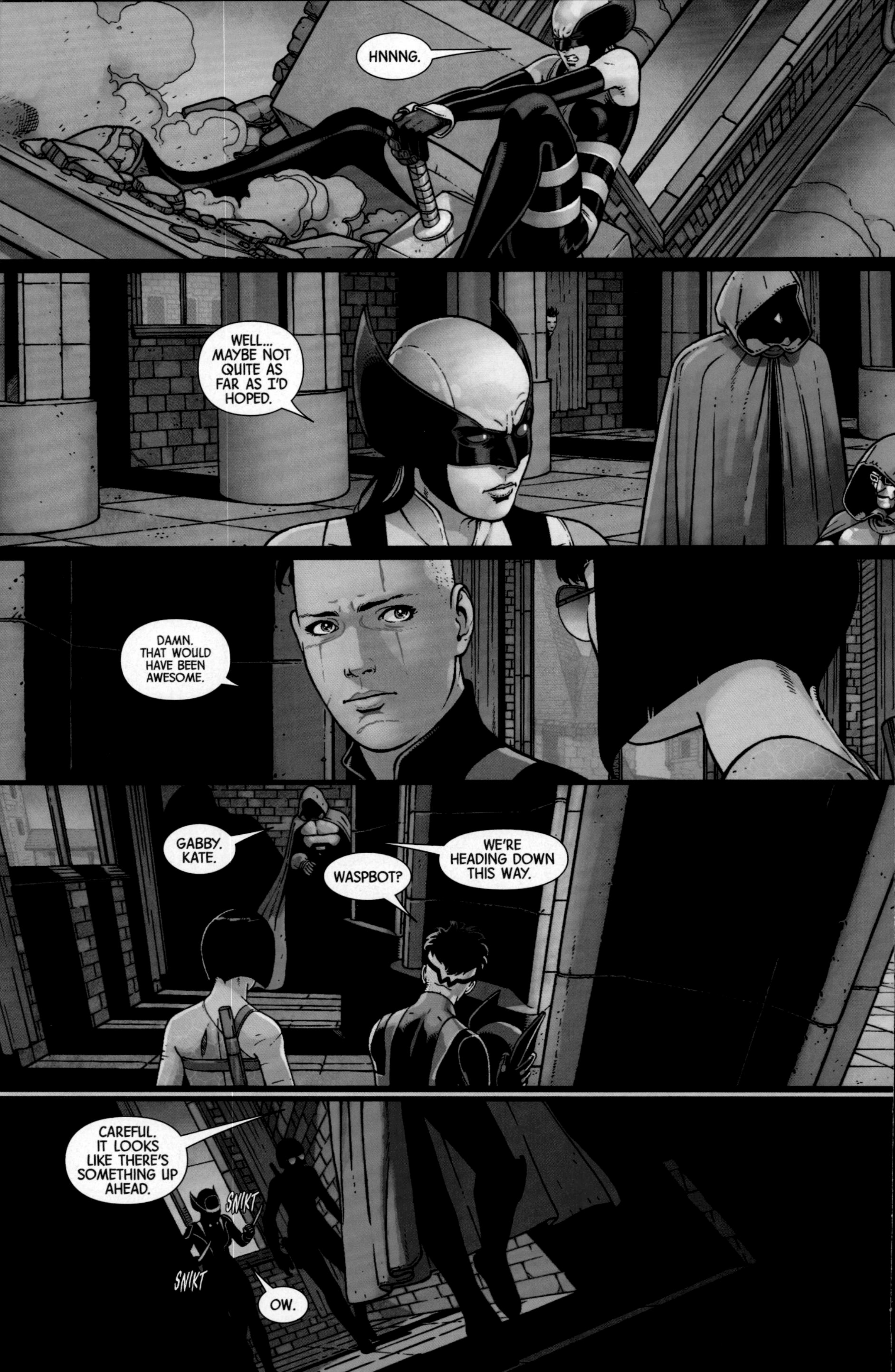
HNNNG.
WELL... MAYBE NOT QUITE AS FAR AS I'D HOPED.
DAMN. THAT WOULD HAVE BEEN AWESOME.
GABBY. KATE.
WE'RE HEADING DOWN THIS WAY.
WASPBOT?
CAREFUL. IT LOOKS LIKE THERE'S SOMETHING UP AHEAD.
SNIKT
SNIKT
OW.

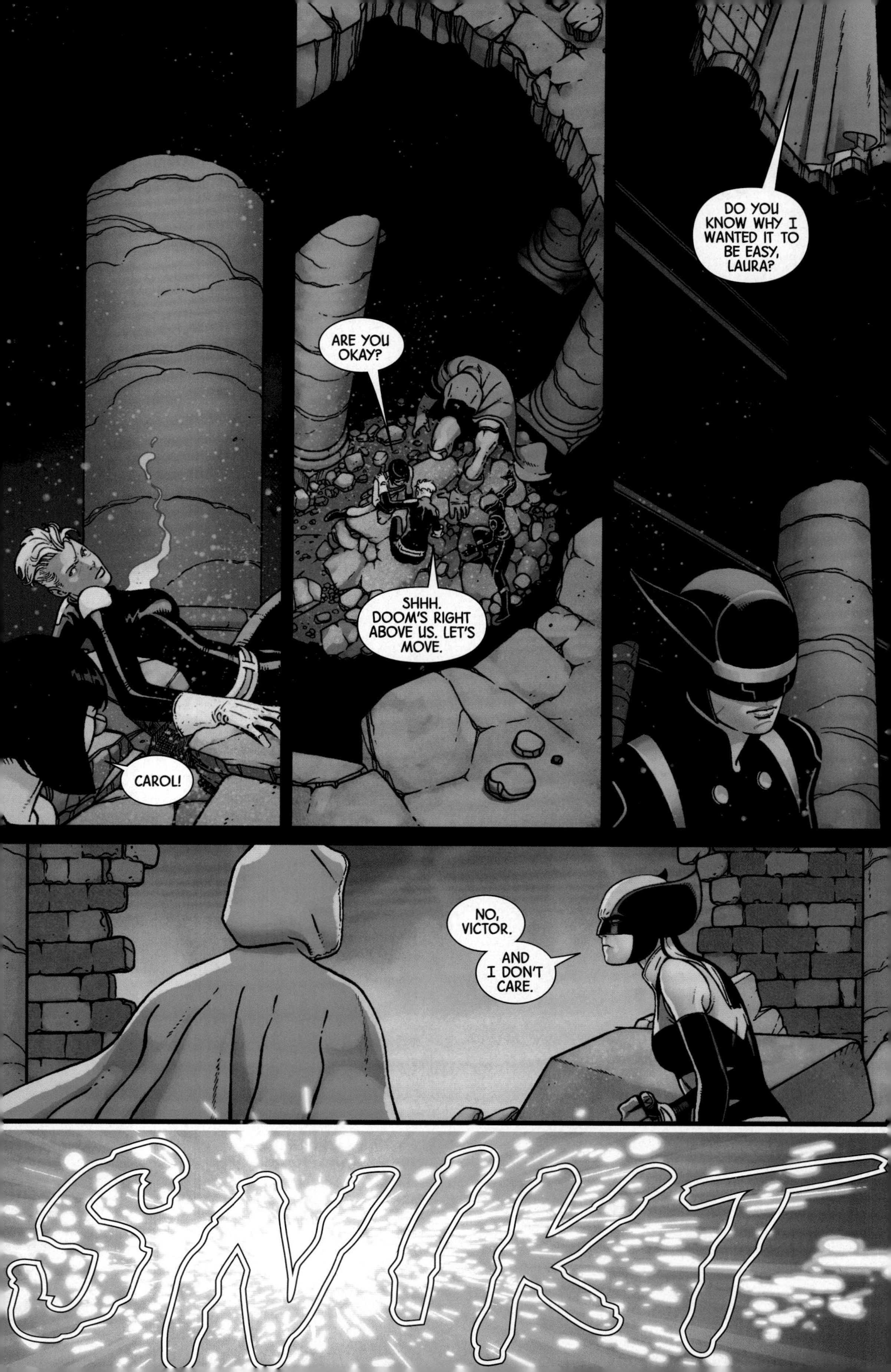
CAROL!
ARE YOU OKAY?
SHHH. DOOM'S RIGHT ABOVE US. LET'S MOVE.
DO YOU KNOW WHY I WANTED IT TO BE EASY, LAURA?
NO, VICTOR.
AND I DON'T CARE.
SNIKT

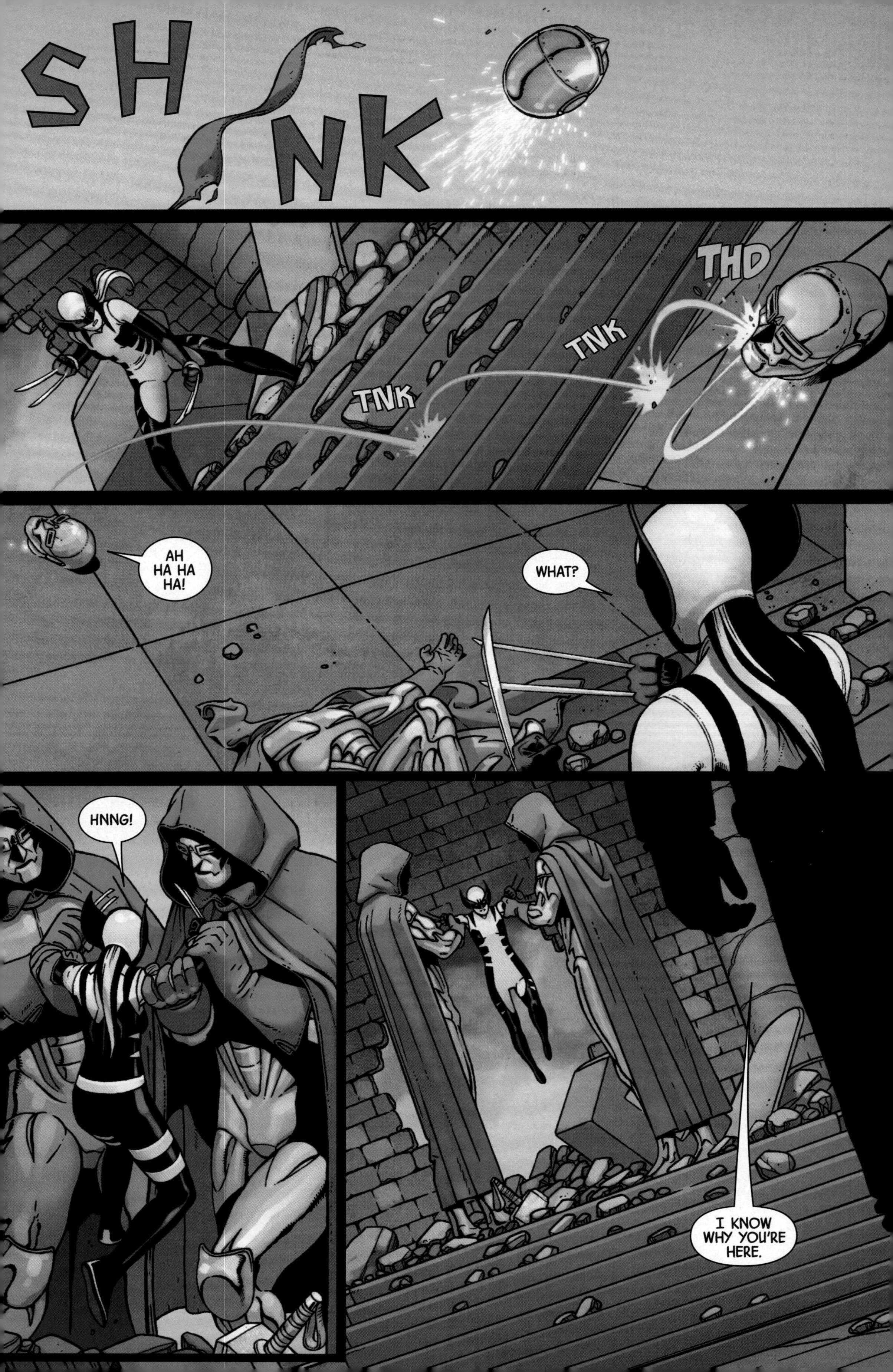
SHNK
THD
TNK
TNK
AH HA HA HA!
WHAT?
HNNG!
I KNOW WHY YOU'RE HERE.

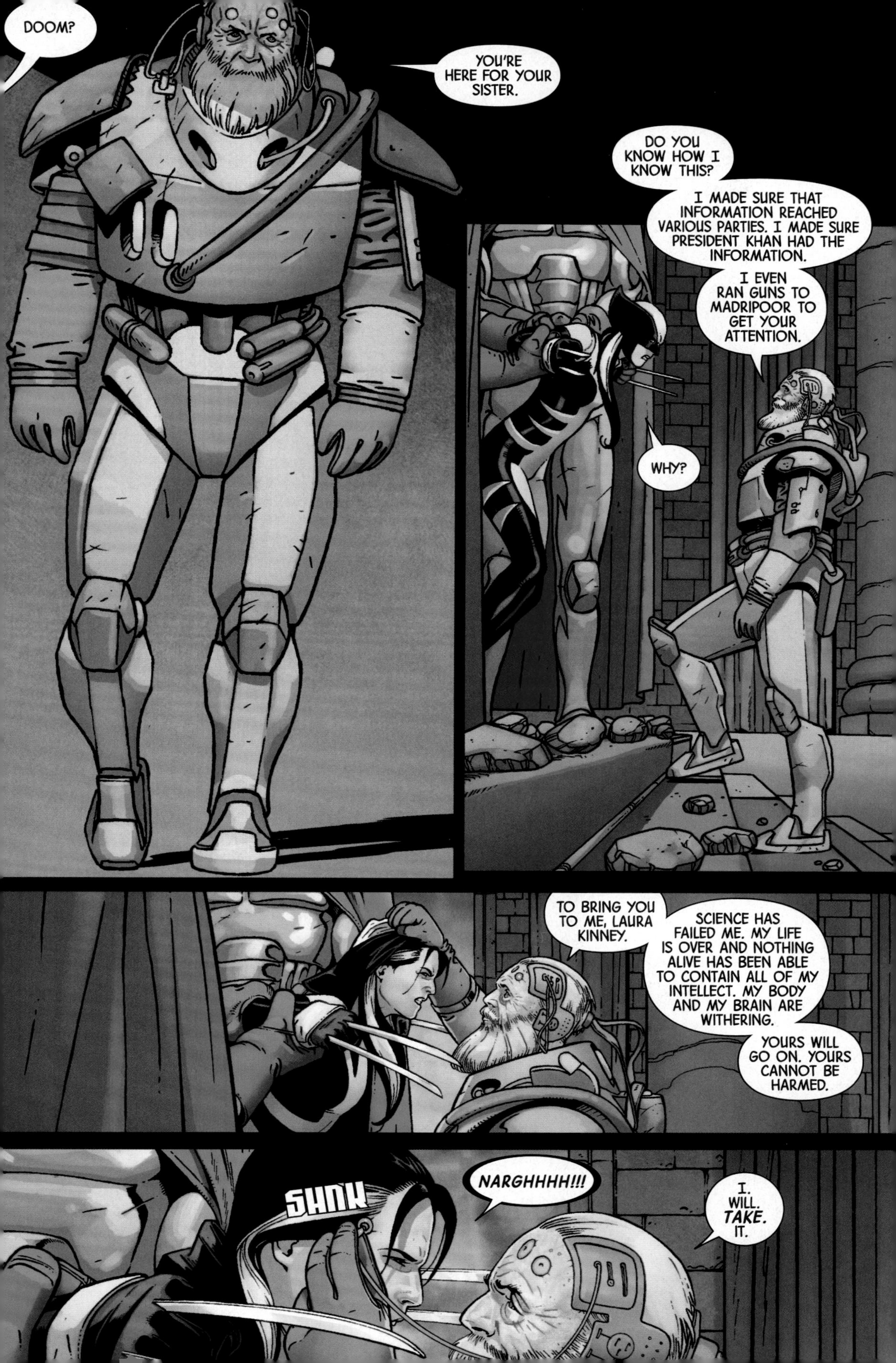
DOOM?
YOU'RE HERE FOR YOUR SISTER.
DO YOU KNOW HOW I KNOW THIS?
I MADE SURE THAT INFORMATION REACHED VARIOUS PARTIES. I MADE SURE PRESIDENT KHAN HAD THE INFORMATION.
I EVEN RAN GUNS TO MADRIPOOR TO GET YOUR ATTENTION.
WHY?
TO BRING YOU TO ME, LAURA KINNEY.
SCIENCE HAS FAILED ME. MY LIFE IS OVER AND NOTHING ALIVE HAS BEEN ABLE TO CONTAIN ALL OF MY INTELLECT. MY BODY AND MY BRAIN ARE WITHERING.
YOURS WILL GO ON. YOURS CANNOT BE HARMED.
SHNK
NARGHHHH!!!
I. WILL. TAKE. IT.

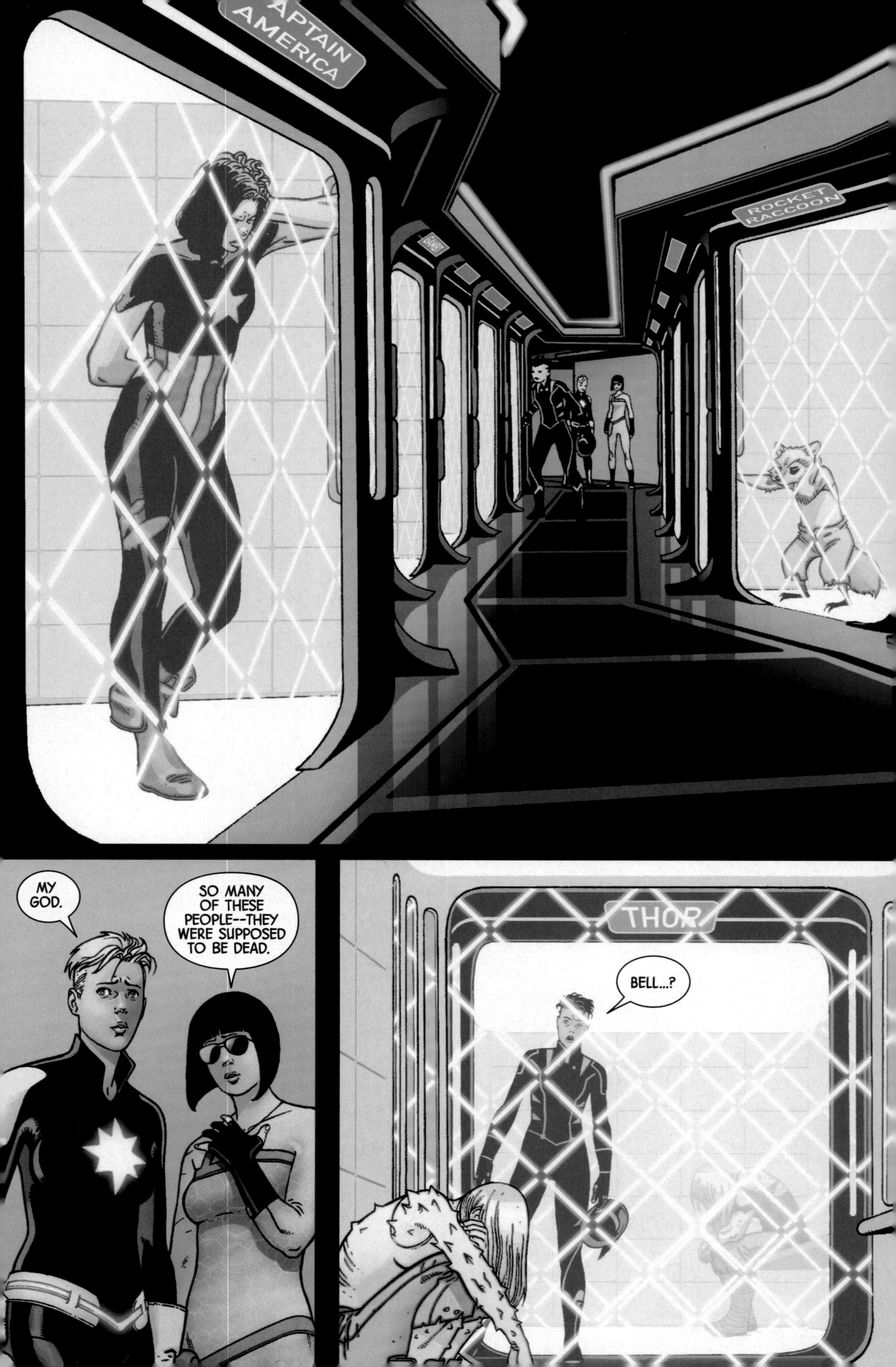
APTAIN AMERICA
ROCKET RACCOON
MY GOD.
SO MANY OF THESE PEOPLE--THEY WERE SUPPOSED TO BE DEAD.
THOR
BELL...?

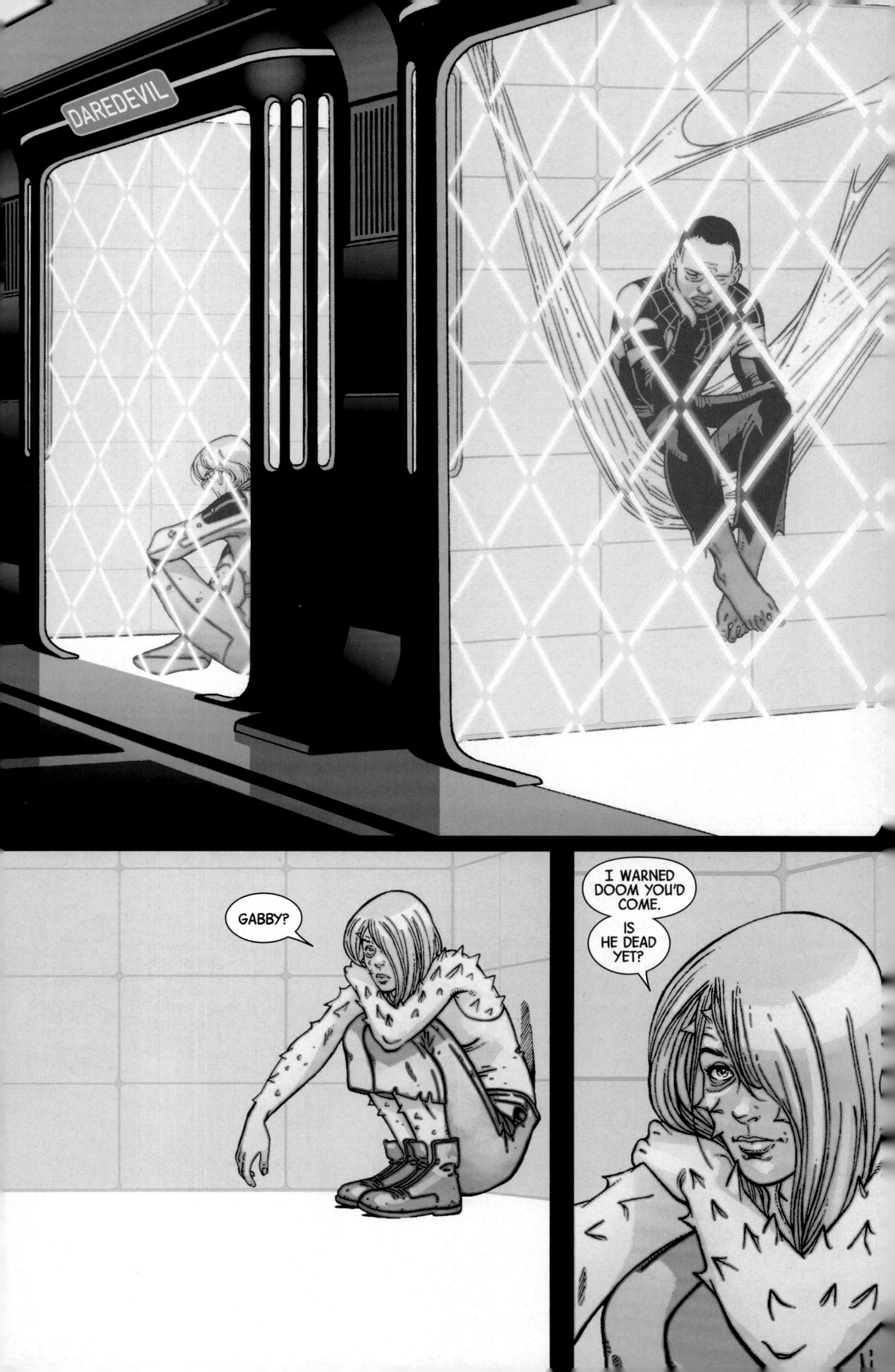
DAREDEVIL
GABBY?
I WARNED DOOM YOU'D COME.
IS HE DEAD YET?

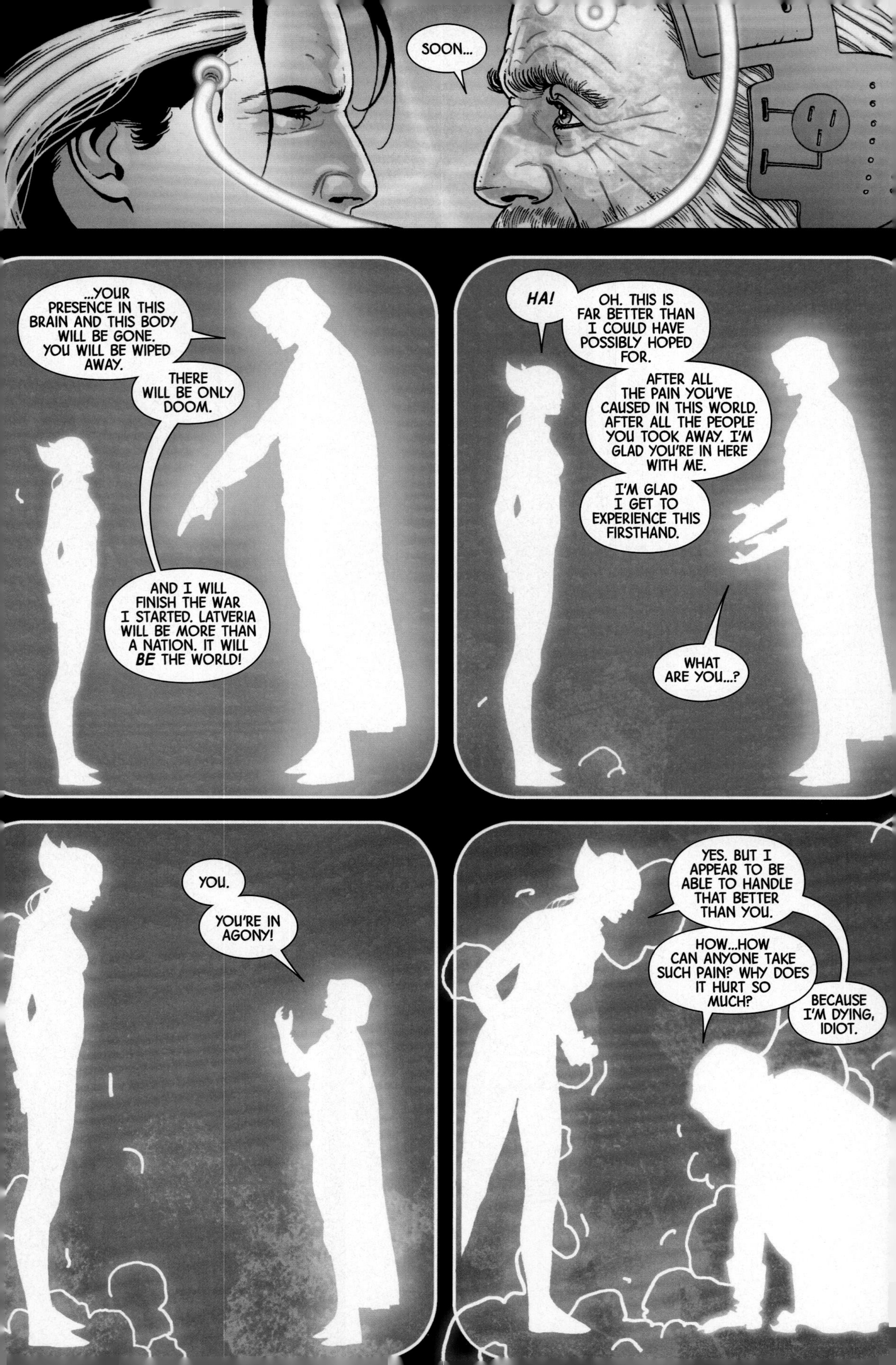
SOON...
...YOUR PRESENCE IN THIS BRAIN AND THIS BODY WILL BE GONE. YOU WILL BE WIPED AWAY.
THERE WILL BE ONLY DOOM.
AND I WILL FINISH THE WAR I STARTED. LATVERIA WILL BE MORE THAN A NATION. IT WILL BE THE WORLD!
HA!
OH. THIS IS FAR BETTER THAN I COULD HAVE POSSIBLY HOPED FOR.
AFTER ALL THE PAIN YOU'VE CAUSED IN THIS WORLD. AFTER ALL THE PEOPLE YOU TOOK AWAY. I'M GLAD YOU'RE IN HERE WITH ME.
I'M GLAD I GET TO EXPERIENCE THIS FIRSTHAND.
WHAT ARE YOU...?
YOU.
YOU'RE IN AGONY!
YES. BUT I APPEAR TO BE ABLE TO HANDLE THAT BETTER THAN YOU.
HOW...HOW CAN ANYONE TAKE SUCH PAIN? WHY DOES IT HURT SO MUCH?
BECAUSE I'M DYING, IDIOT.

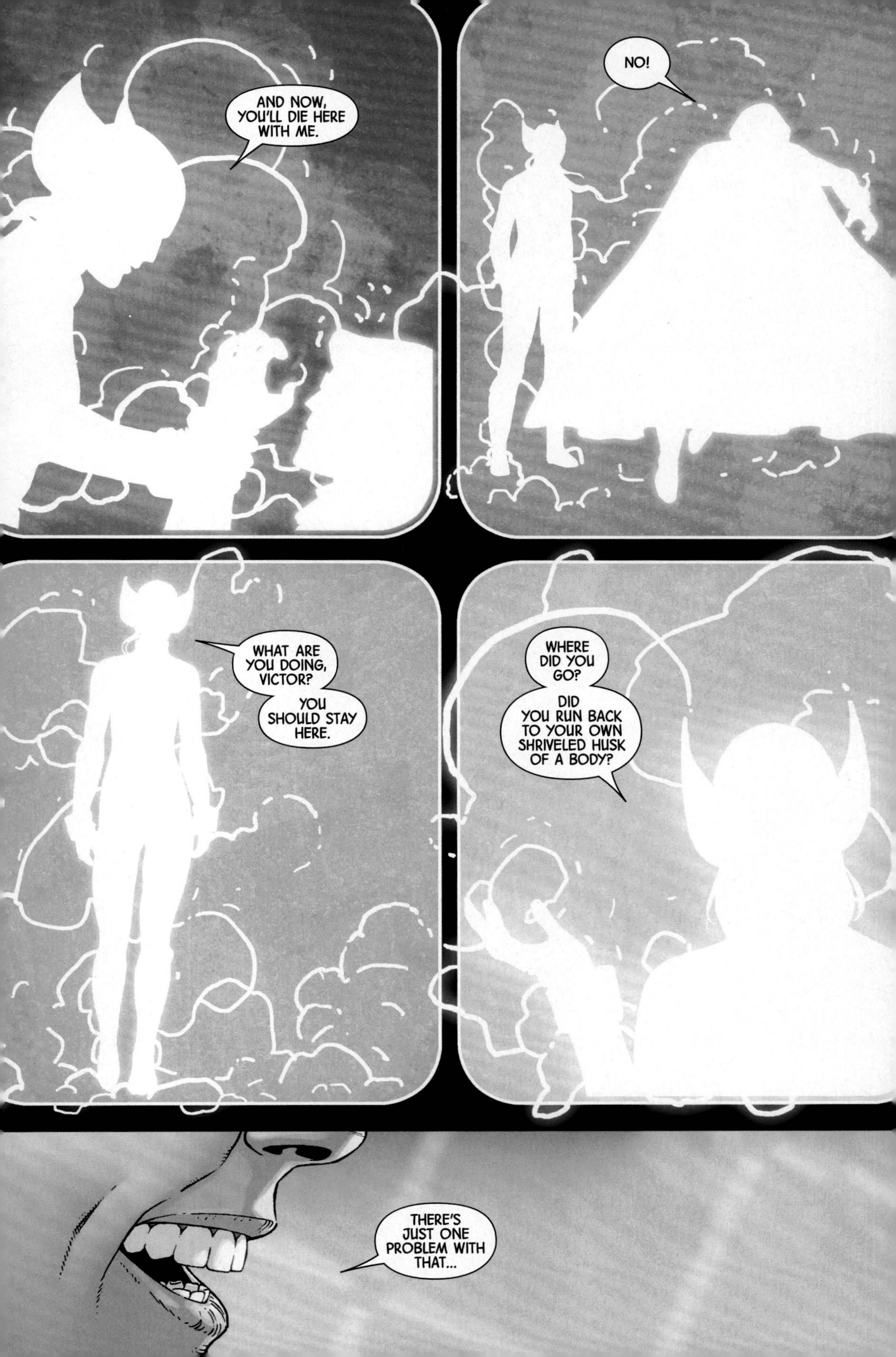
AND NOW, YOU'LL DIE HERE WITH ME.
NO!
WHAT ARE YOU DOING, VICTOR?
YOU SHOULD STAY HERE.
WHERE DID YOU GO?
DID YOU RUN BACK TO YOUR OWN SHRIVELED HUSK OF A BODY?
THERE'S JUST ONE PROBLEM WITH THAT...

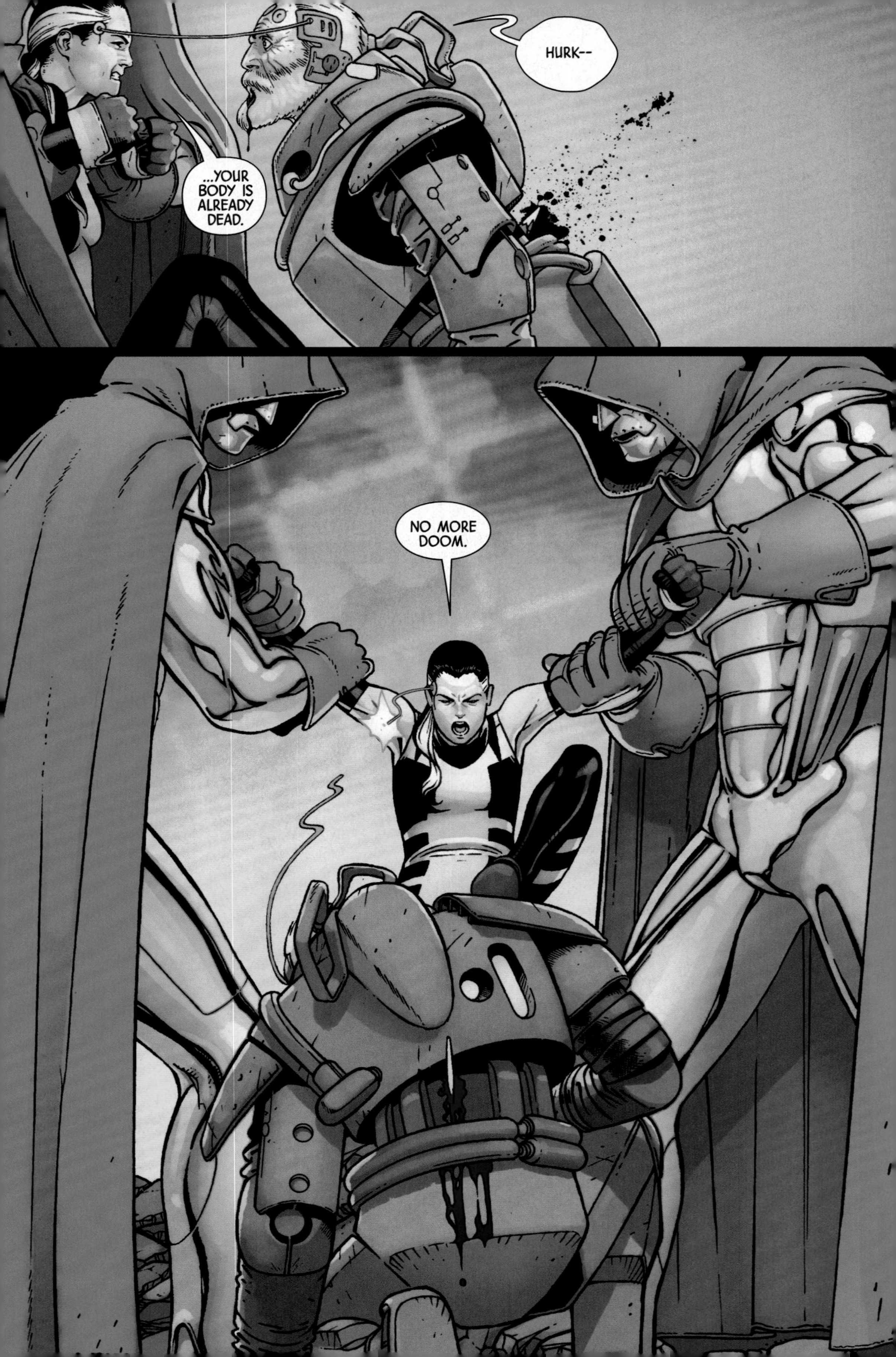
HURK--
...YOUR BODY IS ALREADY DEAD.
NO MORE DOOM.

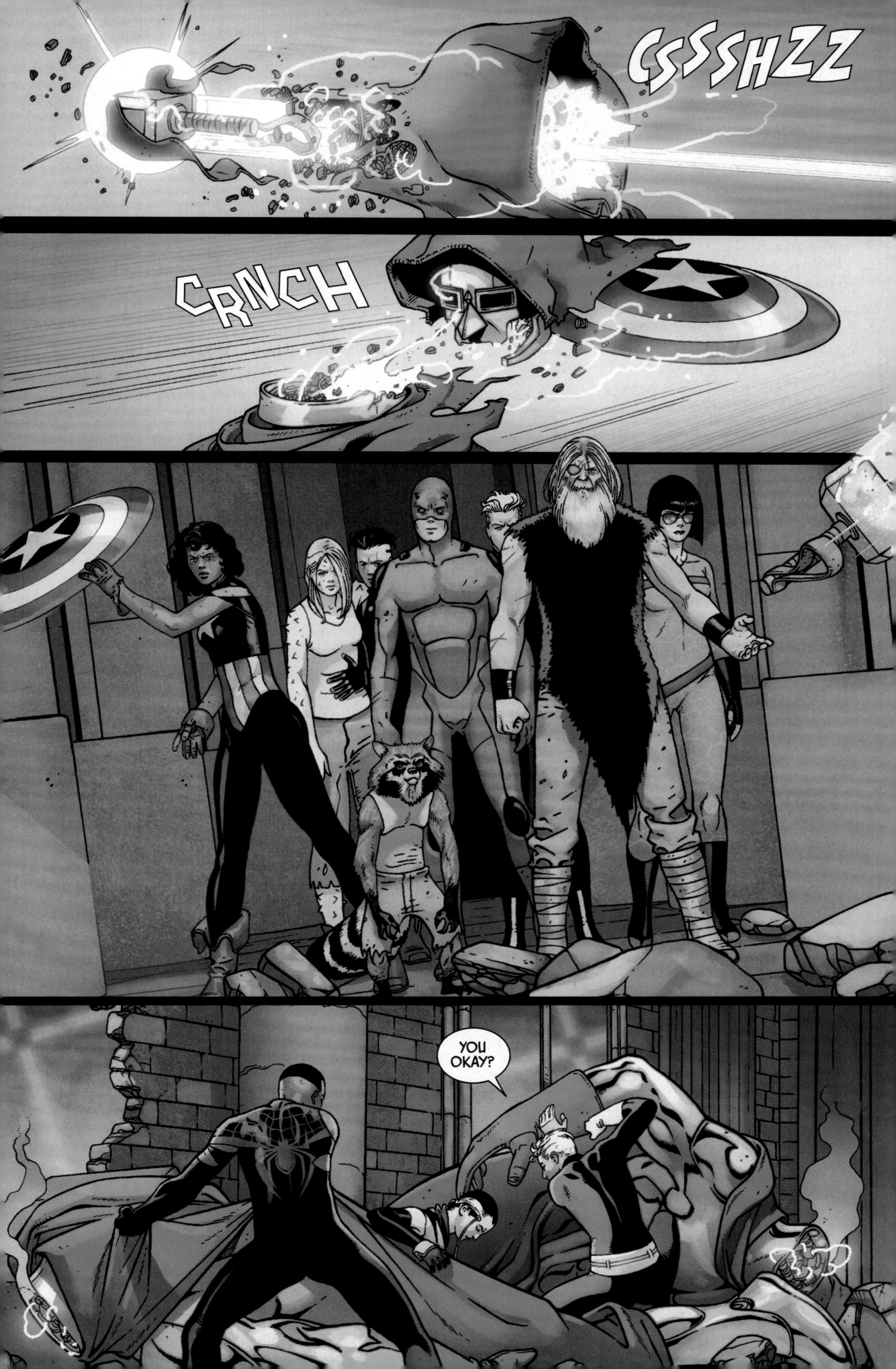
CSSSHZZ
CRNCH
YOU OKAY?

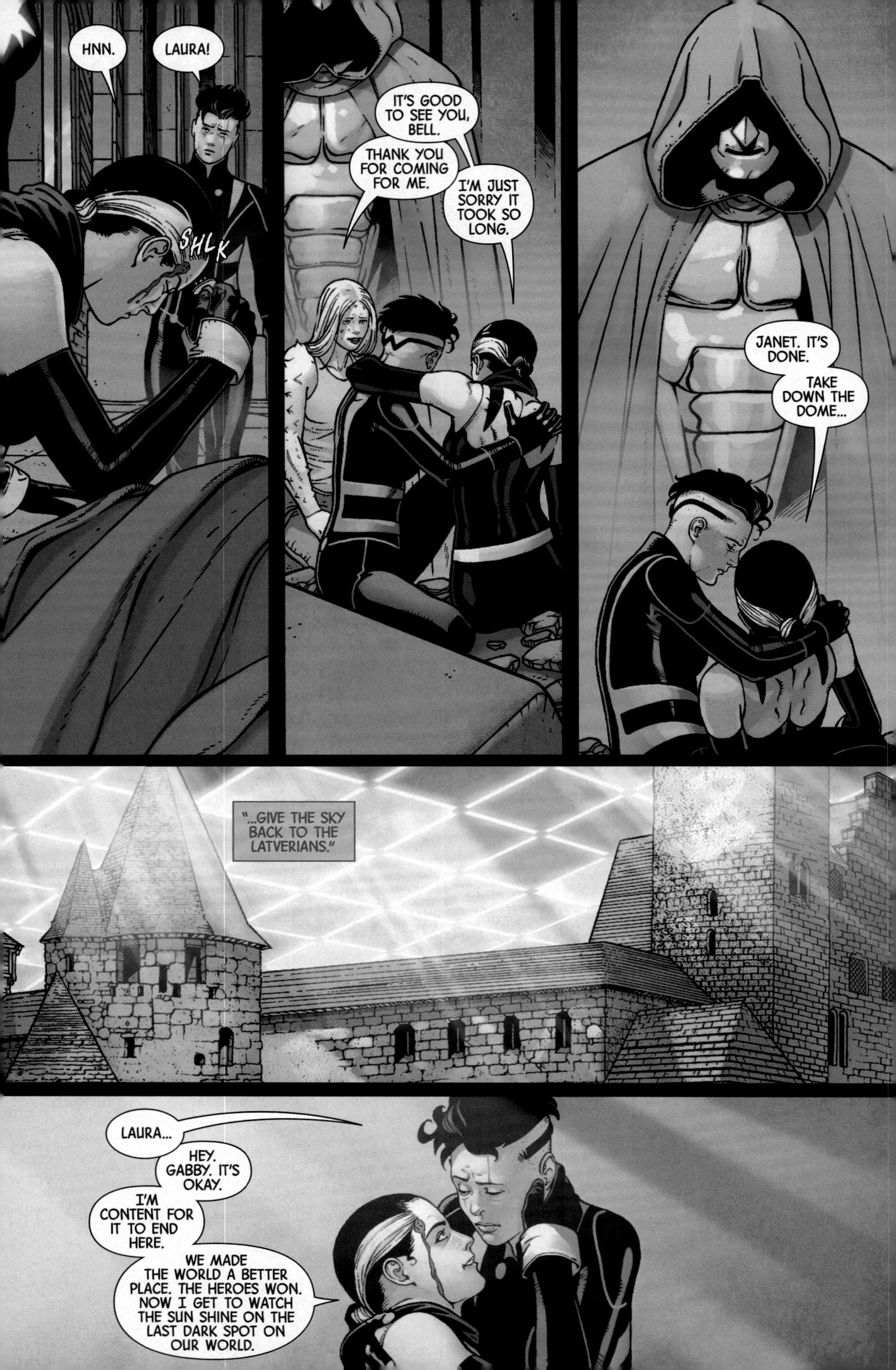

HNN.
LAURA!
SHLK
IT'S GOOD TO SEE YOU, BELL.
THANK YOU FOR COMING FOR ME.
I'M JUST SORRY IT TOOK SO LONG.
JANET. IT'S DONE.
TAKE DOWN THE DOME...
"...GIVE THE SKY BACK TO THE LATVERIANS."
LAURA...
HEY. GABBY. IT'S OKAY.
I'M CONTENT FOR IT TO END HERE.
WE MADE THE WORLD A BETTER PLACE. THE HEROES WON. NOW I GET TO WATCH THE SUN SHINE ON THE LAST DARK SPOT ON OUR WORLD.

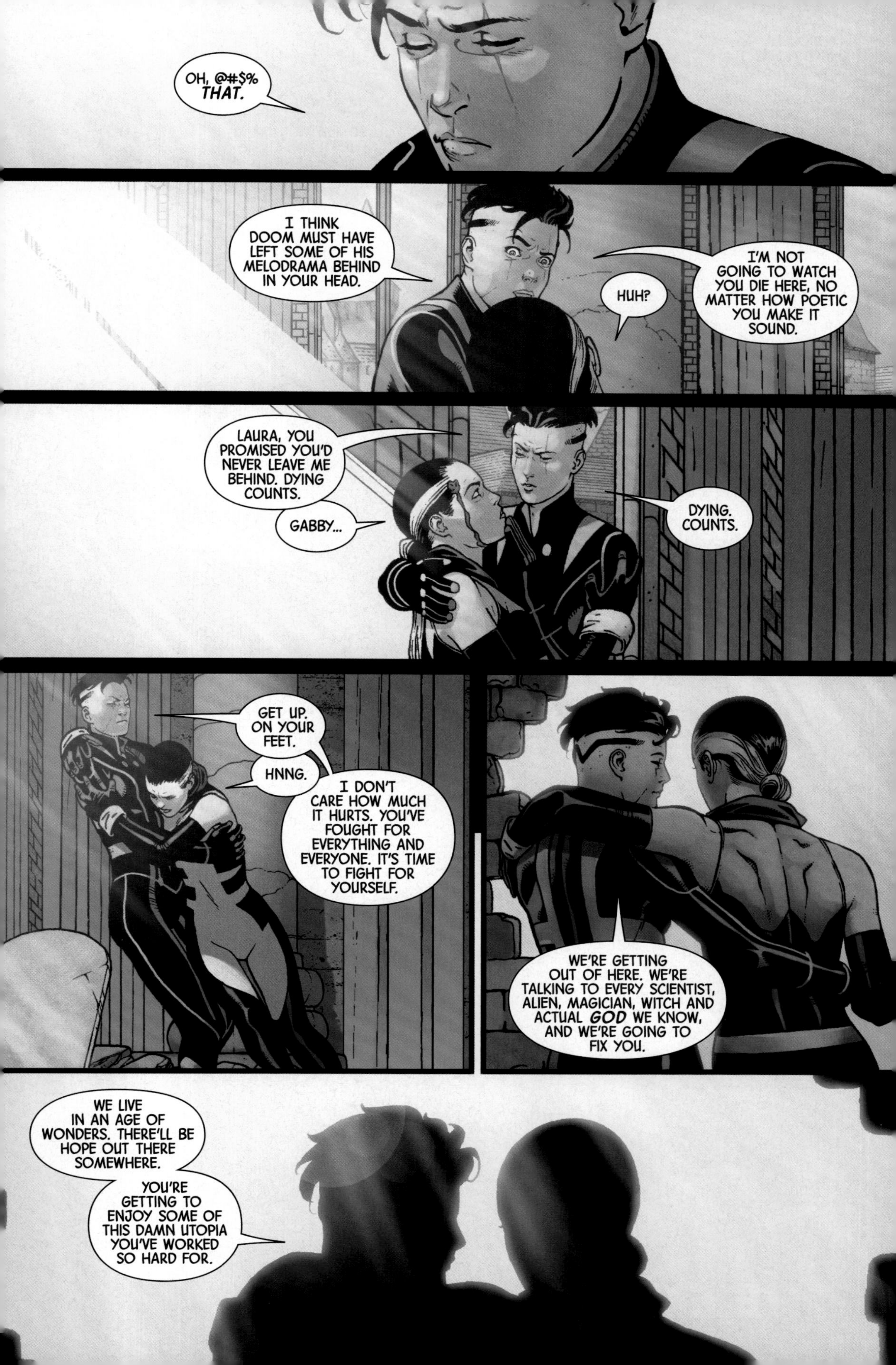
OH, @#$% THAT.
I THINK DOOM MUST HAVE LEFT SOME OF HIS MELODRAMA BEHIND IN YOUR HEAD.
HUH?
I'M NOT GOING TO WATCH YOU DIE HERE, NO MATTER HOW POETIC YOU MAKE IT SOUND.
LAURA, YOU PROMISED YOU'D NEVER LEAVE ME BEHIND. DYING COUNTS.
GABBY...
DYING. COUNTS.
GET UP. ON YOUR FEET.
HNNG.
I DON'T CARE HOW MUCH IT HURTS. YOU'VE FOUGHT FOR EVERYTHING AND EVERYONE. IT'S TIME TO FIGHT FOR YOURSELF.
WE'RE GETTING OUT OF HERE. WE'RE TALKING TO EVERY SCIENTIST, ALIEN, MAGICIAN, WITCH AND ACTUAL GOD WE KNOW, AND WE'RE GOING TO FIX YOU.
WE LIVE IN AN AGE OF WONDERS. THERE'LL BE HOPE OUT THERE SOMEWHERE.
YOU'RE GETTING TO ENJOY SOME OF THIS DAMN UTOPIA YOU'VE WORKED SO HARD FOR.

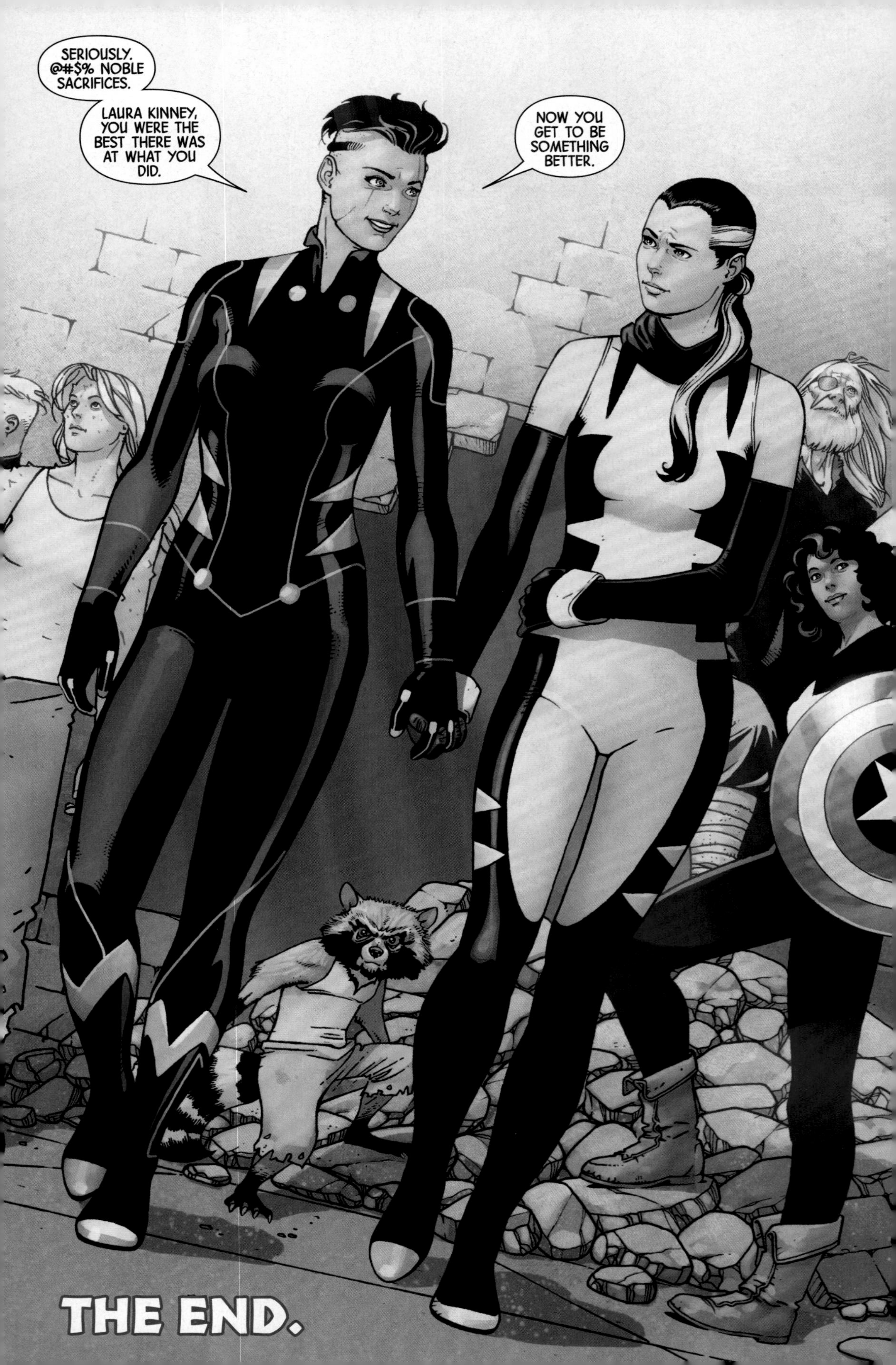
SERIOUSLY. @#$% NOBLE SACRIFICES.
LAURA KINNEY, YOU WERE THE BEST THERE WAS AT WHAT YOU DID.
NOW YOU GET TO BE SOMETHING BETTER.
THE END.

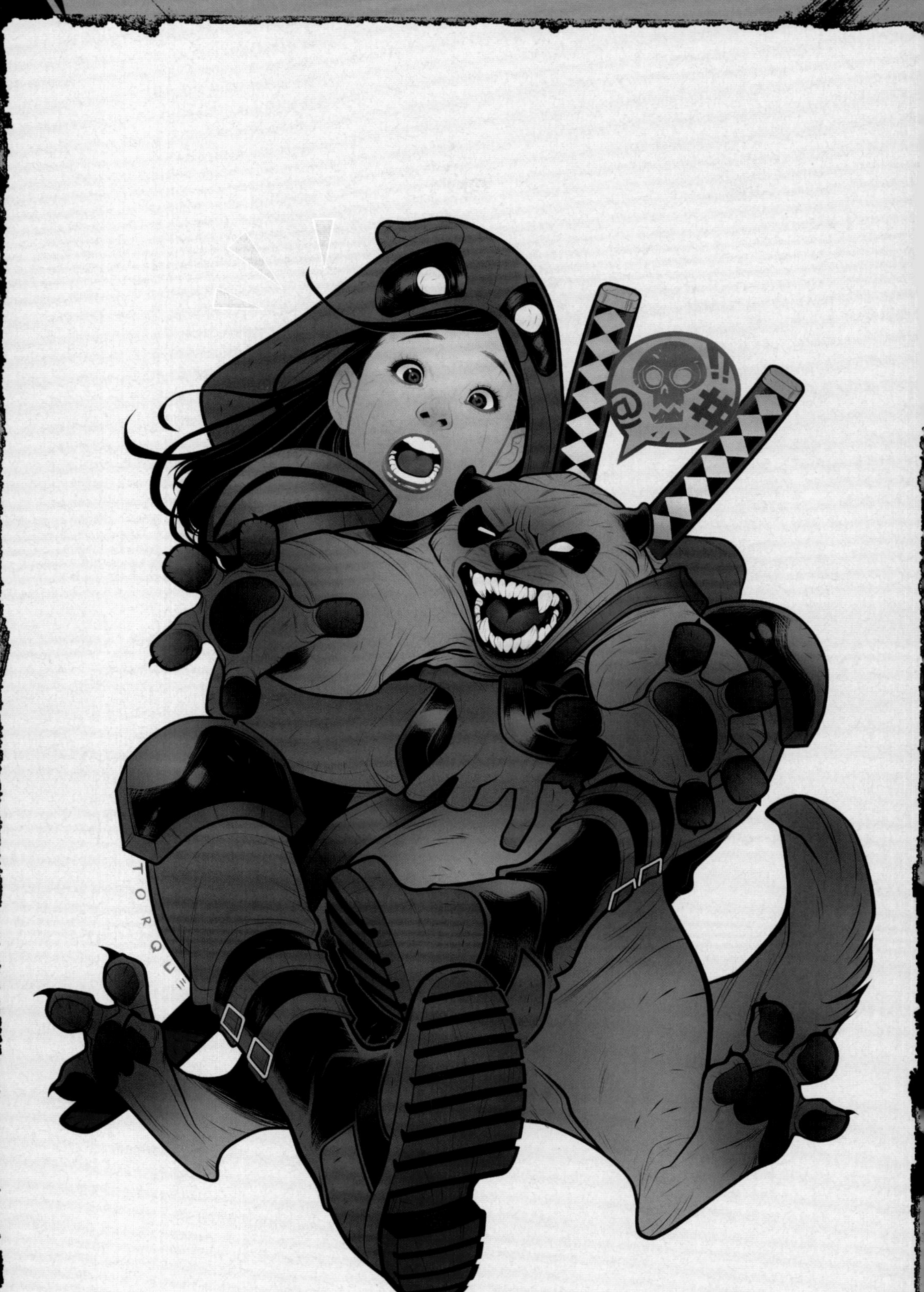
TORQUE
@
#

#35 variant by

ELIZABETH TORQUE

Character designs by
RAMON ROSANAS